DIFFERENT DRUMMERS

Don Caron and Lyle Hatcher

Sound Enterprises inc. Publishing

Publishers Cataloging-in-Publication Data

Caron, Don and Hatcher, Lyle
     Different Drummers / Don Caron and Lyle Hatcher
     1st Edition – Spokane, Washington
     SEI Publishing
     www.seizoom.com

Fiction/Biographical/Christian/Family Life

ISBN 10: 0981963609 (h.c)   0981963617 (s.c)
ISBN 13: 978-0-9819636-0-0 (h.c) 978-0-9819636-1-7 (s.c.)
EAN: 52395 (h.c)   51495 (s.c)
LIBRARY OF CONGRESS CONTROL NUMBER: 2009923323

Editing by Anne MacIver
Cover design and layout by Tami Rotchford
Authors' photograph by Mary Gladhart
Cover photograph by Allison Achauer
Printed and bound in the USA
Special thanks to:
     Jack LaLanne   Derek Kavanagh
     The Dahlke Family   The Caron Family
     The Hatcher Family   Gary and Lisa Marks
     Maria Baker

NOTICES
Excerpts from *The Jack LaLanne Show*, copyright © 2005 BeFit Enterprises. Used with permission. Jack LaLanne photo © Be-Fit Enterprises. Used with permission.

Published and distributed by SEI Publishing
www.differentdrummersbook.com

CONTENTS

PROLOGUE

When the boy and the dog reach the wide expanse of the open meadow, their pace temporarily slows. Lyle stops and bends down, hands on his knees, needing air but not tired. He can see the Log from here, across the meadow, and he keeps his eyes on it, holding his focus. Dino lets loose with an excited bark and runs ahead, already sure of their destination.

Lyle isn't ready. He throws his hands out wide, palms upward, and turns his face into the sun. He stands like that, perfectly still, and then suddenly reaches out and grabs a wild sunflower, crushes it in his fist, and holds it close to his face. He breathes deeply, taking in the pungent odor of the fading summer.

Dino barks again, and Lyle scatters the remains of the flower into the wind and breaks away at a full sprint, pushing until he can no longer feel his legs moving. His eyes squint and his hands stretch open and without slowing he throws his head back and shouts, "You wanna run? Let's run!"

Out of the corner of his eye, he glimpses motion, and he turns to find David catching up to him in smooth, long strides, so easy, so relaxed. Lyle, with his short legs, knows David can easily outpace him, but he doesn't. He matches Lyle's speed perfectly, and as they move in unison, they glance at each other and their faces break into wide grins, uncontainable, both of them reveling in this incomparable sensation, this wild exhilarating freedom.

The sky is a luminous blue, the trees are every green imaginable and the boys are running so fast, the meadow floor has become a magical dazzling haze of all shades and shapes winging past them, gliding beneath their feet. They race toward the Log with a reckless fervor, as if they had waited a lifetime for this precise moment—this one chance.

CHAPTER ONE

FALLING

If a man does not keep pace with his companions,
perhaps it is because he hears a different drummer.
Let him step to the music which he hears,
however measured or far away.

~ HENRY DAVID THOREAU

1965

Nestled at the foot of the Bitterroot Mountains in Northern Idaho along the shoreline of Lake Pend Oreille, is a four-thousand acre refuge known as Farragut State Park. There's a hidden natural wonder in this park: a spacious meadow formed in the shape of an enormous amphitheater, circled by a protective forest of stately pine, aspen and Western larch. It's an ideal location for camping, isolated and sheltered, with plenty of space, and ready opportunities for every conceivable outdoor activity.

One nippy morning in early September, the thirteen members of Pack 221, the Tenderfoots, crawl from their tents and scurry about, starting their fires and preparing their breakfasts.

Mr. Evans, a former Marine turned Scoutmaster, and Mr. Gallagher, his assistant for the weekend, have been up for quite a while. They stand, slumped against the morning chill, sipping their instant coffee and watching the Scouts at work.

"Where's Hatcher?" Mr. Gallagher inquires. "Haven't seen hide nor hair of him since he came boltin' outta that tent a half-hour ago."

"No, and you won't," Mr. Evans chuckles. "I needed a break, so I sent him off for some firewood. That kid is busier 'n two tomcats in a gunny sack."

Mr. Gallagher grins. "Busier 'n a peg-legged pirate in a room fulla rat traps."

"Busier 'n a fart in a skillet," Mr. Evans fires back.

"Why, he's busier 'n a one-eyed man in a—"

"All right, all right, we got kids around here! That little varmint's gotta be kept busy, that's all."

The men enjoy a hearty laugh while Lyle, the Scout they're discussing, scrambles up the steep hill sloping toward the rim above the camp. He sports a flattop crew cut, slight fangs and bright, clear-blue eyes, and he's short for his age of ten—the shortest Scout there. A hatchet in his hand and determination on his face, he moves quickly up the hillside without stopping to rest. It's a long climb and he likes it.

Wood rats last night, and chipmunks at sunup. Squirrels droppin' pinecones on the tent. Bombs away! Rabbits sound like babies cryin' when the coyotes kill 'em. Frankie had to run and sleep in the grownups' tent. The rest of the Scouts stayed awake, but I was too tired to worry.

Crows yellin', "Strange boy, boy in the woods!" The winds cover me up and hide me. I'm safe up here.

Man, I wish Jimmy would quit snarfin' his nose. Quit it! Quit snarfin'! If Mike says, "I can't do it" one more time, dang it, I'll just go help him! I feel bad for him, anyway. He's no crybaby. His dad never goes to any of the Scout stuff. Everybody else's dad goes, why doesn't his?

Crispy burnt bacon, fried potatoes, and little tiny cereal boxes from Kellogg's. I'd like three, please. No, wait! Make it four!

Lyle arrives, breathless, at the top of the hill. There, looming above him, is the reason for his efforts: a colossal standing-dead Ponderosa pine, well over sixty feet high. He spotted it from the camp first thing this morning, and it had "a weekend's worth of firewood" written all over it.

Lyle's eyes travel to the top. He expended a lot of energy on this climb, and the effort triggers self-reflection. He realizes he's completely worn out his welcome with all of his friends. It's not his fault, really. It's simply that people have trouble keeping up with him. But whatever the reason, a guy will do almost anything for friendship, and as he stands gazing up at the giant tree, he thinks, what his friends need right now is firewood, and lots of it. It doesn't occur to him there could be difficulties chopping through the enormous trunk with a tool designed for little more than splitting dry kindling.

He winds up and swings with such force that the hatchet glances off the bark and flies out of his hand. He spins around to check if anybody noticed. A squirrel chatters noisily at him, then scampers up a nearby larch and vanishes from sight.

Lyle retrieves the hatchet, digs his feet in, and hacks away at a frantic pace, switching hands as needed to avoid slowing down. Bark chips and wood shavings scatter to the ground. The distant sounds of the Scout camp float up from the bottom of the bowl and echo back from the opposite rim.

> *Sure glad I'm not down there, fakin' havin' a good time. Tyin' knots, who cares? How to trap and skin animals? If I was hungry, I'd kill a deer. Not sure how, I just would . . . Holey smokes! There's one right now!*

Lyle sights a doe, lying in the tall grass rimming the upper edge of the basin. The camouflaged animal would be invisible to almost anyone else, but to him it stands out as if in thick, dark outline. Colorblind, Lyle knows only shapes, textures, and patterns. "Color" is an indistinguishable muddle for him, with the single exception of blue—that gloriously inviting, drinkable, swimmable, irresistible, blueberry blue—the exact color of this morning's sky.

The sun is high enough now, above the hills, to cast the golden glow of morning down into the camp. The warm air, true to Indian summers in the Northwest, settles onto the forest like a comfortable blanket. Lyle breathes it all in.

Gotta love the smell of those campfires. Smoke follows beauty and me. Mr. Evans says it keeps the mosquitoes away. They don't bite me anyway 'cause I have anti-mosquito blood.

Musty sleepin' bags, canvas tents and propane. It puffs when you light it with a wooden match. Blue flame with a yellow tip like candy corn. Stare right at the lantern and you can't see at all. Watery hot chocolate, graham crackers with Hershey's and burnt-to-a-crisp marshmallows. If you just toast 'em golden brown you're a wuss or a girl.

Repetition has refined Lyle's hacking into actual chopping, and the chopping sends wood chips rocketing in every direction, filling the air and littering the ground. The morning breeze rustles through the trees, drawn from the hills by the warm sunlight striking the cool water of Lake Pend Oreille.

Most people woulda quit by now but this is the easiest way to get a lotta firewood. Besides, the guys'll think this is the coolest!

When a tree falls, wait 'til it almost hits you, then move fast at the last second. Don't be scared 'til I'm scared! I never exaggerate, swear to God!

Lyle focuses on the motion of the hatchet and finds a rhythm, steadier and less frantic. His arms are tired but he doesn't slow down—doesn't even consider it.

CRACK!!!

The sharp noise splits the air like a gunshot and echoes against the opposite side of the meadow. Birds fill the sky in a noisy flurry and swiftly disappear over the ridge. Lyle stops. He waits. He can hear the voices from the camp below, distant and indistinct. He listens, but he can't make them out.

Swinging the hatchet out wide, he puts every ounce of effort into another hit. The tree responds with an unearthly rumble. Lyle waits again, and then lifts his hatchet. As he is about to strike, the tree interrupts, emitting a crackling sputtering groan that starts quietly and quickly crescendoes into a frightening roar.

Lyle leaps up and backs away, awestruck by the immensity and power of the sound. The massive tree slowly leans and twists and begins to fall. The wind takes hold of its boughs and it topples, tearing off the higher limbs of its neighbors, ripping larger and larger branches from the surrounding trees with the enormous force of its descent, finally slamming heavily into the ground and bouncing sideways in a roaring din of breaking branches and splintering wood.

The thunderous noise attracts the attention of the entire camp. Everyone freezes, staring up at the crest of the hill. The tree has landed parallel to the hillside and lies there, in plain view of the Scouts below. Lyle clambers up on top of it, waves the hatchet above his head, and screams out a high-volume Indian war cry. It echoes for miles.

Standing on the downed tree, he goes to work hacking off the branches. The first few come away easily, but when he encounters one of the larger limbs, he struggles. After chopping into it from the top, he attacks it from one side and then the other. Growing impatient, he kicks down at the limb, throwing all of his weight against it. The branch snaps. The tree takes a forward turn and pitches him over backwards onto the ground.

Lyle watches in horror, as the tree meets the downward slope and takes another slow roll . . . and then another, as if testing its newfound freedom. He springs to his feet and tears after it, clinging to the trunk and digging his fingers into the bark in a desperate attempt to stop it.

"No, no, no, no, no!"

The tree flips over, again, then again, gaining momentum. It leaps and bounces down the hill, throwing up chunks of turf and dirt as it rips a fast path through the steep meadow. Lyle chases after it in a panic, waving his arms above his head.

"*Run!* Run for your lives!"

The pine collides with an enormous rock outcropping and the impact launches it into the air. The top snaps off in its own direction while the main trunk smashes into the ground, rolling directly at the camp.

Mr. Evans, alerted by the threatening rumble of the tree's approach, swings around to see a fifteen-hundred-pound rolling pin bearing down on his troop. To the right, he finds all the color drained from Mr. Gallagher's face. To the left, the Tenderfoots are huddled, paralyzed in their tracks.

The sound of a whistle pierces the air. Mr. Evans shouts an order:

"Run for the trees!"

The Scouts waste no time scrambling for cover.

Lyle's feet scarcely touch the ground in his frenzied flight after the tree. He trips and falls but jumps back to his feet, falls again, accidentally somersaults, and manages to land upright, running. Unable to keep up, he's still charging down the hill when the tree reaches camp, blasting through the tents and fires, crushing and mangling everything in its path.

When it finally rolls to a stop, there is complete silence. A single cricket chirps once. It's as if every trace of life in this previously protected place has been swept away. Campfires have been smothered and are mere wisps of smoke. Smoldering ashes scatter about the area and dust drifts up and swirls away in the breeze. Tents are flattened and backpacks squashed and mauled. There's not a sign of a Cub Scout anywhere.

The long silence gives the campers the courage to emerge, cautiously, from behind the trees and out of the underbrush. Mr. Evans rises from his post behind a large rock and storms directly up to Lyle.

"Sac-ra-men-to-Ca-li-for-nia! What were you thinking? Look at this! *Look at it!* Are you out of your mind?!"

"I was gettin' some firewood. For the whole 221," Lyle offers sheepishly, pointing to where the tree came to rest at the opposite side of the camp. "See? It's dead."

"*It's* dead? We could all be dead, for cryin' out loud! Just . . . just put your things in your pack! I'm takin' you home."

Numb, Lyle gathers his camping gear together and stuffs it into his mangled backpack. Mr. Evans opens the trunk of his car and directs Lyle's movements with terse gestures. Lyle tosses his backpack into the trunk, climbs into the passenger seat, and waits there for Mr. Evans.

Seventy-five miles away, Miss Dorothy O'Donnell is alone in her office. She moves about the room with a nervous feminine grace, yet almost manly authority. Late forties, tall and fit, she wears her hair tight in a bun, knotted and pinned stiffly in place. Her clothes are neither designed nor worn with an eye to attractiveness, casting her rightly as a spinster. A radio plays from somewhere in the room. The KJRB newsman's resonant voice relaxes her.

A new package of number-two pencils rests on the desk. While she listens, Miss O'Donnell slips a pencil from the pack, inserts it into the sharpener, and slowly turns the crank. She removes it, confident it will have a perfect conical point, which it does. She cleans the pencil with a quick puff of air and places it neatly in her center desk drawer, where she lines them up like a well organized infantry, awaiting orders.

If Dorothy O'Donnell loves anything, it is this school. Linwood Elementary is her domain, and she runs it not unlike a general. Her strict authoritarian methods have earned her the nickname "DOD Almighty." The teachers whisper it, invariably with respect and admiration, but only among themselves. Despite their efforts to hide it from her, she knows. Nothing escapes her attention.

The newscast ends and the programming shifts to music. Miss O'Donnell switches off the radio, and basks in the silence. Out in the hallways, the doors are closed, as they always are when classes are in session. It is so quiet here, someone entering might think it to be a vacation day. Closed doors and absolute silence are two of her many regulations. This is her school, and those are her rules.

A door opens, and breaks the peace. An eleven-year-old boy exits his fourth-grade classroom, relying on the wall for support. His skin and face shine, practically glow, and his hair is an unusual brownish yellow color, like a perfectly drawn choirboy on a Christmas card. His body is long and gangly, and he has the unmistakable loping stride characteristic of muscular dystrophy.

The journey from classroom to restroom is a long one for David, and today he finds it even more trying. Throwing one leg in front of the other and sliding his hand along the wall, he persists until finally he arrives at the bathroom. The door feels heavier than usual but he wrests his way inside. He balances against the sink to rest.

Glancing up, he catches his reflection in the mirror. Beads of perspiration form on his forehead and trickle down his cheeks. He'd like to reach up and wipe them away, but he's afraid to let go of the sink. Instead, he lowers his head and watches the droplets plop into the bowl, winding around on the smooth surface until they disappear down the polished chrome drain.

David inhales, then makes his way along the row of sinks, using them for support. He stumbles and catches himself, avoiding a disastrous fall, but he's unable to regain his balance. His heart pounds as he struggles .to stand upright, pushing forcefully against the porcelain surface.

Something in his body has changed, and he refuses to give in to it. Holding himself up with his arms, he waits for the muscles in his legs to respond, as they always have before. Arms quivering, he grows even more determined. When the quivering intensifies into spasms, David feels control slipping swiftly away, and despite excruciating effort, his arms and legs give out. He collapses to the floor and lies there exhausted, breathing labored, too tired to move. His clothes are damp from the prolonged exertion. They cling, sticky and heavy to his skin.

David isn't frightened. He knew someday this would happen. The doctors warned he would eventually lose the ability to walk without assistance, and sometime after, the ability to walk altogether. He just hadn't expected it so soon. He hadn't expected it today.

Lying with his cheek to the floor, he contemplates the perfectly straight lines of shiny tiles, and he's grateful Mr. Merrick keeps it so clean. The cold surface feels good on his skin, cooling his body and relaxing him.

Inevitably, energy returns. He rolls to his stomach, spreads his legs apart, and pushes himself up onto his hands and feet. He developed this trick as a way to stand up, but this time he falls. He makes another attempt, then another, and is forced by exhaustion to rest. It's now very clear—he is not going to stand, yet he has to get back to the classroom for help.

David struggles to the exit and heaves his body into a sitting position. He grabs the handle and opens the door, just enough to slip his hand around its edge. He pushes away as forcefully as he can, and falls over onto his side. The door swings back and closes on his body, trapping him.

He waits for his breathing to ease back to normal. Gathering his strength, David drags his legs free. Once in the hall, he rests again, then slides along the floor, working himself forward on his elbows. It's a slow and laborious process, but he focuses on the glow he sees coming from the doorway at the end of the hall. He stops several times to rest, and finally reaches the classroom.

David taps quietly on the doorframe, waits several minutes, then taps again. He taps and waits . . . taps and waits . . . until Mrs. McGuire glances up and notices him. She rushes over and drops to her knees.

"Goodness, gracious! Why didn't you call out?" she exclaims, her voice full of concern and compassion. She lays a comforting hand on his back.

"I didn't want anybody to see me," he admits shyly.

Without getting up, Mrs. McGuire swings around and speaks with hushed urgency to the student in the desk closest to her.

"Jimmy, go get Miss O'Donnell! Quickly, now!"

At the Hatcher residence, in a quiet suburb of North Spokane, Lyle's older sister, Linda, sits on the couch in the living room, doing homework. A car pulls into the driveway, and she unfolds from her comfortable spot. Tall for her age of thirteen, the tallest girl in the entire school, she has perfect posture, which exaggerates her height even more. Linda kneels on the couch by the window, edges the drapes aside, and peers out.

"Mom?" she shouts at the kitchen. "When's Lyle s'posed to get home?"

"Sunday night," Mrs. Hatcher calls back. She winks at her husband. "The calm before the storm," she adds with a grin.

Lyle's younger brother, Steve, hops up next to Linda at the window, excited at the possibility of entertainment. They watch together, as Mr. Evans opens the car door and Lyle climbs out and retrieves his backpack. Pieces fall off and the crushed canteen bounces from the driveway. Mr. Evans, obviously drained, shuts the trunk.

Eight years old, with white hair like Linda's, Steve is something of a sight to behold: skinny and bowl-legged, with corrective shoes shaped in such a way they appear to be on the wrong feet. (The neighbor lady sometimes intercepts him on the way home from school and very helpfully switches them.) He leaps off the couch and rushes to the kitchen to deliver a live report for his parents.

"Well, he's here right now, and somebody squashed his canteen!" Steve announces, as if taking credit for the event.

"That was a brand-new canteen," Mrs. Hatcher frowns. She grabs a dishtowel and hastily dries her hands.

"Yeah, I know—brand-spankin' new!" Steve buzzes back to the window to gather another update.

Linda glares. "Don't have a cow, Steve."

Steve ignores her, reporting again to the kitchen. He raises his volume a notch. "Scoutmaster Evans is mad!" He flies to the couch for another peek and then starts toward the kitchen again, almost shouting this time, "I think he's in really big—"

"Steve! That's enough." Mrs. Hatcher enters the room. "Ron, will you see what's going on, please?"

Linda stays perched at the window as her dad walks out the door and down the sidewalk, with Steve tight on his heels.

Mr. Hatcher stands in the driveway talking quietly to Mr. Evans. Steve gloms onto Lyle, who drags his backpack toward the house.

"Hey, what happened?" Steve asks, following him through the front door.

"Nothin'."

Linda's tone is gentle, concerned. "You okay, Lyle?"

"Did ya get in trouble? Huh?" Steve demands.

Suddenly, Mr. Hatcher looms in the entryway. He closes the door a bit louder than necessary. It gets everyone's attention.

"Dad, it wasn't—"

"I don't even want to hear it."

"But Dad," Lyle explains, "all I was doin' was gettin' some firewood and the wind—"

"Mr. Evans tells me you cut down a tree right on top of the Scout camp." Mr. Hatcher shoots a look at his wife.

"No, no, that's not how it happened. I didn't cut it down on top of the camp, Dad."

"You're grounded for a week."

"But Dad, I—"

"Did you hear me?! One more word outta you, and it'll be two weeks."

"Okay, Dad, I know, but I'm tryin' to tell ya—"

"Two weeks, then! Now go to your room!"

Lyle slumps down the hallway.

"And take this thing with you!" Mr. Hatcher grabs the backpack off the floor as if it weighs no more than a feather and holds it out in Lyle's direction. Lyle turns back, takes the crumpled pack from his dad, and drags it down the hall into his bedroom, closing the door.

Mr. Hatcher thrusts a forefinger in the direction of his two other children. "You two. Go to your rooms. Go on!"

Linda immediately obeys.

"But Dad, I wanna listen," Steve objects. "Anyway, I—"

"To your room!" Mrs. Hatcher halts him mid-sentence.

The parents wait for the bedroom doors to close. Mr. Hatcher, six foot two and over two hundred pounds, strong as an ox and towering in the small kitchen, leans and puts his hand on the table, waiting. His wife stands ramrod-straight, sixty-one inches of fearless authority. He admires her in so many ways, and at the moment can't help notice that the pretty Mrs. Hatcher has a perfect hourglass figure.

Her words yank him back to reality. "What next?"

Mr. Hatcher's frustration floods back. "Why doesn't he ever think about the consequences?"

"Because he's ten years old?"

"I don't care if he's ten years old. He could have seriously hurt someone. You don't see any of those other Cub Scouts cutting down trees on top of the camp, do you? They're ten years old!"

"You're always telling our kids, 'Don't be a sheep, don't be a follower.' At least he gets that part right." She stifles a grin. He's not amused.

"There's gonna have to be some changes." Mr. Hatcher grimaces. "This kinda thing can't keep going on like this."

David sits on his living room couch, observing, as Dr. Metcalfe carries a brand-new, folded wheelchair through the doorway and leans it against the wall. The doctor kneels in front of David and methodically checks the flexibility and muscle response in his legs.

"David, we need to talk about where this is going."

He flexes the boy's foot. David searches the doctor's face.

"Did my mom tell you what happened at school today?"

"Yes. She did. It's something we've been expecting. Your muscles continue to grow weaker. Tell me about your exercises. Have you been good about those?"

"We never miss a day, right, Mom?" David responds, incongruously upbeat.

Mrs. Dahlke smiles.

"You've done a great job, no doubt about it." Dr. Metcalfe agrees. "I want you to keep that up, and we'll be adding a few more. Now. I need you to promise me something." Dr. Metcalfe rises. He opens the wheelchair, and pats the seat cushion into place. "Promise me you're not going to get any speeding tickets in this thing. What do you say?"

Mrs. Dahlke hurries in to help, as Dr. Metcalfe maneuvers David into the chair, swings the footrests into position, and lifts David's feet, placing them on the rests.

"Why don't you take it for a test drive? I need to talk to your mom for a minute. Okay? Be careful now, son."

David slides his hands over the wheels, as Mrs. Dahlke and Dr. Metcalfe step onto the front porch and close the door. Mrs. Dahlke stares at the sidewalk, deep in thought. Dr. Metcalfe waits, aware that she wants to say something.

"Will he ever walk again, Doctor?" she eventually asks, meeting his eyes.

He hesitates. "No, Mrs. Dahlke, he won't. Not without help."

"When I took him to Salt Lake City," she begins, tentative, "the doctors there said they'd have a cure in eight years. It's been seven, now. Have they been able to . . . ?"

"It's tough, Mrs. Dahlke. Believe me, I know. But hang in there. The research is ongoing, and you never know."

He pats her arm, and moves down off the porch.

"Dr. Metcalfe?"

He stops, turning back.

"Thanks for stopping by. And . . . thanks for bringing the wheelchair."

"No problem. I was on my way home. If you need anything at all, give me a call. Oh—Mrs. Dahlke?"

He pauses.

"I've worked with a lot of patients over the last thirty years. That boy of yours?" Dr. Metcalfe smiles kindly. "He might surprise us."

CHAPTER TWO

THE TROUBLE WITH DANCING

I have learned to use the word "impossible"
with the greatest caution.

~ WERNHER VON BRAUN

The gymnasium at Linwood Elementary is busy, as it is every Tuesday morning at ten o'clock. This is a time every child in the school anticipates with great enthusiasm. This is the day Mrs. Maxfield teaches dancing.

Mrs. Maxfield sashays into the gym with striking grace and elegance, a flamboyant, energetic woman in her mid-forties. She wears a full-bodied midi-skirt lavishly decorated with hand-painted flowers, and her jet-black hair is neatly wrapped into a French bun. As she sets her portable record player on the stage, her smile—today as every Tuesday—betrays the absolute delight she feels . . . for Mrs. Maxfield has a secret.

When she interviewed for her post as the fifth-grade teacher at Linwood Elementary, she was prepared to be persuasive. Her husband was out of work and she was desperate to be hired. But when Miss O'Donnell informed her they were searching for someone who could also teach dancing, Mrs. Maxfield's persuasiveness astonished even herself. She didn't hesitate to proclaim that *she*, Madge Maxfield, had the background and experience for the job.

For Miss O'Donnell, finding a qualified teacher who could also cover dancing was an enormous relief. What she didn't know—what brings the smile to Mrs. Maxfield's face this and every Tuesday—was that Mrs. Maxfield had never danced a step in her life.

Hired on the spot, she wasted no time ensuring she could deliver on her claims. She rushed home and rifled through *The Spokesman–Review* in search of a coupon she had noticed when she read the morning paper.

> **Learn to dance in twelve easy lessons**
> **at the Universal Dance Studio**
> **in Downtown Spokane.**
> **Twelve classes**
> **for only twenty-five dollars.**

The following Monday, she signed up at Universal and took her introductory dance lesson, and the next morning stood in front of her new students in the Linwood gymnasium, ready for her first session as a dance instructor. She fell in love with the teaching, with the dancing, and with the children. Mrs. Maxfield was hooked.

Today, hardly any of the students notice Mrs. Maxfield's entrance because they're captivated instead by Jason's attempt to conquer the peg climb. Resembling a gigantic, horseshoe-shaped cribbage board fastened to the wall, the climb has holes running up the left side, across the width and down the right; the challenge is to use the two pegs as movable hand-holds while attempting to navigate the entire route.

Jason is dangling part way up, his legs flailing as he struggles to yank out a peg, insert it in the next hole, and make his way to the top.

"Come on, Jase!" George encourages.

"He ain't gonna make it," Billy predicts. "No way."

Billy, utterly convinced neither Jason, nor anyone else in the class, can complete the peg climb, has confidently bet a pack of Red Hots on the outcome. Jason manages to move up to the next notch, eliciting yet another rallying comment from George. He hangs there for a while, but his legs aren't moving anymore. He falls to the floor, and the kids respond with screams and groans.

"I told ya." Billy says. "Nobody ever does it. It's impossible."

Lyle steps up and jumps at the pegs but he's too short to reach them. Jason and Billy make stirrups with their hands and give him a boost, and he just manages to get the pegs inserted back into their starting positions when Mrs. Maxfield interrupts. She claps her hands together sharply to get everyone's attention. Billy and Jason drop Lyle to the floor, and the three of them hurry to join the other students.

"Good afternoon, ladies and gentlemen," Mrs. Maxfield sings in her Southern Belle lilt.

"Good afternoon, Missus Maxfield," the children sing back to her in unison.

Unison, that is, with the exception of one—that one being Lyle. His full attention is on Sharon Anne, a cutie with mousey brown hair and a pretty smile.

"Now children, please line up. We have an exciting hour of dancing before us. Can you feel the energy? I can. Good posture, now, big smiles!"

As Mrs. Maxfield speaks, she demonstrates clearly and precisely what she expects from the children. At Universal Dance Studio, the instructors, whether dance experts or not, know how to act the part. She faithfully imitates what she has seen there, giving the children the full benefit of her observations. She stands with her back erect, head up, shoulders down, and chest lifted.

"Puff up like a bird," she says, and does so herself.

In fact, she does look like a dancer and the smile comes naturally as she gazes around the room, checking to see how well the children emulate her. They love her, and even Lyle would normally be trying very hard to please her, if he weren't so distracted by Sharon Anne.

Mrs. Maxfield removes the sleeve from the record that she uses for class: *Blame it on the Bossa Nova.* Lyle pays close attention as she eases the disk over the spindle and lifts the needle.

He's figured out a plan, and he's confident he's positioned himself perfectly for it. His feet are already moving in short kicks and pops, and he's vigorously shaking his hands, like he's trying to dry them. He's ready to dance . . . with Sharon Anne.

Mrs. Maxfield places the needle onto the record and the familiar choir of scratchy static warms up the speakers.

She claps out the count, "And five . . . six . . . seven-and-eight-and . . ."

The dance begins. Instantly, Sharon Anne is swept away and disappears into the throng of weaving and bobbing heads. Lyle tries to keep track of her, but it's like watching a teacup ride at an amusement park.

> *Dang it! I can't see her. Oh, wait! Here she comes. Nope, there she goes. Now she's gone. Oh, there she is! Here she comes, closer and closer and . . . dang it! Where'd she go this time? Where did she go? Oh! Yes, yes! There she is. This time for sure. Yes! Whoops! You gotta be kiddin' me! Gone again?*
>
> *Bam! Bama-rama-ding-dong! Holey smokes, I'm dancin' with her! I'm dancin' with Sharon Anne!*

He fixes his gaze on the blue barrette in Sharon Anne's hair. It plays a familiar trick on his eyes. She seems to be standing motionless, as the rest of the room swirls around them.

> *She's got those tiny hamster ears. Freckles on her nose. C'mon hands, warm up! I swear I can't hear anything. No sound. Say somethin', you dope. My heart's gonna jump right outta my chest and hit her*

square in the eye like a frog's tongue! Gross! Good gravy, focus. What would Fred Astaire say?

She smells like ivory soap and powder, she smells like a warm wind and flowers. I don't know what kinda flowers. Just some flowers that smell really, really, good type smelling flowers.

Her breath is like steam out of an iron. It's milk in the morning, warm toast with homemade strawberry jam. Her breath is like . . . it's like . . . it's like Cocoa Puffs. Yeah, that's it, Cocoa Puffs. Man-oh-man, I love chocolate!

Lyle bumps into the dancers behind him, and it snaps him out of his daydream. He's clutching Sharon Anne in a clumsy grip, almost a bear hug, and he stumbles over her feet, causing a traffic jam.

Sharon Anne tries diplomatically to extract herself, but finally has to say something to get him to release his hold.

"Do you mind?"

The music ends and she scuttles to another part of the gym, straightening her dress and hair, searching for her friends.

Eyes on fire, Lyle races toward the cinderblock wall at full speed. He takes a giant leap and smacks into the peg climb as he grabs both of the pegs in his fists.

"Got 'em!" he exclaims, only to himself.

He swings his body recklessly, inserting a peg and lifting himself up, yanking the other peg out, hitting the next hole, and lifting, again and again. He's completely focused and fully engaged in his wildly fun private party. He reaches the top, easily navigates across to the other side, and starts back down. By now, all the kids are gathering to watch.

He finishes without a miss, pops both pegs out at the same time by pushing his feet against the wall, and drops to the floor, pegs in hand. He indulges in a ridiculous victory dance while the kids go wild, screaming and shouting and dancing along with him. There's no stopping him now. He puts the pegs under his shirt, imitating Mrs. Maxfield's posture and physical stature.

He puffs up like a bird, and with his peg-breasts and best Southern Belle accent says, "Can you feel the energy? I can. Good posture, now! Big smiles!"

The other kids respond with gleeful shrieks. Sharon Anne turns away in disgust. She isn't the only one who is unimpressed.

A voice cuts through the din.

"Mis . . . terrrr . . . Haaaatcher!"

The gymnasium is instantly silent. Lyle glances around and startles to see Miss O'Donnell hovering over him, arms folded in front of her like General George Patton. Lyle has noticed she has an uncanny way of showing up at the precise times he'd prefer she did not.

"Mr. Hatcher?" she says firmly, "I have a plan for you."

Lyle stares at her, slowly lowering his left hand, causing his pointy left breast to sink to his waist.

"Are you listening to me?"

Lyle nods.

"Good! You will be running to school in the morning. The bus is off limits to you. And I don't want to see you walking, either! You will be running! Is this clear?"

"Yes, Miss O'Donnell!"

Lyle tries to extract the other peg but it's so tightly wedged against his skin, his efforts make it appear there's a wild guinea pig loose under his shirt. Miss O'Donnell winces at the sight of it. She reaches out her hand, impatiently snapping her fingers.

"Hand over those pegs, before you put somebody's eye out," she demands in a stern voice.

Lyle works the peg free, and hands it to Miss O'Donnell, who's clearly relieved to have it over with.

"And another thing," she continues. "Tomorrow you'll spend recess in the boiler room! And right now, two laps around the playground!"

Lyle doesn't move a muscle.

"Now!"

He jumps and bolts out the door.

Down the hall in the fourth-grade classroom, Mrs. Stewart, familiar to the students as an occasional substitute-teacher, sorts through neatly organized stacks of papers on Mrs. McGuire's desk. Tonight, she'll write to her husband at his post in Vietnam, and let him know of her good fortune in landing a temporary teaching job. But right now she is preoccupied as she prepares to teach on very short notice.

Mrs. Stewart has taught Mrs. McGuire's class before, and she particularly enjoys it, though she's aware she has big shoes to fill with this job. She knows how much the children adore Mrs. McGuire—not only the fourth-graders, but all of the students in the school.

The only other person in the room with Mrs. Stewart is David Dahlke, sitting in his new wheelchair near the window. An opened book lies on his work tray, and David contemplates a full-color rendition of the solar system while he draws his own version on a sheet of blue-lined notebook paper. He stops working for a moment to listen to the noises drifting down the hall—children laughing and playing in the gym.

"Sounds like they're having fun," he comments to Mrs. Stewart.

"You may wheel down there and watch, if you want to," she offers.

"No, it's okay, Mrs. Stewart. I really want to finish this."

David returns to his drawing and then interrupts himself again. "Mrs. Stewart?"

"Mmm?"

"I'm really glad we have you for a teacher when Mrs. McGuire's not here."

"Why, thank you, David! So sweet of you to say. I'm sorry she's gone today, I know you're all awfully fond of her. She's not feeling well. Something's going around, I guess. We'll make her a card this afternoon, how would that be?"

David nods.

"Have you had the flu yet this year, David?"

He shakes his head.

"No, I don't usually get sick like that."

He turns to the window and spots Lyle on the perimeter of the playground, running, with several dogs chasing behind him. Lyle stops, picks up a pinecone, and throws it straight up in the air. The dogs bark wildly and dart in circles, ready to pounce on it the moment it lands. Lyle gazes upward, and lets the pinecone fall directly toward his face. At the very last second he moves out of the way, and zooms off again, dogs in hot pursuit.

David cranes forward to keep Lyle in sight . . . and loses him as he and the dogs round the corner of the building. He angles his wheelchair to see if Mrs. Stewart witnessed this peculiar bit of theatrics. She did not. Her attention is on the children flooding back into the room, energized from their dancing, faces flushed.

Moments later, Lyle charges in. The exertion doesn't seem to have slowed him down. Mrs. Stewart intercepts him before he gets far.

"Lyle, you have a new desk. I've got you up here, in the front row."

"Did I do something wrong, Mrs. Stewart?"

"Please collect your things and bring them with you."

Lyle gathers up everything in his desk, wanting to be sure he only has to make one trip. One is more than enough, when you're suddenly the center of this type of attention. As Mrs. Stewart leads him to the front of the classroom, he turns his head toward the windows and squints at the playground, pretending there's something intriguing out there, hoping everyone will wonder.

Tile, tile, tile. Step on a crack, break your mother's back. Black shoe scuff. Mom always says, "Pull your shoulders back and walk like a king. People will think you're important."

I'm thinkin' I hate the front row. The front row is for teacher's pets, and for kids who need glasses, and for cheaters . . . or kids with a problem. Does Mrs. Stewart think I cheat?

The teacher helps him get situated in his new location, next to David. Lyle adjusts the desk to make it perfectly square with the tiles. He arranges his things and takes inventory. Pencils are sharpened and sit small to tall.

"We'll pick up right where Mrs. McGuire left off. Page twenty-seven in your history books, please," Mrs. Stewart announces to the class.

"Dang it. I forgot mine," Lyle blurts out, actually surprised he can't find it.

Mrs. Stewart steps over to David's desk and says quietly, "David, would you mind sharing your book with Lyle today?"

David shakes his head, and Lyle scoots his desk closer.

Satisfied the issue has been resolved, Mrs. Stewart continues with her lesson plan. She writes a question on the chalkboard in large block letters, all capitals.

She presses too hard on the chalk and makes a screechy noise. Why does she do that? Mrs. McGuire never makes that noise when she writes on the board. Those letters are way too up-and-downie. Her fingernails are all chewed. I wonder if she knows what she's doin'.

Lyle starts to feel anxious. Mrs. Stewart moves away from the chalkboard, her question completed:

WHO INVENTED THE VACCINE FOR POLIO?

She turns back to the class and says, "Please read, beginning on page twenty-seven, and quietly raise your hand when you know the answer."

Lyle's apprehension grows. The question on the chalkboard looms, rolling itself into the room, taking over the space, demanding to be answered. Lyle's eyes are intently fixed on David's book, but he can't concentrate. The letters will not form into words. His eyes feel lazy.

> *Stale air in here, rose perfume and oatmeal stinkers. Tap-tap of pencils, snarfin' sounds, and the pages shooshin' when they turn. I can smell tunafish sandwiches.*

Hands pop up all around the room as the faster readers find the answer. Mrs. Stewart waits for everyone before she continues.

> *Michael breathes too loud. He always sounds that way. Why does he leave his crayons on his desk like that? They're gonna roll off. Nerdling, put 'em away! You're not colorin' anything! I had special crayon holders in the second grade with the colors written on 'em in big letters 'cause I'm colorblind. That was the year Suzy wet her pants. Nobody ever forgets that.*

David leans over to Lyle and whispers helpfully, "Are you done yet?"

David's words, even with his gentle delivery, strike Lyle's ears like an accusation from a judge in a big black robe. He thinks of *Perry Mason*, not one of his favorite shows.

"No, I'm not done!"

"Do you need some help?" David asks.

Irritated, Lyle shakes his head and makes another effort to read. He can make out the first word, "the", and then his mind drifts back to the Suzy incident.

> *It sounded like spilled milk at the dinner table, runnin' to the center where the big crack is, drippin' down and puddlin' on the floor. It was an awful lot once she started and she kept goin' and goin'. Good gravy, Suzy . . . you're makin' us feel weird . . . can you just clench?!*

"Are you having a problem with it?" David inquires politely.

"I don't have a problem. What's your problem?"

"What do you mean, what's my problem? Are you talking about—?"

"I mean, what's your problem?!"

"Shhh. You're going to get us in trouble. We're supposed to be reading."

"Readin'? Hey, I can read. I have a focusing problem. Not a stupid problem. Focusing."

Mrs. Stewart glances over at them and shakes her head.

"That's not what I meant," David tries to explain, "and now you got us in trouble."

"Did not."

"You did."

"Did not."

"Yes, you did."

"Not!"

David squirms in his wheelchair.

"Shhh. Okay. You didn't. Please be quiet."

"You be quiet."

"Excuse me, Mrs. Stewart?" David says quietly.

"Yes, David?"

> *Oh, great! That's just great! Here we go again!*

"Are you squealin'?" Lyle whispers at him, worried.

David ignores him.

"May I go to the restroom, please, Mrs. Stewart?"

"Of course. Lyle, would you go with him?"

Lyle sits, staring after David as he wheels himself away from his desk.

Wow, he's not a squealer!

"Lyle, did you hear me? Go with him, please!"

David is already at the door. Lyle springs to his feet and catches up with him.

Outside the classroom with the door closed behind them, Lyle scans for opportunities—so much freedom, so many possibilities—until he realizes there's nothing here but an empty hallway with no one in it, and his attention shifts back to the only thing of interest: David's wheelchair.

"Hey, how fast d'ya think this'll go? Like maybe twenty miles an hour?"

"It's not for racing," David replies, patient and matter-of-fact.

"I know. I know that! But what's the fastest you've ever gone? I mean if you're really goin' fast, like super-fast, how would you stop it?"

"It has brakes, right here." David points out the handles, situated above each wheel. "But it's not for racing."

Lyle jogs backwards up ahead, facing David, already filled with his own ideas, an enormous grin on his face.

CHAPTER THREE

THE FEELING

True friendship is a plant of slow growth.

~ GEORGE WASHINGTON

*T*a-tap. *Ta-tap.* The distinct echo of high heels drifts from down the hall and around the corner, breaking into Lyle's reverie.

"Oh no!" he exclaims.

"What?" David worries, mainly because of the look on Lyle's face.

Lyle yanks open the bathroom door, and whispers urgently, "Get in there. Fast!"

Again they hear the shoes, closer this time. *Ta-tap, ta-tap.*

They hustle into the room, and Lyle drops to the floor. He scopes out the perimeter from under the door, watching as a pair of high heels passes by. Abruptly, he jumps up, startling David.

"Duke!" he shouts into the corner of the room.

"Duke . . ." The tiled wall responds.

Obviously, he's done this before.

"Puke!" he shouts.

"Puke," echoes the wall.

He throws his voice into the corner, with staccato force, singing his improvised lyrics to the popular tune, *Duke of Earl.*

"Puke-puke-puke, puke of hurl, puke-puke, puke of—"

David glances around the room, shifting nervously, as though he expects Miss O'Donnell to beam herself into the urinal stall.

"Don't worry. She's not gonna come in here. Miss O'Donnell. Ughh!"

"I like her. I think she's nice."

"Why don't you just marry her then?"

David rolls his eyes.

"That's what I thought," Lyle grimaces.

David chooses to ignore the comment.

"Hey, I was just wonderin', how come you were walkin' at the beginning of school and now you're in a wheelchair?"

"I have muscular dystrophy."

"So you can't walk anymore?"

"I can still walk, but I have to have help with it."

"What's gonna happen?"

"Nothing. I just have to do my exercises every day. Hey," David says, intentionally changing the subject, "I saw you running out there on the playground during dance class."

"Oh, that. It's not what everybody thinks. I'm not in trouble or anything."

"You're not?"

"Heck, no. See, I got this thing. It's kind of a problem. My brother calls it *the feeling*."

"Okay, well, I was wondering about it. I mean what's it like?"

Lyle thinks for a moment.

"You know those little drummers? The kind you wind up?"

"Yeah," David says. "I have two exactly like that at home. They're dogs."

Lyle stops short. "Are you sure they're not bears? I mean, I've seen wind-up bears but I've never seen wind-up dogs. You sure they're not bears? 'Cause if—"

"They're dogs," David insists.

"Okay, fine then. You know when you wind 'em up, and you wind 'em, and you wind 'em, and you wind 'em?"

Lyle demonstrates the winding with quick flicks of his wrist.

"And then, when you let 'em go, they go like this?"

He moves his arms in a slow jerky robotic style, getting faster and faster until he works himself into an insane seizure of frantic, flailing air-drumming. When he stops, David stares at him in disbelief.

"That's what it's like? Are you kidding me?"

Lyle widens his eyes and stares directly into David's pupils.

"Nope, I'm not kidding. That's exactly what it's like."

David shakes his head. "How could it be like that? It doesn't look anything like that when you're doing it."

"Doin' what?"

"Running," David replies, astonished that Lyle has already forgotten what they're talking about.

"Running?" Lyle asks with surprise. "I thought you were talkin' about *the feeling*. You don't know what running's like? Haven't you ever run before?"

"Not really. I mean not like you do. I always walked kind of funny, you know, because of the muscular dystrophy. You run more than anybody I've ever seen."

"Oh, anybody can do that."

"Even me?"

"Oh yeah, you could do it! Definitely!"

David suddenly remembers why he needed to come to the restroom in the first place, and squirms.

"Would you please hand me the tube? In the green thing?"

Lyle checks the back of the wheelchair and locates a green fly-rod sleeve. Curious, he slides it out, opens one end and peers inside. He removes a long neoprene tube, and brandishes it overhead, like a swordsman testing a new blade. As he swings the hose, the motion creates a distinctive sound and pitch, feeding a sense of power and excitement in him. He swings it faster and faster, trying to force the sound even higher.

Shwoop. Shwoop! Shwoop!

"Don't move," he commands David. "I promise I won't hit you."

David, immediately nervous, sits with his back erect, completely immobile.

"Stop!" he says stiffly, moving only his lips. "I need that!"

Lyle misinterprets the calmness of his response as encouragement. He whirls the hose even harder.

Shleeep, shleeep, shleeep, shleeep!

Now it's moving so fast it's almost invisible and it sounds like a dangerous power tool on the loose.

"Stop it! Please!" David begs.

Lyle stops, but instead of handing it over, he puts it to his lips and sings into it, half megaphone, half trumpet.

"*Puke-puke-puke, puke of hurl—*"

"Stop it. Please give it to me!" David insists.

"Sorry. I was just havin' fun. What's it for, anyway?"

Lyle holds the tube out to David, an apology on his face.

"It's my urinal tube. Give me a sec, okay?"

David takes the tube from him and proceeds to use it for its intended purpose. As comprehension dawns, Lyle puckers. He spits and wipes his mouth on his sleeve, making a face as if he bit into a raw lemon.

David diplomatically changes the subject.

"Hey, I was talking to Mrs. Stewart, the substitute teacher, this morning while you guys were dancing in the gym."

"Yeah?"

"Yeah, she's nice."

"I like Mrs. McGuire better. She's actually my favorite teacher . . . ever," Lyle replies wistfully.

"Me, too," David agrees.

Lyle opens the door to the hallway and holds it while David wheels himself through.

"She's pretty, too," Lyle reflects.

David and Lyle are certainly not alone in their feelings regarding Mrs. McGuire. She *is* a very pretty woman, and has a bright smile she wears often, but those are merely hints of a deeper attractiveness, an almost magical quality, that makes children want to be close to her. If she is on the playground during recess, a crowd of kids always swarms her.

"I wonder when she'll be back," Lyle ponders.

"She's sick."

"Yeah, I know. What's she got?"

Lyle lets the door swing closed. The boys move slowly down the hallway in the direction of the classroom, in no particular hurry to get there.

"I don't know what she has," David tells him. "But . . . I know she's not going to make it."

"Not gonna make it to what?" Lyle asks, confused.

"Oh," David says, turning his face to Lyle, with a sudden expression of sadness. "What I meant was . . . umm, she's going to die."

A peculiar sensation stabs Lyle, a dull prickly vibration. It travels through his entire body, from his scalp to the bottoms of his feet, leaving an unpleasant and sickly feeling in his chest area. A frown clouds his face.

"What . . . are you . . . *talkin'* about?!" Lyle challenges David angrily. "That's the craziest thing I ever heard. Nobody can tell that. You don't know! Anyway, who told you that? The doctor?" Lyle pauses for a quick breath. "Did the doctor tell you that? What's his name? I wanna call him, right now!"

"It wasn't a doctor." David says, surprised at Lyle's outburst.

"Okay, then," Lyle says.

David isn't certain he should share how it is he knows about Mrs. McGuire. He thinks about it and hesitates, but decides it's the right thing to do.

"God told me," he says simply.

Lyle is stunned. He's never had to take on God before.

"Wait a minute. God told you?"

David nods, slowly.

"Mr. McGuire called me last night, and told me she was in the hospital. And he asked me to pray for her."

"Why would he call *you*?"

"I don't know."

The answer pacifies Lyle, easing his anxiety about David's dire proclamation.

"People call me, too," he tells David. "To find lost stuff in the woods, 'cause I can see everything. I found two watches, a wallet with seventy-eight dollars—seventy-eight, can you believe it? And I found earrings, and keys, and money, and I even found a diamond ring once. Oh no, wait a minute. I didn't find the wallet with seventy-eight dollars in it. Actually, my brother, Steve, found that . . . umm . . ."

Lyle pauses, deep in concentration. David waits patiently. Lyle blurts out, "But I *was* the one that pushed him into the bushes where he found it, so . . ."

David bursts out laughing. Lyle laughs too, choosing to believe the laughter is David's admission he's mistaken about Mrs. McGuire.

In the classroom, Lyle plops into his seat next to David. The two of them go back to reading from the history book, but neither is thinking about history. David considers telling Lyle the rest of it—about how people call him to pray for them because they believe he has a "special relationship with God."

Doris Greer was the first to call, a few years back, when she learned she was dying of cancer. She requested David pray for her, sharing that she desperately wanted to live long enough to raise her two boys. David went into his room and turned out the lights. Later that night, he assured his mother that Mrs. Greer was going to be fine.

He wonders what Lyle would say if he told him about that. David clearly remembers the surprise on his mother's face, even if she did try to hide it, when at the age of four he explained to her that God talked to him. He glances over at Lyle, who is wiggling in his chair.

Mrs. Stewart notices. "Lyle? Please try to sit still," she warns, though her tone is gentle.

Lyle tries, but he can't stop thinking about what David said. He wants to, but he can't.

> *What did he say about Mrs. McGuire? What were his exact words? "I don't know what she has. But I know she's not going to make it."*

Lyle shakes his head, trying to force the thought to leave him alone.

> *That was just crazy! People can't say stuff like that. He doesn't know. Nobody can know that! Not even doctors.*

Lyle sneaks a look at David, who is now deeply engrossed in the history book. Lyle squirms again, and the words he doesn't want to hear—or even think—come to mind despite his efforts to hold them down.

> *"God told me." Ergghhhh! Well even if God did tell him, there's still gotta be a way to stop it!*

"Dang it!" Lyle blurts out, thumping his fist on his desk.

"Lyle!" Mrs. Stewart scolds in a forced whisper. "I warned you once."

"I'm sorry, Mrs. Stewart."

"Do you need something?"

"No, thank you. I'm sorry, Mrs. Stewart."

Lyle forces himself to hold very still in his chair, but he can't keep his mind from racing.

A fter school, Lyle beelines for home. There are questions to be answered. Big questions!

At the crosswalk, a happy-looking yellow lab, panting with his tongue hanging out, sits across the street next to the fire hydrant, waiting patiently.

Lyle lets out a high-pitched whistle, giving the dog permission to bound across the street and jump on him. He showers Dino with a good scratching, not even slowing down to do it.

"Hey, boy. C'mon!"

When they reach the Hatcher house, they charge across the yard, leap onto the porch and burst through the door into the kitchen. Lyle's mom juggles the last-minute dinner preparations. She doesn't miss a beat.

"Hey! Slow down and put the dog back outside. I don't like him begging. And then go wash your hands and help your brother set the table." She sips from a spoon to taste-test the sauce she's preparing.

"Mom, do you believe in God?" Lyle dives in.

Mrs. Hatcher chokes on the sauce, spilling some on the stove's burner where it sizzles as she spins to face him.

"Lyle, what have you done?!"

"Nothin', Mom. That's not what I meant. I just need to know 'cause this kid at school says God talks to him! I'm not makin' this up. He really said that!"

Relieved, she regains her composure and snaps back to her tasks.

"Well, honey, then I think you should ask your friend at school more about it. How would I know if God talks to him or not? I can tell you one thing I do know. It's time for dinner, and I'm saying it for the last time. Wash your hands and help your brother set the table!"

"But Mom—"

Mr. Hatcher's voice booms out from the next room.

"Lyle! You heard your mother!"

Lyle shoots from the kitchen, question unanswered.

CHAPTER FOUR

THE WEASEL

*Don't think to hunt two hares
with just one dog.*

~ Benjamin Franklin

Lyle wakes up feeling out of sorts. It's not clear to him what he's troubled about, though he knows he didn't sleep well. He plods quietly into the kitchen, thinking no one else will be up, but Mrs. Hatcher is at the kitchen table, studying.

"Hi, Mom."

She reaches out and gives him a hug, still engrossed in her studies. Lyle drops into a chair and watches her, knowing better than to interrupt. Early morning is her private study time, and she has often made it clear that without it she will never earn her teacher's certification.

Footsteps sound in the hall, and Mrs. Hatcher tilts up her gaze with a smile. Typically, by this time of the morning, Mr. Hatcher has been at work for several hours, milk truck loaded, delivering his route, but not this week. Every six weeks he has five days off, the result of his six-day work week. More often than not, he works these days for the extra money, but today he shuffles into the room to enjoy the luxuries of sitting at the breakfast table and reading the paper.

In no time, the kitchen buzzes with morning activities, as Mrs. Hatcher deftly manages the challenge of getting the children off to school.

"Mom?" Linda asks. "Can you give me a ride to the leadership conference after school tomorrow? I've been nominated for treasurer."

"I'll pick you up at three." Mrs. Hatcher says, drawing Linda close. "Good job, I'm so proud of you."

This bit of extra attention to Linda does not go unnoticed by Steve. "I need a ride to Jo Albi Stadium on Saturday. I'm gonna win the punt pass and kick again this year!" he proclaims with confidence.

Mr. Hatcher delivers Steve a stern gaze. "Son, we've talked about this before. You shouldn't get so cocky. Practice and hard work. That's the ticket, and you know it."

"Okay, Dad."

Lyle digs in his pocket and comes up with a brand-new, yellow merit badge. He holds it out proudly.

"Got my survival badge. What d'ya think of that?"

Linda pats Lyle's flattop haircut, as if he's a good luck totem of some sort.

"G'bye Mom, 'bye, Dad," she says, as she gathers her things and slips out the door.

"I thought you got kicked outta the Cub Scouts," Steve challenges Lyle, trying to start something.

Mrs. Hatcher quickly interjects. "Let's not even get into that. Steve, go to your room and get your shoes on. You're going to be late."

Steve moves to do as he's told, but Lyle stops him.

"For your information," he tells Steve, "I didn't get kicked out. I'm just takin' a break. I'm kinda busy with other stuff right now."

"Yeah? Like what?" Steve grills. "Sharon Anne?" Steve packs his voice with as much ridicule as his eight-year-old imagination can muster. He plugs his nose when he says her name, for extra effect.

Lyle can't let it go. He grabs Steve around the neck and administers a noogie.

"Ow, Lyle!" Steve whines, loudly. "Ow, ow, ow, ouch!"

"That's enough!" their dad snaps. "And by the way, Lyle, if we get one more report from Miss O'Donnell about trouble at school, you can forget about any fishing trips to Pend Oreille!"

"Dad! I don't mean to do it."

"Yeah," says Steve, his voice spooky. "It's *the feeling*."

Steve apes an exaggerated version of a frustrated Lyle, wrenching his face up like a bulldog, stiffening his neck and face muscles, and wildly flexing his fingers.

"Nice, Mr. Funny Pants," Mrs. Hatcher observes dryly.

Steve embellishes his imitation even further. She suppresses her laugh.

"Now that's enough of that! I know what it's like. I have the same thing only I get it in my feet." She points a slender finger at Lyle. "But it doesn't mean I go around stomping on people."

"That's funny, Mom," Lyle grins.

Steve darts to his bedroom and back, shoes on his feet, says his goodbyes and wanders out the door. The television in the living room is on, and Mrs. Hatcher warms up for her daily exercises with *The Jack LaLanne Show*, stretching while listening to the fast-paced, high-energy coaching.

Everyone knows better than to mess with Mom's "out of the house by eight o'clock" routine. Lyle is the exception to her rule. He stays, mesmerized by Mr. LaLanne's voice, and watches right along with her, up to the very last minute. At 8:15 sharp, he'll dart out the door, arriving at school seconds before the final bell rings.

Jack LaLanne captivates and motivates people merely with the sound of his voice, as millions of women across the country—

at this moment foregoing coffee and donuts for morning exercise—can attest. But this isn't why Lyle loves his show.

Lyle's fascination stems from the stories he's heard about Mr. LaLanne, such as his swim across the Golden Gate channel while towing a 2,500-pound cabin cruiser, and another from Alcatraz Island to Fisherman's Wharf he accomplished while handcuffed. In Lyle's eyes, these are feats that would challenge even the characters in his favorite comic books.

More importantly, Lyle feels a strange kinship with Mr. LaLanne, possibly because he promotes many of the same lifestyle choices Lyle is familiar with through his mom's rules: no sugar, lots of exercise, regular sleep, and healthy food.

If this was just some boring old guy crusading against junk food, Lyle would be down the street faster than you could say "Twinkie." But in Lyle's mind, Jack LaLanne is a true-life hero: a living, breathing example of How Anything Is Possible. As Lyle listens, he thinks of what happened yesterday in school.

"If you want a miracle, you have to have the intestinal fortitude and willpower to do the right thing. But you have to do it. I promise if you will just dedicate a few minutes a day, you will get results. A few minutes. That's all I ask.

"And please, please remember, if you're going to improve yourself there's only one time that's important. You know when that is? It's not Christmas. It's not New Year's. It's NOW! N-O-W! Are you with me? All right.

"And I want you to remember this, too. When you set a goal for yourself, get that picture in your mind and focus on it every single day when you get up and every night when you go to sleep. You let your mind and your body know that's the picture you want for

yourself. That's what you want to be able to do.
That's who you are going to become."

"Lyle, I'm not writing a note," Mrs. Hatcher prods, focusing on her leg-lifts. "Inhale . . . exhale . . . inhale . . . exhale."

"Get going!" Mr. Hatcher orders from the kitchen.

Lyle snatches his books and the grocery bag containing his rather large lunch, and sprints out the door.

"Everyone pay attention, now. I have some ve important news!" Mrs. Stewart announces, p to view the pond of faces staring back at her.

When they're all listening, she moves throu passing out sheets of paper, laying one on eac

"All right, then. Once again, it's the ti begin our Science Fair projects."

A unanimous buzz of favorable through the class.

"Please read this care be aware of the such as . . . n

"Wha
hand

their substitute teacher. But she instantly regretted bringing up the subject of rule number five, and she has no intention of allowing a full-on debate about burnable versus combustible. Those are not the images she wants in their heads when choosing a science project.

"Now, you can do your project alone, or you can get together with a friend," she continues. "Or it's just fine to have a family member help you. But it has to be finished by ＿rent Night, because we'll be putting all the projects on ＿y in the gym for the parents and other students to see."

＿es around the room to make sure everyone is ＿e she goes on.

＿falls on the second Wednesday of November ＿vember tenth. So be sure to circle the date ＿ home. It's eight weeks away. Fifty-six ＿xact."

＿ation in the top lefthand ＿ly beneath where she

'11

explanation he swings around in his chair, stretches over, and triumphantly slaps his paper down on David's desk with a self-satisfied grin, as though it contains the solution to world peace.

"What d'ya think?" Lyle demands in a whisper.

David gazes down at the paper. It's blank. He glances up at Lyle, perplexed.

"Oh, sorry," Lyle says, reaching out and flipping the paper.

On the opposite side is a drawing of a stick figure riding in a wheelchair, with a second figure riding on the back. It's a fairly good rendering of the chair, but there's something not quite right about it. For one thing, some unidentifiable parts have been added under the seat area.

"Okay," Lyle says. "I've been thinkin' about how fast your wheelchair goes, and well, I figure if we put a bigger sprocket on it . . ." Lyle's voice trails off, and he waits, expectant.

David studies the picture, then gives Lyle a puzzled stare.

"For the . . . Science Fair!" Lyle exclaims, dismayed that David isn't tuned into his brilliant plan.

"That'd be great," David replies, nodding respectfully. "But me and my brother are stuffing a weasel."

"Stuffin' a weasel! Are you kiddin' me? That is crazy. Where did you get a weasel? I've never even seen one in the wild. Do you actually have a weasel?"

"Yes, we do have one," David assures him.

"Are you sure you don't want me to help you? I will, you know."

"No! Thanks, though. My brother's helping me," David replies, ever polite.

"I know, I know that, but what I mean is, I'm really good with animals. Even the wild ones."

"The weasel's already dead. He's in the freezer right now. My brother Dennis froze him last week. He does taxidermy."

"You are so lucky," Lyle murmurs, with genuine envy.

It takes Lyle a few minutes to recover. He was certain David would want to do a project with him, and his disappointment is greatly intensified by this surprising news about a weasel.

He gathers his confidence and saunters down the center aisle, canvassing the classroom in search of a different accomplice. It appears everyone has already made their choices. Then he spots Paul, alone at his desk. He wanders over, knowing better than to seem too eager.

"Hey, Paul. Can you believe it? David's gonna stuff a weasel!"

"Whoa, totally wicked!"

"You wanna do a project with me?" Lyle inquires casually.

Paul doesn't even glance up from his reading.

"Nope. My dad's helpin' me. We're doin' electromagnets."

"Electromagnets? Dang it!" Lyle mutters.

Greg is alone and appears to be unoccupied, so Lyle squeezes through a group of kids to get over to the next row of desks.

"Excuse me, 'scuse me. Hey, Greg, you wanna—"

"My old man said I can't ever do another one with ya. Never. Ever. That's what he said."

"Are you kiddin'? You mean 'cause of last year? That wasn't my fault!"

"It was a perfectly good volcano 'til you stuffed all your leftover fireworks in there," Greg reminds him.

"Those were Piccolo Petes, Greg. You were the one who said to put 'em in. And anyway, what good is a volcano if it doesn't erupt? I mean, they're s'posed to do that. It's why they call it a Vol-can-ic E-rup-tion." He enunciates clearly, for emphasis.

"What I said was, 'Let's put *one* in,'" Greg corrects him, holding up his index finger. "One."

"Remember Mr. Merrick?" Johnny chimes in from over in the next row of desks. "His eyebrows got torched. Boy, did he go ape. What a riot!"

"Hey, Johnny, did you hear about the weasel?" Lyle aims to boost his credibility by riding on David's popularity, connecting the weasel to his own search for a partner.

Johnny shakes his head.

"David's stuffin' it for his science project, and I'm lookin' for somebody to—"

"I got Doug helpin' me," Johnny interrupts him. "We're meltin' a nail in soda pop."

"Dang it," Lyle grumbles, "Everybody's stealin' my ideas!"

"I think we got a pretty good chance of winnin' this year," Johnny speculates.

"Sure," Paul scoffs, "now that Darin's goin' to St. Thomas More."

"Darin only won 'cause his dad works at Hollister-Stier. He had connections," Derek informs them with authority.

"No kiddin'," Johnny adds. "He came up with a lot of way cool stuff."

"My dad always says it's not who you know, it's what you know," Paul explains in a wise voice. "Uh, something like that."

"Yeah, if you don't got connections, you don't got . . . nothin'," Derek concurs.

"Connections," Lyle says nodding. "That's right."

> *Connections? I don't have any of those! Dad works at the dairy. It's not like I can make cottage cheese for a science project!*

Lyle decides a better use of this time might be to strike up something with Sharon Anne. He roams past her desk, pretending to be cool and aloof. Her Pee Chee folder is covered with an elaborate display of noodlings and doodlings. He steals a quick glance out of the corner of his eye, hoping she'll notice him. She doesn't. She's busy talking with Francine. Lyle definitely does not want Francine to notice him. He's sure she doesn't like him, and anyway, the two seem deep in discussion about their science project. He listens, pretending not to.

"He was so, sooo dreamy," Francine observes.

"I know," Sharon Anne answers in a throaty whisper. "I really, really wish he hadn't transferred to St. Thomas More."

Lyle zeroes in on Sharon Anne's folder. Amid a lot of decorative swirly-girly stuff, right smack in the middle of it all, is a big heart with an arrow through it. Neatly printed in the center, in heavy letters, drawn and redrawn, wearing through the cardboard, are the words, "Sharon Anne loves Darin."

The recess bell interrupts, and Mrs. Stewart quickly takes charge again.

"Class! Those of you who have decided on partners and projects need to write them down and turn them in by the end of the day. The rest of you only have 'til Monday. Now, please put your books away and clean up around your desks before you leave."

Mrs. Stewart approaches Lyle, who's busily organizing all of his papers and books. He likes his desk to be neat.

"Did you find someone to work with, Lyle?" she inquires.

"No. Not yet."

Mrs. Stewart eyes the back of the room where Melvin Schmeck sits alone, perfectly content to be working by himself. His desk is already littered with sketches and scale drawings of a volcano, and he studiously checks and rechecks his angles and measurements with a professional-looking transparent protractor.

Mrs. Stewart calls out to him. "Melvin, have you decided on a project yet?"

Melvin calls back in a voice too high-pitched to tolerate for more than a sentence or two.

"Yes, Mount Vesuvius. The destruction of Pompeii. It'll be glorious!"

Melvin pushes his glasses back up on his nose and wipes the spit from his desk with his sleeve. He salivates when he says words like "Vesuvius" or "Pompeii."

"Melvin, that sounds fascinating. Don't you think so, Lyle?"

"Um, that's okay. I did a volcano last year."

Mrs. Stewart smiles privately.

Lyle hurries off in the direction of the exit, nothing on his mind now except the thought of joining in the fun he can already hear coming from out on the playground—and perhaps the possibility of catching another glimpse of Sharon Anne.

"Where are you going?" Mrs. Stewart inquires.

He glances at her over his shoulder. Where else would he be going? It's recess.

"You're headed to see Mr. Merrick, are you not?"

Lyle comes to a full stop.

"Did you forget what Miss O'Donnell told you yesterday?"

"Oh, yeah," Lyle nods, dejected. "I forgot."

He changes course, and heads for his punishment with Mr. Merrick. And even though he doesn't actually blame Mrs. Stewart, as he steps outside into the warm sun, he suddenly misses Mrs. McGuire.

CHAPTER FIVE

TESTING EVERYTHING

Question with boldness, even the existence of God;
because if there be one, He must more approve
of the homage of reason, than that of blindfolded fear.

~ THOMAS JEFFERSON

Mr. Merrick sees Lyle coming, and his eyes brace ever so slightly for the onslaught. Mr. Merrick may be the janitor, but the life-lessons he offers rival those of the best teachers at Linwood. And Lyle's penchant for getting in trouble has made him into Mr. Merrick's star pupil.

Growing up in the Great Depression prepared Mr. Merrick for most anything, and every hard-earned dime shows on his face. His has been a life of hard physical labor, from ranch work throughout Idaho and Montana to a lengthy stint with the Burlington Northern Railroad. "There's no free lunch," he's fond of saying, with a shake of his head to drive the point home. A tough life has produced a gentle philosophy, however, and Lyle doesn't *really* mind punishments in the boiler room, since it's an excuse to spend time with this man.

As Lyle runs up, Mr. Merrick scarcely moves other than to take the pipe from his mouth to say, "There's a box in there waitin' for ya."

Lyle doesn't hesitate, tromping straight to the boiler room. Before his eyes can adjust to the dim light, he nearly trips over a large box of dirty erasers. He sniffs the air.

It's warm in here like Jim Reeves and bluegrass music. It's always cold outside after bein' in here. Bomb shelter! Lock the door, no teachers allowed! Jiggling, jangling key-chains warn you when they're comin'.

Giant club wrenches and bars of Lava soap and the furnace hum-m-m-m-ming along. Coffee in a thermos, a damp mop, and stinky chemicals. This one time, me and my brother mixed all the chemicals we could find in the toilet and the fumes made us really dizzy. My mom was so upset she started to cry. Sorry, Mom, I would never hurt your feelings. Never!

Smells like a factory and a gas station all mixed together. Rubber hoses, and clove gum, and big hands with dill pickle fingers and hair with way too much butch wax. And tobacco—it smells really good in the pouch, kinda sorta okay in the pipe and terrible in the garbage. It smells safe in here. This is a man-place.

Lyle heads straight for the sink and drinks out of the faucet by filling his palm with water and slurping it up. Mr. Merrick hears the water running and yells at him.

"Use a cup!"

Lyle wipes his face with his hands and shakes them dry. "That's okay! I'm done."

Outside, Mr. Merrick discreetly eyes Mrs. Maxfield, who approaches the boiler room on her way to playground duty. She arrives within earshot.

"Mornin', Mrs. Maxfield. Or should I say, Ginger Rogers?" His voice is friendly, with a pleasant edge of teasing thrown in.

She responds to this harmless flirtation by letting her normally slight accent drift farther South.

"Why, that's ever so sweet of you. And to loan me your hi-fi for my dancin' classes, as well. I'm sure I've mentioned it before, but just in case, let me say thank you so kindly, Mr. Merrick."

"Another one of your masterpieces?" he asks, admiring her dress.

With a dramatic flourish, Mrs. Maxfield fans out the folds of her skirt to reveal hand-painted birds and flowers.

"Why, yes. Yes, it is! They're lilacs. Bless Miss O'Donnell's heart, but I think it's just hateful we aren't allowed to display our paintings in the school!" She caresses the word "hateful" to make it sound almost complimentary. "Why, art is the very essence of individuality! So I just painted this skirt last week, and next week, well—"

"Well," Mr. Merrick interrupts, "DOD Almighty might have stopped you from hangin' your paintings, but she can't very well stop you from gettin' dressed, now, can she?" He laughs, delighted to share a bit of rebellion, and Mrs. Maxfield blushes.

"You absolutely must forgive me. I should learn to keep my mouth shut," the dance teacher says, genuinely contrite.

He smiles warmly, showing support and absolution. Mrs. Maxfield tenders a smile of her own, and moves away in her typical stylish manner, just missing Lyle as he trudges from the boiler room lugging the box of erasers behind him.

Mr. Merrick pops a Sen-Sen into his mouth and shakes a few into Lyle's outstretched palm as though he's done it a hundred times before, which he has.

"Mr. Merrick, can I ask you a question?"

"Fire away."

"What happened to your ear?"

Mr. Merrick tugs on his right ear. The earlobe is missing and the ear itself is like a wrinkled potato chip.

"I was born with it like this."

"Can you hear out of it?"

"Yep."

"Can I touch it?"

"No! It's just an ear. So what're ya in for today, Sparky?" Mr. Merrick asks, moving things along.

"Dancin'," Lyle replies, staring at Mr. Merrick's ear.

"Yeah, I heard all about ya doin' the hootchie-kootchie with the climbin' pegs."

"It doesn't matter. I get in trouble for everything, anyway. Even stuff I don't do."

"Maybe it makes up for the times ya don't get caught. Ya spend way too much time in here. And ya got nobody to blame but yourself!"

Mr. Merrick picks up two erasers and plops them in Lyle's hands. "Here ya go, dancer-boy. Why don't ya hootchie-kootchie with these for a while?" he smacks the erasers together.

Lyle laughs, shutting his eyes against the cloud of dust. He attacks the job aggressively, but after only a few minutes, he stops.

"Mr. Merrick? Can I ask you another question?"

Mr. Merrick raises his eyebrows. "Is it about my ear?"

"No. But it is kinda weird, though," Lyle qualifies.

The janitor takes a couple puffs on his pipe, observing Lyle out of the corner of his eye. Lyle appears to be thinking.

"I'm waiting," Mr. Merrick says quietly.

"I was wonderin'. Is there such a thing as God?"

"Is there such a thing as God? Do ya lay awake at night thinkin' up these questions?"

"No, I just wanna know."

"What do *you* think?"

"I don't know, Mr. Merrick. That's why I'm askin' *you*. 'Cause last summer when I was fishin' with my grandpa, they got a cabin on Twin Lakes, you know, over in Idaho right by Rathdrum—that's a funny name, Rathdrum. Rath . . . drum. Why would they name it that? It doesn't make sense. Anyway, we were across the lake, by the point, where all the rocks are, you know, right out there by the big—"

"Land the plane, boy!"

"Okay, Mr. Merrick—I'm hurryin', I'm hurryin'—so like I was sayin', we're out in the boat, me and my grandpa are, and a deer comes down to the water, and then a rabbit, and grandpa didn't see it, but I did 'cause I'm—"

Mr. Merrick widens his eyes, and loudly clears his throat, demanding a point get made, immediately.

"Okay, so anyway, and I see that stuff, and it was super-cool, so I look over at my grandpa, and I say, 'Isn't it amazing that God made all this?' and my grandpa looks at me, and he goes, 'Who says there's a God?'"

Mr. Merrick waits a moment to make sure the convoluted story is complete, and when Lyle doesn't continue, Mr. Merrick ventures a guess at the purpose behind it. "So you think your grandpa doesn't believe in God, is that it?"

"I don't know. I mean, he takes my grandma to church every Sunday. But he never goes in."

"It doesn't have anything to do with church. That's a different subject altogether."

Lyle gazes at him.

"Do *you* think there's a God, Mr. Merrick?"

Mr. Merrick is conveniently distracted by a loose machine screw on one of the furnace pipes. He picks up a screwdriver and tightens it, then jiggles the pipe, testing to be sure it's secure. When he finishes, he turns his attention back to Lyle, hoping the boy has lost interest in the conversation.

"*Do* you, Mr. Merrick?"

Mr. Merrick empties the ashes from his pipe and fills it with fresh tobacco from his pouch.

"Doesn't matter what I think . . . or what anybody else thinks," he says. "This is one of those things everybody has to figure out on their own—pure and simple. Got it?"

He throws Lyle a very serious expression, almost a glare, raising one eyebrow and putting the pipe back in his mouth, to signal the end of discussion.

"You don't think there's a God, do you, Mr. Merrick?"

"Doggone it. Don't try that on me," Mr. Merrick growls. "You gotta quit this constant testin' of everything and everybody. It's part of why you're in here so much, always testin' people like ya do. Ya can't trick people into sayin' what ya think ya need to hear. Like I told ya, some things ya have to figure out on your own!"

"Okay, I was just askin'," Lyle says sheepishly.

He digs into the box and finds two more erasers caked with chalk. He claps them together fast and hard, and the air is soon dense with dust; he chokes on it and stops again.

"Maybe I could use that for my science project. What d'ya think about that?"

"Use what? The fine art of cleanin' erasers?"

"No, Mr. Merrick! That's not what I'm talkin' about. What I'm sayin' is I could test to see if there really is a God or not. That's what I'm sayin'!"

"You could what?" Mr. Merrick stops what he's doing and turns to Lyle.

"I was thinkin' I could test to see if there really is a God."

Lyle likes the way this sounds. He enjoys the brilliance of his new idea and the way it makes him feel—as if some element of control is returning to his life.

Mr. Merrick bursts his bubble. "Ya can't do God for a science project."

"Why not?"

"It won't work."

"Why not?"

"Well, for starters, when d'ya gotta have this done?"

"Fifty-six days from today, to be exact," Lyle informs him confidently.

"Well, here's the situation. People've been tossin' that question around for thousands of years and they're still bickerin' over it, so I don't think it's likely you'll be gettin' it figured out this month, next month, or even the month after that." Mr. Merrick punctuates his point with a hard stare.

The recess bell rings, and the children file back into school.

"Better get goin'. I don't want ya gettin' in trouble for bein' late on top of everything else," Mr. Merrick says quietly. "And see what ya can do about comin' up with a science project ya can actually finish in fifty-six days. And not a volcano!"

He points to his eyebrows.

"Okay, I will. That's exactly what I'm gonna do. Thanks, Mr. Merrick."

Lyle pops his two erasers together one last time, intentionally sending a cloud of dust in Mr. Merrick's direction. Lyle laughs and tosses the erasers in the box. Mr. Merrick watches him sprint for the classroom.

"Fifty-six days," he muses to himself, shaking his head. Mr. Merrick is thoroughly played out.

The day drags by slowly for Lyle. He has no space for the classwork, as his mind races with a disorganized muddle of new information: Science Fair, needing a project partner, fifty-six days, Sharon Anne, God, and David's frightening (though surely inaccurate) prediction about Mrs. McGuire. It all bangs around in his head like a half-dozen tennis shoes in a clothes dryer, and the more he dwells on it, the less sense it makes.

When the final bell rings, he follows David out the door, only inches behind his wheelchair. David, unaware Lyle shadows him, wheels himself onto the sidewalk and situates by the school wall, in the sunlight. Lyle scrutinizes his every move as David digs a book from his bookbag and immerses himself in the pages.

"What are you doin'?" Lyle loudly interrupts.

David startles. "Oh! Hi. I'm reading."

"I know that. What, though?"

David holds up the book so Lyle can see the title: *The Prophet*, by Kahlil Gibran.

"It looks like a good book," Lyle comments. "I like Thor, Son of Odin."

"What?"

"You know, the Viking God of Thunder. With his hammer Mjöllnir. No matter how many enemies come after him or how many ice giants have him down, he never, ever gives up. Never!"

"Well, you know," David observes thoughtfully, "ice giants can be a huge problem."

"How come you're readin' out here?" Lyle asks.

"I'm waiting for my brother to come get me."

"Where do you live?"

"Right over there," he says, pointing, "just a couple of blocks from here."

"Hey! I could walk home with you. It's on the way to my house and I just got un-grounded, so that'd be great!"

David's never been grounded, so being-grounded and getting-ungrounded are subjects of interest to him. He lowers the book onto his lap.

"What'd you do to get grounded?"

"Oh, nothin'. Somethin' that happened at the Scout camp. But I'm not a Cub Scout anymore so it doesn't matter."

"Did you quit?" David inquires, curious.

"No, I'm just takin' a break. Maybe focus on some other things for a while."

"You got kicked out, didn't you?"

"Who told you that? Was it Daly? 'Cause if it was—"

"Nobody told me. I figured maybe you got kicked out. You know, because of *the feeling* and—"

"Okay, here's what happened," Lyle interrupts. "I cut down a huge tree."

"What's wrong with that?"

"Exactly."

There's a long pause . . . and then Lyle launches into it.

"Okay, so there I was, up on this super-steep hill gettin' firewood, and everything was goin' just fine, and then the wind made this enormous bull pine fall over sideways. And that never happens, does it?"

Lyle pauses, but not long enough for David to respond.

"No!" Lyle emphatically answers for him. "Then it rolls over this big ol' rock that shows up right outta nowhere, and that made it go shootin' down the hill right smack on top of all the tents. Wham! Boom! Bang! Flatter'n a pancake!"

Lyle waits, expecting David to dispute the story.

"Flatter than a pancake," David says, impressed. "I wish I could've seen it."

"Hey," Lyle says, sensing an opening, "You wanna do that science project together?"

David stares at him to be sure he's not joking. It doesn't appear he is. "Didn't you already ask me?"

"Did I?" Lyle asks, knowing full well he did.

"Remember? For the third time? My brother's helping me. We're stuffing a weasel."

"Oh, yeah," Lyle recollects. "Stuffin' a weasel."

He distorts his face, one feature at a time, until he achieves all the characteristics he imagines a stuffed weasel would have. He puffs his cheeks full of air, makes his eyes big and round, juts his front teeth out as far as possible, and stares straight ahead like a zombie.

"Nice face!" a voice interrupts.

Lyle spins to see a tall, skinny young man standing there. His hair is long and wild and his face has a reckless appearance, in a comical sort of way. He resembles Merlin the Magician, with a trick or two up his sleeve.

"Hi, there," he says, offering his hand. "I'm Dennis, but you can call me Dennis." He cracks a grin. "David's brother."

Lyle shakes his hand.

"My name's Lyle and you can call me . . ." His voice trails off in confusion. "Uh, Lyle."

"Let's go, guys," Dennis urges. "Can't keep a lady waiting."

David throws a sidelong glance at Lyle.

"Girlfriend," he explains.

"Right on," Dennis affirms.

Dennis and David approach the Monroe Street intersection with Lyle traipsing after them. They reach the crosswalk, where the yellow lab waits across the street by the hydrant. For the benefit of his new friends, Lyle replaces his usual whistle with a deafening shriek.

"Diiiiiii-nnnooo-oooohh!"

David and Dennis jump, startled, and Dino comes running.

"Good grief! You scared me half to death!" David exclaims.

"Hey, David," Dennis jokes. "What happens if you get scared half to death twice?"

The brothers fall out laughing.

Lyle ignores them. He's busy giving the dog his after-school rubdown. "Yesh, dat's a goo' boy, ishn't it? He wikes dat, doeshn't he. Ooo, yesh."

The dog wags his tail so hard his whole body is in a twist.

"This must be your dog, huh?" Dennis asks.

"Yeah, ah . . . I mean no," Lyle stammers. "He's the neighbors' dog, the neighbors two doors down, the Crumbs. But he's always followin' me. His name's Dino, you know, like the Flintstones' brontosaurus. We hike and stuff. This one time we were playin' hide and seek, and we crawled under a bush to hide. It was all pitch-black and dusty and he's whinin' and shnuffin' around. You know why? Why d'ya think? Huh? Why?"

He waits a few seconds, as though expecting an answer, and then continues, like a professor who thinks he's managed to mentally outmaneuver a class of geniuses.

"Because there was a porcupine, that's why! A huge porcupine! This big!" Lyle holds his arms out wide, indicating a size significantly larger than any porcupine could ever be.

"And we were under the shrubs with it, like nose to nose. This close!" Lyle shoves his face an inch away from David's, and then just as quickly goes back to plodding along next to him.

David has never been around behavior of this sort, and he finds it slightly unnerving. But Lyle doesn't notice, or doesn't mind, and he races forward with his story.

"We caught him, and put him in the stationary tub, and we named him Porcus. We'd just sit there and watch him, and watch him, and watch him, all day long."

"Not much else you can do with 'em," Dennis agrees. "It's not like you can throw 'em a Frisbee. I've got one in the deep freeze right now and I'm plannin' to stuff it, if my mom doesn't come across it first and make meatloaf out of it. Porcupine meatloaf. That'll stick to your ribs!"

The boys all get a good laugh.

"Do you like to swim?" Dennis asks Lyle.

"Sure thing. I'm a great swimmer. I can swim like a fish."

"Groovy. We got a pool at our house. Why don't you come over and swim for a while?"

"Okay. I just need to call my mom," Lyle says. "Oh, wait! I can't. I don't have a swimming suit."

Dennis transforms, seemingly changing not only size and shape but facial characteristics as well. He holds an invisible microphone up to his mouth.

"Ding-ding, ding-ding! Howard Cosell here, live at the Monroe Street crosswalk with two pint-sized pugilists, asking the difficult, the tough question. Mr. Lyle, given the chance, the opportunity, to swim in the dazzling crystal-blue waters of the famous Dahlke family pool, what would you say?"

Dennis shoves the invisible microphone up to Lyle's mouth.

"Ah . . . I don't uh, have a swimming suit?" Lyle ventures.

"At a glance, based on your size, your quick feet, your razor-sharp cheese-grated crew cut, I'd say we have some trunks, swimwear, if you will, that would fit you like a glove. What do you say to that, Champ?"

It's a good imitation and David and Lyle both laugh.

Ten minutes later, Lyle is decked out in an enormous pair of Bermuda shorts decorated with garish orange and red flowers. The swim trunks belong to Dennis, who is over six feet tall, so on Lyle they're more like ridiculously large, baggy clown pants reaching to his rib cage and hanging to his knees. Lyle is indifferent to fashion issues right now. His attention is consumed by the promise of a swim.

He charges out the basement door leading to the pool area, and Dennis follows with his girlfriend, Jenon, navigating David and his wheelchair through doorway. When they catch up with Lyle, he's standing in the Dahlkes' backyard in a trance, awestruck.

Where Lyle expected to find a swimming pool, there is instead an enormous structure unlike anything he's ever seen in his life. It covers nearly half the backyard, and stands almost as high as the house. It weaves and bobs and pulsates like an enormous, oddly shaped jellyfish.

"Holey-moley!" Lyle cries. "What *is* that thing?"

CHAPTER SIX

THE BUBBLE

Truth is tough. It will not break, like a bubble, at a touch;
nay, you may kick it about all day like a football,
and it will be round and full at evening.

~ OLIVER WENDELL HOLMES

ennis grins. "Why, that's a little something we call the 'Bubble.' Go on in."

He fully understands Lyle's fascination, since he remembers well the first time *he* saw it. His dad acquired the Bubble not long ago, from Lloyd's Sales and Service, where they used it for their outdoor winter and fall parking lot sales. When they no longer needed it, Mr. Dahlke was in the right place at the right time to load it up and haul it home, one of many benefits he enjoys as a highly respected and trusted hardware salesman in the community.

Lyle opens the wooden outer door and encounters a canvas wall with a large zippered flap. He eagerly unzips it and steps inside the chamber. It's so steamy he can scarcely see. He pads around the pool, waiting for the others while he explores this peculiar place. He runs his hand along the heavy canvas wall, and in the dense fog almost trips over a large fan, part of a system that keeps the Bubble filled with air.

Dennis and Jenon wheel David in, and Dennis lifts him from the chair and sets him in the water at the deep end.

David rolls onto his back and bobs in the pool like a cork.

"Hey Lyle, if you need a life jacket, grab onto David," Dennis jokes. "He's unsinkable."

Lyle dashes to the pool's edge and leaps into the air, limbs sprawling in every direction. Seconds before hitting the water he rolls himself into a compact ball, sending a splash to the top of the Bubble, drenching the pavement. His suit balloons up like a puffer fish, but even with the additional buoyancy, Lyle sinks to the bottom like a rock. He decides to hang out there.

"Dennis! Is he all right?" Jenon exclaims.

Dennis peers over the pool's edge. They both study Lyle for a while . . . quite a while.

"He's starting to freak me out. Are you sure he's okay?"

"Yeah, he's fine," Dennis reassures her. "Looks like maybe he's a bottom dweller."

Lyle finally pops out of the water right next to David, who floats near the edge.

"It's really deep!" Lyle belts, digging water from his ears.

For the first time, he notices they're not alone. In the shallow end, David's older sister, Dena, wades among a group of preschool-aged children. Twenty this year, she looks like a grown-up to Lyle. Her ash-brown hair, normally worn in a flip, is neatly tucked under a swimming cap. She's intense and enthusiastic, and her charges squeal in delight.

Dena notices Lyle's interest, and calls out, "Hey David, come here for a sec!"

David travels to the shallow end, and the little swimmers jump up and down, excited. They know what's coming. David is a Pied Piper of sorts for small children. Everywhere he goes they gather, and won't leave until their parents coax them away with the promise, "You can talk to David again next time."

Dena now has the unwavering attention of every child there, as she knew she would. David drifts up next to her on his back. She pushes him under water, all the way to the bottom, and the children wait, breathless, until she lets go and he pops right back up. The kids shriek with laughter and demand to see it over and over again, and then want to try it on him themselves. David lets them push him down repeatedly, until Dena announces it's time to get back to the swimming lessons.

David swims smoothly over to where Lyle has been waiting and observing.

"Hey, David—I just noticed something about you. About your legs."

David figures he knows what's coming. He's heard all the comments before.

"They're long as the dickens, and your feet are huge! Their like fins with toes. You're a giant toad."

David mouths the word "toad," attempting to process it. Lyle doesn't give him time.

"Yeah, you've got big ol' toad legs. Look at mine. Look at 'em! I have short wiener dog legs. Have you ever seen a wiener dog huntin' for ducks? No! You and me, we're opposites—total opposites. I can't float and you can't sink. Isn't that crazy?"

David hasn't heard *that* before, and it takes a moment for him to adjust to the tempo of Lyle's one-man conversation.

"Hey, who are all those kids?" Lyle presses.

David blinks before he answers, wondering if he's supposed to talk yet. "Oh, those kids . . . they're all from . . . from all around the neighborhood."

"I know. I know that. But what I'm askin' is, what are they doin' in your pool?"

David laughs. "My mom makes sure everybody can get swimming lessons if they want to," he explains, proud of his mother. "Some moms can't pay so she lets them trade stuff like ironing and sewing and knitting . . . Hey, once we even got a whole year supply of dill pickles."

"Cool! So that's a class?"

"Yep. The tadpoles."

"Tadpoles?"

"Yeah." David smiles. "We have grades for all the swimmers. Instead of first grade, second grade, and all that, we have tadpoles, frogs, fish, seal pups, seals, porpoises, dolphins, and swimmers. My mom and Dena and Ella teach, so with three teachers we can do a lot of classes."

"Which group would I be in?" Lyle wants to know.

"We'll have to make a new group for you, one *before* tadpoles," David needles. ". . . Okay, I know. You're an egg sack."

"Hey! You're an egg sack," Lyle shoots back.

"Listen, egg sack," David says. "Do you know how to do the backstroke?"

"No."

"The breast stroke?"

"No."

"How 'bout the butterfly?"

Lyle shakes his head.

"Can you do the crawl?"

"Yeah. I can crawl. I can crawl like crazy."

Lyle drops to the bottom of the pool, and crawls around like a crawdad for a very long time before coming up for air. When he pops up, David is shaking with laughter.

"You told my brother you could swim like a fish."

"I took lessons," Lyle defends himself.

"No way."

"Yeah, I did."

David shrugs in resignation.

"I flunked the test," he admits.

"How can you flunk a swimming test?"

"They made us swim at least ten miles. All the way out to the dock at Wandermere Lake. I almost made it, though."

"How far did you get?"

"Halfway. Then I had to turn around and swim back."

"If you were halfway, and swam back, it's the same distance," David points out.

"The same as what?"

"The same as making it."

Lyle gets perturbed. "I didn't make it, all right?"

Lyle heaves himself out of the pool and jumps to his feet. He runs to the fence, turns, and races back at the pool, executing another cannonball. It drenches David and Dennis, and Jenon screams and scrambles to a dryer spot.

An hour or so later, David and Lyle, soaking wet and wrapped in towels, drip all over the Dahlkes' basement. Lyle wanders about the room, examining things while David dries off.

The basement resembles a museum: it's packed with stuffed animals, antiques, books, old furniture, toys, and an enormous array of unusual knick-knacks. And—most curious—there appear to be no less than thirty living creatures down here, not including humans. Lyle has never seen anything like it.

Wow! Wow! Unbelievable! This is Wild Kingdom *and the Cowles Museum all mixed in one. It's the outdoors indoors. When you come in here, you can hear critters, everywhere, shiftin' around. Mice divin' under the leaves and paper. And the rats quit racin' on that Ferris wheel and stare at you. Two huge snakes in a glass box never move. Nothin'. Lizards hidin' in the sawdust and pretty soon all the things that are alive look dead, and all the things that are dead look alive.*

Creepy puppet on top of the cabinet! David calls him "Charlie." His eyes follow you around and he never, ever blinks. His hair shines from the light in the fish bowl. I have one like it, but I keep mine in a box where he can't bug me. Holey smokes, look at that bug collection. It's a giant goldmine!

"That's my *coleoptera* collection," Dennis says, when he sees Lyle staring. Dennis grabs Jenon around the waist. "And this is my *pulchella puella*."

"Pretty girl," David whispers to Lyle.

Jenon snuggles up to Dennis. "Whoo," she purrs, "handsome and smart."

Yikes! She's a . . . whatever it was he said. This science guy stuff sure is the ticket!

"If you think those beetles are cool, wait'll you see the killer coyote I'm workin' on," Dennis says.

An enormous tarantula scurries across the terrarium glass, less than two feet away. Lyle jumps, freaked. "I love that thing!" he shouts, trying to save face.

"That's Huge," Dennis tells him.

"No kidding," Lyle agrees. "The biggest spider I ever saw!"

"That's his name," Dennis laughs.

Lyle has already lost interest.

"Hey, what's that white scar on your leg?" Lyle asks David. "It looks like a sticker-bush slice."

"When they tested me for muscular dystrophy they had to take a piece out of my leg. We went to a hospital in Salt Lake City."

"Did it hurt?"

"I don't remember it much. I was little. My mom says I used to tell people that's where the doc-odile bit me."

"Doggone it," Lyle empathizes, his eyes locked onto the scar.

Muscular dystrophy is a mystery to Lyle, but as he learns and absorbs and observes, it takes shape in his mind as an adversary. His heroes come primarily from comic books, where the foes are monsters and phantoms, and ultimately you must do battle.

"I've got a big ol' scar on my leg, too," Lyle tells him. "I was buildin' a snow fort last year, and makin' it really cool. And Michael Miller, this kid next door, kept messin' with it and messin' it up, so we got in a big fight and I got him down on the ground and I was standin' up and he bit right into my leg. I couldn't get him off me 'cause he was hangin' on with his teeth! I was yellin' at him to let go—'Let go,' I said—but he wouldn't.

"So I dragged him by his teeth clear across the yard, and I picked up the coal shovel and whacked him over the head. He let go all right, but he chomped down when I hit him, and he bit a chunk right outta my leg!

"When my mom saw the big hole in my leg, she goes, 'Where's the rest of it?' I told her I didn't know. And she goes, 'Well, maybe he ate it.' Ha! Pretty funny, huh?"

Lyle glances around at his audience. He gets a chuckle from Dennis and David, but Jenon lapses into a fit of giggling she can't get under control. She leaves the room and on her way accidentally disturbs Puff, the badger, who skitters across the floor in front of Lyle.

What?! Can you believe it? A badger! Sniffs all around me and unties my shoe. She squints. What's wrong, Roadhog, lose your glasses? She sniffs me again. "You're good," she says, and she jumps up on a soft chair to snooze. Look at all this stuff! Butterfly net, and a smoke bellows, and a beekeeper's mask, and sprayers, and jars, and a microscope and slides and—

"Holey-moley macaroni. What is *that?*"

Lyle's attention fixes on a strange, half-mechanical, half-electrical device, all decked out with tubes and wires.

"That's the Wizzard XL 2000," Dennis tells him. "Step aside, and I will demonstrate."

Dennis flips a switch and the machine emits a loud steady hum. He sets some metal letters in a short, shallow tray, picks up a small bronze plaque, and clamps it onto a compact moveable platform. As he pushes the platform into the machine, it whirs and grinds, and dust flies up from the stylus in a streaming golden cloud. Lyle is mesmerized.

Dennis flips off the machine and removes the plaque. He polishes it on his shirt and hands it to Lyle. Then he takes Jenon's hand, and they slip out the door, on their way back to the Bubble.

Lyle admires the creation, which has the name "Dino" neatly engraved on it.

"Cool!" Lyle whirls to David, excited. "Hey, about the Science Fair. I know about the weasel and all that. But I was thinkin' maybe you and me could do a giant bug collection. And you could do cool labels like this."

Lyle waves the Dino plaque in the air.

"We could win for sure! Maybe we could even go to State. It'd sure be cooler than anything Darin ever did."

"Who's Darin?" David asks.

"Oh, he's nobody."

"Well, me and Dennis have already—"

"If you're afraida bugs, that's okay," Lyle interrupts.

"No, I'm not afraid of bugs."

"My sister's afraida bugs. So if you *are* afraida bugs that's fine. 'Cause that's nothing to be ashamed about."

"I'm not afraid of bugs! I live in . . ."

Mrs. Dahlke has made her way quietly down the stairs and stands in the doorway, listening to David and Lyle. Their conversation ends abruptly as they look at her. She didn't do anything to attract their notice, but they felt her presence, and recognize something is wrong.

"David. Lyle." Her eyes take in both of them. "There's something I need to tell you."

A stretched-out silence ensues. Lyle shifts uncomfortably.

"It's about Mrs. McGuire," Mrs. Dahlke says quietly.

Lyle's heart beats fast; he can hear it and feel it in his ears. David is still, his eyes on his mother. His face whitens, and tears well up.

"You know she's been ill," Mrs. Dahlke continues. "Miss O'Donnell called. She wanted you to know before you went to school tomorrow. I'm very sorry boys, but Mrs. McGuire passed away."

David's hands creep slowly up and cover his face. Lyle's features cloud into a dark frown. There is another lengthy silence. Lyle is the first to speak, and his voice is flat.

"I need to go home now. Thank you, Mrs. Dahlke, for letting me go swimming. 'Bye, David."

He turns to leave, and bumps into a chair. He eyes it angrily, as though challenging it for getting in his way. He treads up the basement stairs, through the kitchen and living room, and out the front door, closing it silently.

Standing on the front porch of the Dahlke house, Lyle feels a sickness in his stomach, slowly spreading through his entire body, and with it a sensation of being utterly lost, with no sense of direction. He felt this once before, when David first told him Mrs. McGuire was going to die, only this time it's stronger and it actually hurts. He feels an overwhelming urge to escape. He doesn't want to see anyone, or hear any voices. He wants to be alone.

"C'mon, boy," he mumbles to Dino.

The two of them skirt around the Dahlkes' VW bus, and race hard and fast down the street. As they turn onto the road leading to the school, Lyle cuts into the vacant lot. They scramble to the top of the ridge and race through the scattering of pine trees.

Something about being among the trees, and running on bare dirt instead of pavement, changes things. Lyle and the dog both stop at the same time.

"I'm very sorry boys, but Mrs. McGuire passed away."

Lyle wants to fight this strange demon that effortlessly keeps pace no matter how fast he runs and overtakes him with sadness and confusion. He steps on a pinecone, crushing it, and then kicks it hard, sending it flying down the hill.

David did know! How did he know? I'll bet they said somethin' to him. No, that's not it. They said somethin' to his mom and he heard it. She didn't wanna hurt his feelings. She's nice. I like her. But she shoulda told him. She has the coolest house ever. What if my mom gets sick and they don't say anything? That makes me mad! Really mad!

Lyle wishes he knew what had taken Mrs. McGuire. Whatever it was, he wants to get even with it. He picks up a stick and brandishes it with threatening gestures. Dino knows Lyle isn't in the mood to play. He sits down very close to his boy, and a tiny dog complaint escapes him: a sad sound. Lyle whips the stick at some bushes and severs the branches. It feels good to inflict damage.

That Wizzard machine of Dennis' was crazy! I wonder if I can borrow that thing. That'd get me a blue ribbon for sure.

"I wanna win that Science Fair!" he blurts out, almost mad.

The disturbing sensation hits him again, like an electric shock. This time it's almost overwhelming.

"Mrs. McGuire passed away."

He sits in the weeds for a long while. The sun sinks below the cliffs of Five Mile, and the dusk rolls evenly into darkness. The temperature drops rapidly but Lyle doesn't care. A series of unresolved issues have ganged up on him, and his ten-year-old mind lacks the experience to wrestle them into submission.

Getting in trouble at school and being sent to the boiler room doesn't mean much. That's normal, everyday material for him. Impressing Sharon Anne, that's a big deal, and there's the Science Fair, and that's big, too, for the same reason. Deep down, he needs David, but he wants to believe David needs him. It's not that Lyle can't do a Science Fair project on his own. Naturally, he can, but that's about as fun as catching a trophy bass when you're the only one on the dock. David might be his last chance. And besides, there's the weasel, and the Wizzard XL 2000 and the Dahlke basement—full of all that . . . stuff.

> *Mrs. McGuire died. And David knew. That's just crazy. How could he know? If there is a God, I wanna know!*

> *Maybe David just imagines that God talks to him. He's in a wheelchair, and Jack LaLanne says the Good Physician above will make you whole again if you just have the intestinal fortitude to do the right thing.*

> *Why wouldn't David know about that whole intestinal fortitude thing? Why isn't he doing the right thing? He needs help. And Mr. Merrick knows a lot of stuff, but he didn't say there was a God.*

Lyle wants this to be the final word on the issue and for a few minutes he successfully pretends it is. But a clear picture persists in his mind of the white scar on David's leg, and now, in his active and vivid imagination, it takes on the shape of a monster he has to do battle with and conquer.

> *Who does know, if David doesn't? Well, if there really is a God, then David should be able to walk . . . no, he should be able to run! He needs all the help he can get, if he's gonna whip that scar. He's gotta run, or he can't get away, or chase bugs, or . . . or run some more!*

> *I've gotta help David do the right thing like Jack LaLanne says, and then if there is a God he will be able to run. He needs me!*

"C'mon, boy!" Lyle shouts at Dino, as he springs to his feet and sprints down the street.

Moments later they fly past the VW bus and up to the Dahlkes' porch. Lyle rings the doorbell and waits. The door opens a crack. There's some rustling and banging before it swings all the way open, and when it does, there's David, thoroughly surprised to see Lyle.

"All right, here's the deal," Lyle launches, realizing he needs to do some fast talking. "See, what we're gonna do is . . . well, you're gonna do a huge bug collection with me and we're gonna win the Science Fair. And I'll show you everything I know about running, and I know some stuff nobody else knows. But you gotta promise, I mean it, you gotta promise you're not gonna tell anybody I'm teachin' you to run. Not a soul. That's the deal. Deal?"

Lyle snaps his fingers, and offers his hand. He waits. David sits there, not moving. A moment before it reaches the point of being unbearably awkward, David swings his chair back into the house.

"Mom!" he calls. "Can Lyle stay for dinner?"

He angles back to Lyle, reaches out his hand, and they shake.

CHAPTER SEVEN

THE QUEEN

Consider the black widow spider:
the poor thing has the fatal misfortune of possessing
enormously too much power for its size.
So everybody kills it on sight.

~ ROBERT HEINLEIN

Thursday, September 16
55 days to Parent Night

Steve and Linda have left for school, and Lyle stands in the living room, lunch sack in one hand, books in the other, staring at the television, once again entranced by Jack LaLanne's words.

"*Most people are going in the wrong direction. Every day, they lose something. Every day, there's some tiny thing their body can't do that it could do the day before. We've got to switch that around, and get it going in the right direction.*

"*Like we talked about yesterday, it's you who can make a miracle in your life, and if you want that miracle, you have to have the intestinal fortitude and willpower to do the right thing. But you have to do it.*

"*So folks, every day I want you to make sure you do something you couldn't do the day before. That's right! You have to take that first step. But you have to start NOW! N-O-W!*"

Mrs. Hatcher turns and gives Lyle a meaningful stare. He's out the front door in seconds, racing down the street with Dino. When they reach the intersection at Monroe and turn north, Lyle stops, staring into the distance. A few blocks away someone pushes a wheelchair at the cross-street by the school, and Lyle figures it's Dennis pushing David.

"C'mon, boy!" he spurs Dino. "We can beat 'em!"

Lyle and Dino take off, sprinting toward the school. They catch up with David just as they reach the front entrance. To Lyle's surprise, it isn't Dennis who's with David, but an older man in a suit and tie.

"Hey, Lyle." David smiles. "This is my dad. Dad, this is my friend, Lyle Hatcher. Lyle and I are working on some stuff together."

Mr. Dahlke gives Lyle a warm, broad smile and offers his hand. "Pleasure to meet you, Lyle."

Lyle shakes his hand. "It's nice to meet you, too, Mr. Dahlke."

David's dad turns the wheelchair handles toward Lyle.

"Would you like to take over for me, here?"

Everything in Mr. Dahlke's mannerisms, from his handshake to the way he talks, makes Lyle feel grown-up, manly. He likes it.

"You gentlemen have a good day. And good luck with those projects you're working on. I'll see you tonight, David."

"Okay, 'bye, Dad."

Lyle wheels David up to the door and opens it.

"I got our toolkit right here," David announces, patting his backpack. "Dennis helped me put it together last night."

"Your dad's nice," Lyle says.

David nods, as he wheels himself through the doorway.

They start down the hall toward the fourth-grade room—and sense something is very different here. There's a somber tone, and it's everywhere: in the classrooms and the hallways, even out on the playground. News of Mrs. McGuire's death has already spread through the school.

Miss O'Donnell has never had to deal with the death of one of her teachers. In her mind, the magnitude of the event somehow requires action. She is in charge; she needs to do something. Last night, after careful thought, she decided to call all the families of Mrs. McGuire's students.

Her decision was based at least as much on what she personally needed, as it was on her compassion for the children. The one thing she is consistently incapable of doing, is nothing. This morning she moves from room to room, on a mission to talk to each class.

As Miss O'Donnell speaks to the fourth-graders, a hailstorm begins pelting the school. It serves as a good distraction and acceptable ending to Miss O'Donnell's stiff attempt to explain death to ten- and eleven-year-olds—who already understand it, in their own way.

The children crowd around the windows and watch the pea-sized balls of hail pour down, and Miss O'Donnell listens to them marvel at the way the hailstones bounce and dance off the sidewalks and playground equipment. With a nod to Mrs. Stewart, she slips from the room.

After the excitement of the storm, the remainder of the morning seems uneventful by comparison. Melvin raises his hand and asks if he can change the Parent Night countdown on the board. With Mrs. Stewart's permission, he erases the "56" and writes in "55".

Mrs. Stewart regards her disoriented bunch. She tells them they can take until recess to draw a picture, or write a poem or essay, as a way to express how they feel about Mrs. McGuire. Lyle can't think. He makes an extra effort not to disturb the others but he can't help squirming in his chair. He checks out what David is doing: writing and rewriting something on small sheets of brown notebook paper.

I don't wanna draw a picture and I don't wanna write anything. I wonder if she was alone. Karl's dog, Rags, had somebody there when he got run over by that semi truck. Karl was holdin' him when he died and Rags looked right at him—I saw it.

Nobody should ever be alone. I miss her. I bet Karl misses Rags.

David finally finishes and invites Lyle to check out the poem he's written.

Time

The time is passing ever so fast.

Before you know it, the days are in the past.

So live every moment, and remember this day.

And you will be very happy and gay.

Lyle politely nods his approval, a bit envious of David for coming up with anything at all, and he feels lame about not having done something himself. As always in situations like this, he makes a stab at self-redemption. He checks to be sure Mrs. Stewart's attention is elsewhere, and he leans over.

"We're havin' our first lesson today. Be ready."

David's eyes light. "Running?"

Lyle nods. "Be ready."

David is more than ready. As Lyle elaborates, the intercom speaker, centered on the wall above the blackboard, crackles to life, and Miss O'Donnell's voice fills the room.

"Attention, students. The hail has not yet melted from the sidewalks on the north side of the school, so be very careful when exiting the classroom for recess. The sidewalks are slick. Exit the school in a slow, orderly fashion. There will be absolutely no running. I repeat . . . *no running!* That will be all."

Lyle doesn't hear a word of it. He's far too busy using sign language to clarify for David the details of his first running lesson. With two fingers as legs, his hand scampers across the desk. Lyle—inspired by even an audience of one—soon has his finger-legs leaping imaginary obstacles and being attacked by a pencil.

The recess bell rings and Mrs. Stewart reminds the students to put away their books and clean up around their desks before they leave the room.

"And be very careful as you go out to the playground! You heard what the principal said," she emphasizes.

Lyle hurriedly arranges his papers and books in his desk, while chattering his version of a Jack LaLanne lesson to David.

"Okay, now watch me. You need to get the picture in your mind and focus on that picture every single day when you get up and every night when you go to sleep. Let your mind and your body know that's the picture you want for yourself. That's what *you* want to be able to do."

"What am I supposed to do?" David asks, anxious, scarcely comprehending what Lyle is saying.

"Watch!" Lyle pontificates. "You want to get this picture in your head."

"I just watch?" David asks. "What's that going to do?"

"No, you don't get it. That's only the first *step*. Then you have to make sure that every day you do something you couldn't do the day before."

"Oh!" David says, nodding.

Lyle eyes Mrs. Stewart. He checks the door to the playground. His gaze travels back and forth from Mrs. Stewart to the door, from the door to Mrs. Stewart. She turns her back to the classroom and begins to erase the blackboard.

Lyle makes certain he has David's undivided attention.

"David! Are you watching? Five, four, three, two, one . . . *blast off!*"

Lyle bolts for the door.

"Lyle!" David cries in a loud whisper, realizing too late what the plan is.

Outside the school, Miss O'Donnell stands where the walkway from the fourth-grade classroom intersects with the main sidewalk. She surveys the field, her whistle at the ready, prepared to put a quick stop to any and all infractions. The children stream out the doors, moving far too fast in her estimation.

She blows her whistle and shouts, "Slow down there! Slow down!"

She puts the whistle back in her mouth in case of another transgression. Lyle fires like a shot through the doorway, prepared to sprint the length of the playground and back, as an inspiring demonstration of how this running thing works—and instead hurtles into an all-out slide down the hail-covered walkway.

Miss O'Donnell sees him coming, but she can't move in time. He smacks straight into her, and they both go down. Her back slams into the ground, knocking every bit of wind from her lungs. The whistle in her mouth emits a series of wheezing sounds as she struggles for air.

Lyle gawks, frightened to see her gasping in those short quick breaths. He gets down, very close to her face.

"Miss O'Donnell, are you all right?"

She doesn't respond.

Oh no! She's a big ol' suckerfish floppin' around on the dock. And she's not breathin'. She's havin' a heart attack and she's dyin' right here on the sidewalk, and I'm gonna be the one that killed her!

His eyes dart around, panicked. To his great relief, Miss O'Donnell spits out the whistle and sucks in a near-normal breath. She wheezes, but he's pretty sure she's not going to die. Lyle tries to assist her as she struggles to her feet. She crouches, winded, and glares at him from under her lids.

"I specifically said . . ." She inhales sharply, straightens her back, and completes her sentence. "No . . . *running!*"

With a couple of breaths, she draws herself up, rising to her fullest authority. The principal looms over him and has no trouble delivering her final message.

"Recess in the boiler room! Now!"

Lyle vanishes almost instantly. Miss O'Donnell tugs a white, embroidered handkerchief from her skirt pocket and dabs at her eyes and mouth. Making a quick assessment of the playground, checking for witnesses, hoping not to find any, she fights off a disagreeable mixture of emotions and struggles to relocate her familiar composure. It's good he's gone. She'd like to strangle him.

A few minutes later, the romantic strains of *La Traviata*, scratching away on Mr. Merrick's hi-fi, drift from the boiler room with the soft *clap-clap-clap* of erasers struck together. Inside, Lyle dutifully cleans a large box of them, while outside, Mr. Merrick puts a new coat of paint on the metal door. David's wheelchair is parked on the sidewalk and he's busy, too, smacking an eraser against the wall.

"Did he rope ya into this?" Mr. Merrick asks.

"Nope. I'm just helping out, Mr. Merrick. Lyle's teaching me some stuff, that's all."

"Is that right? 'Some stuff,' huh? Did this 'stuff' have anything to do with Miss O'Donnell endin' up flat on her back on the ice?"

David gives it a few seconds of serious thought.

"It was an accident. I saw the whole thing," he explains, whapping his eraser against the cement wall. "He was showing me something, so I could get the picture in my head. It's the first step."

"The first step to what?"

David shrugs. "I promised I wouldn't tell. Lyle and I made a deal."

"Oh, so that's how it works." Mr. Merrick chuckles, but with an edge to it.

He sings along quietly to the aria on his record player, *"Libiamo, libiamo ne'lieti calici che la belleza infiora. E la fuggevol, fuggevol ora s'inebrii a—"*

A loud yell erupts from inside the boiler room. "Hey! Mr. Merrick! I'm done! Where should I put 'em?"

Mr. Merrick yells back. "You know what to do! The empty wastebasket! Over in the corner!"

"Oh, yeah!"

Mr. Merrick and David hear a scuffle inside, followed by some loud thumps and a distinct scraping sound. There's a brief silence. Suddenly, Lyle appears at the door, wild-eyed and wound-up for action.

"Guys? Do not panic. You are not gonna believe what I've got in there. It's a really good thing you're here, David, 'cause we are open for business! We're gonna need a jar, a big one."

Lyle signals for them to follow him back into the boiler room. David digs a jar from the backpack hanging on his wheelchair.

Mr. Merrick cocks an eyebrow. "Ya just happen to have a jar in there?"

"We're working on a science project and I'm the parts manager."

"Well, then grab your tools and let's have a look."

Lyle waits at the door, gritting his teeth.

"Slow," he says. "Very, very slooow."

David and Mr. Merrick cautiously follow Lyle into the boiler room. Lyle points to a dark corner where the wastebasket is turned upside down.

"It's right there!"

David hands Lyle a quart mason jar, and Lyle holds it down on the floor, up against the wastebasket.

"Boy?" Mr. Merrick says. "You're makin' me real nervous."

Lyle slowly tips the wastebasket and quickly slams the inverted jar to the floor.

He lets loose with an exuberant shout. "I got it!"

He slips the lid under the jar, tightens it down, and holds it up for Mr. Merrick and David to see. Before they can even catch a glimpse of what he has, he turns and shoots out of the room and into the bright sunshine of the playground. Mr. Merrick and David hurry after him.

Squinting against the light, Lyle holds the jar high in the air and makes a proclamation to the entire world.

"BLACK . . . WIDOW!"

The kids on the playground rush in and crowd around.

Lyle gets in very close to David's face, teeth clenched.

"Can . . . you . . . believe . . . we . . . caught . . . her?" he says, shaking and rattling David's wheelchair.

David laughs, nervous but excited, taken aback by this outburst. He digs around in the backpack and finds an entomology book, borrowed from Dennis' workroom. He searches through it.

"Here it is," David announces. "*Latrodectus hesperus*, black widow."

"And here I thought it was just a spider," Mr. Merrick reflects.

"She's not just a spider," Lyle clarifies. "She's the Queen."

"Wow," David observes, "we got a good start on our project, don't we?"

"David, listen! You shouldn't get so cocky. Hard work. That's the ticket," Lyle tells him, quoting his dad.

By now, the entire playground has converged on the boiler room and the kids crowd in, pushing and jostling, trying to get a good look at the Queen.

Lyle hoists the jar above his head so the red hourglass is visible to everyone. As if on cue, the kids fall suddenly quiet, and join in a murmured chorus of soft oohs and ahs. They make their observations in hushed voices, as though they're in church.

"Look't her red belly," someone says.

"It is called an hourglass," Melvin Schmeck clarifies. "It is the distinguishing mark of the—"

"Why's she got 'n hourglass on her belly?" someone else asks.

"Probably 'cause when you get bit you don't have a lotta time," David speculates.

Melvin offers more of his extensive knowledge. "The reason that particular shape is located—"

"How long d'ya think ya got?"

"Not very long," David replies.

Melvin gives up. Everyone is so engrossed in the exhilaration of the capture that Miss O'Donnell's approach goes unnoticed. She weaves through the crowd of children, and when David does see her coming, he takes the jar from Lyle and holds it up for her inspection.

"It's for our bug collection, for the Science Fair. We caught her in the boiler room," David proudly announces. "Isn't she a beauty?"

"Hand me the jar and I'll see to it," Miss O'Donnell says curtly, reaching for it.

Mr. Merrick casually lifts the jar from David's hand.

"I'll tell ya what, boys. Why don't I keep an eye on her 'til after school?" he suggests.

"No, Mr. Merrick. I will attend to it. Give me the jar, please," Miss O'Donnell insists.

Mr. Merrick hesitates, then reluctantly hands it over.

"Now, Mr. Hatcher," she says. Her voice is kind, but there's a condescending undertone. "There are methods which must be observed in the capturing of dangerous insects. You need to take your project more seriously and learn these methods first, so no one gets hurt. Or, you could choose a project which doesn't require such a high level of preparation. Perhaps this would be best for you."

"Yes, Miss O'Donnell," Lyle replies, politely. He suddenly realizes she's about to walk away with the Queen.

"Miss O'Donnell?"

She turns and gives him a hard stare.

"Can we have the spider back after school?"

"The correct way of saying it is 'May we,'" she responds.

"May we have the spider back after school?" Lyle says clearly, a bit louder, almost as if he's challenging her. The fuss and attention engendered a sense of power in Lyle and he won't surrender it easily.

The principal knows exactly what he's doing.

"Now, you think about it, Lyle. You did not go about this correctly. You wouldn't want any part of your project to be the result of sloppy work and poor preparation, would you?"

"No, Miss O'Donnell," Lyle cedes. He has no idea what she's talking about.

"Well, then you know the answer to your question."

She shifts her attention to Mr. Merrick and admonishes him with a glance. "And please turn that thing off."

Mr. Merrick ducks into the boiler room. The opera music stops with a sharp scrape, as he lifts the needle.

The children scatter about the playground. Miss O'Donnell strides back to her office, intending to phone Lyle's mother right away. David and Lyle are left alone, quite despondent about the loss of the Queen.

Mr. Merrick steps out of the boiler room. "Don't worry, boys," he reassures them. "Just stop by my office after school tomorrow."

He winks and goes back inside, closing the door behind him.

Lyle and David eye each other skeptically.

"She'll never give it back to him," David shakes his head. "No way."

Lyle is aggravated.

"That didn't last very long. And black widows are hard to come by. Dang it! One goldmine . . . gone. Just gone!" He kicks the air.

"We can find another," David offers, recovering his usual optimism.

"David, this is not just any bug collection. We need all the bugs, mostly the crazy ones, and a black widow is super-crazy!"

They stare at each other for a moment, and they're both thinking the same thing.

They're afraid they've seen the last of the Queen.

CHAPTER EIGHT

THE LOG

There is nothing more inspiring than seeing a spider working her web, her craft, many times a day, with such perfection and careful patience.

~ SUNIL KHEMANEY

Friday, September 17
54 days to Parent Night

True to his word, Mr. Merrick signals Lyle and David over to the boiler room as they're leaving school, and hands them the jar with the black widow spider in it.

"Wow, Mr. Merrick," Lyle exclaims. "How'd you do it?"

Lyle waits expectantly, hoping for an epic tale filled with aggressive phrases such as, "So I looked her right in the eye, and I told her in no uncertain terms . . ."

"Well," Mr. Merrick replies, "I do empty the garbage. Now keep it under wraps. This is just between us."

The boys eagerly nod their agreement. Having a secret with Mr. Merrick is like being in a club for guys only, and it has added importance because it involves information they're hiding from Miss O'Donnell.

As they head for home, David brings up an issue beginning to nag at him. "How many bugs do we need? Because we only have fifty-four days left, you know. And so far we barely have one bug. If we keep this up, we'll only have eighteen by Parent Night. Is that gonna be enough? Eighteen?"

"Heck no, that's *not* gonna be enough." Lyle frowns at David in reprimand. "What're you even thinkin', David?"

"Well, I . . ."

"This is gonna be, flat-out, the biggest, gnarliest bug collection ever, with every different kinda bug there is! Here's the plan."

Lyle takes an enormous breath.

"We'll put 'em in groups. Spiders over here, and then beetles, then butterflies and moths, dragonflies, grasshoppers will take up this corner, 'cause there's a lotta different kinds of those, and water bugs, but we'll have to go to the fish hatchery to catch 'em—I've seen giant water bugs out there—and let's see, stink bugs and potato bugs, and ladybugs, how many is that?"

"Gee whiz, Lyle, I wasn't really—"

"And we need you to find all the names and make the labels—that's your job . . . since you know Latin."

"What are you talking about? I don't know Latin."

"You knew about the pulla-jello-woolah-woolah thing Dennis said to his girlfriend."

"I only knew because Dennis says it about every day, and he told me what it means. And it's not pulla-jello. It's *pulchella puella*."

"See? There you go. So anyway, you're in charge of labels," Lyle goes on, "and I'll get the hard-to-catch bugs. Like the robber fly. Those are almost impossible. And you never, ever see a praying mantis. Have you ever? No! And the skimmer dragon fly—you gotta find 'em right after they eat, then they're slow, slow-mo. Sometimes it takes days to catch 'em."

"Days? Are you kidding me?" David asks, his eyes wide.

"Scouts' honor. And it's the same thing with the red-winged grasshopper. You gotta run 'em to death. They're the smartest grasshoppers in the world. The grey and yellow ones are nothin'.'"

Lyle lets this sink in and then continues. "This isn't gonna be easy, David. We got some serious work to do. But don't worry. We got a secret weapon!"

"We do?"

"Yeah, we do!" Lyle says, surprised David doesn't know about their secret weapon, when it's so obvious. "Me!"

"You?"

"Yeah, me. Who found the first praying mantis in Spokane? Me. And who found the porcupine in the Preckergies' backyard? Okay, sure Dino smelled it before I did, but it was me! And what about the full-grown robin I caught in my baseball cap, even if nobody believed me except Mom, because she saw me do it! That's right, me!"

"We don't need porcupines and birds."

"Well, it can't hurt, and anyway, I got a super-*super*-secret weapon! I know a place."

Lyle moves in close to David's chair and whispers, "The *Log*. There's a ton of spiders out there. It's bug city."

He resumes his walking. "This weekend I gotta go to Twin Lakes to visit my grandma and grandpa. But next Saturday? All day at the Log."

"Okay, but we'll only have . . ." David does some mental math, "forty-six days left by then. And you know, it's getting colder every night. If it freezes, we're not gonna find *any*thing."

"Good thinkin', David," Lyle muses. "Any time you see a bug, and I mean any kinda bug, nab it. Are you with me?"

Saturday, September 25
46 days to Parent Night

David is up early, eagerly anticipating a day at the Log. Waiting for Lyle to arrive, he works at the Wizzard XL 2000, diligently making brass labels to identify the various bugs he and Lyle expect to find.

Earlier in the week, they thoroughly reviewed the pictures in Dennis' entomology book, which contains details on a couple hundred of the most common insects in the Pacific Northwest. Relying on Lyle's extensive experience with wild things, they divided the bugs into three distinct categories. David painstakingly wrote it all down on several pieces of college-ruled paper, and now has the completed lists spread out on the table before him, for easy reference. Each bug has been placed into one of the three groups:

I.   *Bugs we for sure can find.*

II.   *Bugs we probably can find.*

III. *Bugs we probably can't find.*

At first, they had a fourth category which was called *Bugs we for sure can't ever find*, but after a long discussion, they decided this was not a useful category and it would only create extra work, so they dropped it.

They agreed it would be smart to make the labels for the first group in advance, and get a head start. Dennis told them they could use all the brass plaques they needed, but to be very careful not to waste them.

"They're kind of expensive," he cautioned.

Taking the warning seriously, they are being very careful to avoid the risk of engraving a plaque they may not end up using. David has the reference book open on the table, and he copies the Latin and English names of each insect, then meticulously sets the type on the Wizzard.

The basement is a quiet place to work, with the obvious exception of the proliferation of animals sharing the space. Today the critters are exceptionally calm, intimidated by the aggressive sound of the engraving machine. Indeed, the only animal in the basement making any noise at all is the turkey in the laundry room. She emits a series of soft gobbles, as if trying to calmly resolve a disagreement with the Wizzard.

Lyle charges into the room and skids to a stop.

"First place! Grand prize! Blue ribbon!" he shouts when he sees the labels.

They're neatly lined up on the table: green darner dragonfly, European honey bee, tiger swallowtail, praying mantis, damsel, assassin, two-spotted stink bug, lady beetle, black widow, monarch butterfly, red-legged and band-winged grasshoppers, and the mourning cloak butterfly.

"I knew this was gonna work," Lyle tells him. "Now we have to find all those bugs, or Dennis is gonna kill us."

Before long Lyle wheels David across the bumpy terrain of an expansive meadow, determined to push his wheelchair all the way to the Log. Dino trots along beside them, occasionally running off to take care of some dog business.

They move along at a worthy clip, until Lyle stops so suddenly it pitches David forward and nearly sends him flying from the chair. Fortunately, he's strapped in.

"Okay, this is it. What d'ya think?" Lyle asks him.

David cranes around to survey the area. They are in a large meadow surrounded by pine trees, and directly in front of them is the Log. It's a large tree which fell quite a few years earlier by the looks of it—probably the result of a wind storm or lightning strike. Its branches have snapped off, and the bark on the lower end has started to peel. The wood is pock-marked from the work of bugs and birds, and portions of the Log have been ripped away by the sharp claws of animals in search of food. The high surrounding grasses, yellow and dried this time of year, are a hiding place for grasshoppers and butterflies, and they take to the air as David and Lyle approach.

David nods his head in approval.

"So this is what you've been talking about. This looks perfect!"

Lyle grins. "Yep, this is definitely spider territory!" He gazes around. "Let's get crackin'!"

Lyle pushes the wheelchair in closer to the Log. "Look, here's one," he says, pointing out a spider web to David.

David leans in as close as he can.

"I don't see the spider."

"Get the jar!" Lyle orders.

David scrambles to get a mason jar from the backpack. When he finally finds it, he holds it out to Lyle, but Lyle is nowhere to be seen.

Then he spots him, leaping up from a crouched position about a hundred feet away, chasing about the field, wildly swinging a tumbleweed. David stares, wondering what on earth he's doing out there.

A few minutes later, Lyle comes charging back, and proudly shows David a small grasshopper he's holding very gingerly, between thumb and forefinger.

"I thought we were hunting for spiders," David objects, with a trace of disappointment.

"It might look like a grasshopper, but I call it D-I-N-N-E-R. And I found one the perfect size," Lyle says. "Get the jar ready. C'mon, get it in close to the web. Ready?"

David nods nervously. Lyle throws the grasshopper into the web, and they watch in amazement as the spider appears out of nowhere and encases the grasshopper in its webbing.

"I kind of feel sorry for it," David says, awestruck.

"Quick, get her now," Lyle whispers, as if he doesn't want the spider to overhear.

David scoops the spider and the grasshopper into the jar and hastily replaces the lid.

"You nailed it, David!" Lyle shouts.

David grabs the bug book and searches through it.

"Here it is. Hey, Lyle, it's a garden spider, *argiope aurantia*."

"I know that," Lyle sighs.

"Well, did you know this? There's thirty-four thousand different kinds of spiders!"

"So we've only got thirty-three thousand nine hundred and ninety-nine to go!" Lyle shouts, as he grabs the back of the chair, swings it around, and launches it in a new direction.

"Hang on. Four-wheel drive!" he yells.

And indeed, for the rest of the morning the wheelchair is transformed into a versatile, indestructible, all-terrain vehicle. They get stuck, dig the wheels out, and almost tip over several times. They slog through mud and water, struggle over berms and across ditches, and race over flat stretches.

David willingly goes along with it all, only objecting when Lyle eyes the basalt cliffs of Five Mile and wonders out loud if perhaps they could navigate them if they only made a few modifications to the chair's design.

Lyle scarcely acknowledges the wheelchair as an impediment. It's a minor inconvenience at most, and only because it rules out certain activities such as scaling trees, climbing cliffs and fording rivers. But Lyle perceives those to be temporary obstacles he plans to overcome later, perhaps on their next outing. And in spite of the limitations, he continues doing everything necessary to keep his new partner actively involved. By noon they have accumulated a jar full of spiders, and decide it's time to take a rest. They get situated in the sunshine on the south side of the Log.

"I'm sure glad Mr. Merrick got the Queen back for us."

"Yeah," David agrees. "I wonder if he got in trouble for it."

"No way." A stalk of chickweed hangs from the corner of Lyle's mouth and bounces when he talks. "He's tough as nails. I wouldn't wanna mess with him. Would you?"

"I guess not," David agrees.

Lyle opens his Cub Scout backpack and lugs out a full grocery bag with the top neatly folded and creased, the way he likes it.

"What's that?"

"A snack," Lyle informs him, spitting out his chickweed. "My mom packed it for us."

Lyle pokes his nose into the bag and takes inventory.

"Three peanut butter and jelly sandwiches with homemade strawberry jam with big ol' chunks of strawberries. Yeah!"

He lifts his head from the bag, eyes on David.

"Heavy on the peanut butter, extra jam," he clarifies. His head goes back in the sack. "Two apples, sliced, two gigantic dill pickles, a couple of carrots, four hard-boiled eggs, and a bunch of . . . homemade oatmeal raisin cookies."

His head comes out of the bag again, this time with disappointment written all over his face.

"What? That's it? No fruit pies? Mom!" Lyle dives back into the bag and digs around, checking under the napkins on the bottom. "Found 'em!" he announces, relieved. "Close one!"

"Wow," David says. "We'll never eat all that."

"Are you kiddin' me?" Lyle hands David a sandwich and takes one for himself.

The boys eat for several minutes until Lyle, having finished two of the sandwiches, breaks the silence.

"Hey, David, when God talks to you, how do you know it's God?"

David contemplates this for a few minutes. Normally Lyle wouldn't allow him time to think, but Lyle's busy eating, and there's something about chewing food that transforms him into a perfect student: quiet and attentive.

Finally, David says, "I guess I don't know how I know. I've never thought about it before, because I've always known it, since the time I was little."

Lyle swallows hard, emptying his mouth so he can deliver the next barrage of questions.

"What's it like? Can you see Him? How big is He? Does He glow?" Lyle digs in the bag and finds a pickle.

"I never see Him. I just talk to Him."

"What's He sound like then?"

"He doesn't sound like anything."

"That doesn't make any sense. How can He not sound like anything?" Lyle asks, finishing off the pickle, and starting in on a carrot.

"It's really hard to explain."

"Try," Lyle insists. He produces the other carrot from the bag and hands it to David.

"Well, I go into my room and I sit in the dark, and I ask Him something and then I wait. After a while, He just comes into my head, and I know."

"That's it?" Lyle asks, disappointed. He comes up with a Hostess apple pie and attacks the wrapper.

"Should you be eating those?" David asks him.

"Hey, this isn't for me. This is yours," Lyle says, instantly changing course. This whole talking-to-God thing is not nearly as glamorous as he'd hoped. But he's taking in every last detail and he'll be thinking about it, a lot. He hands David the unwrapped Hostess pie.

It isn't long before lunch is over and the grocery bag is folded up and stowed away in Lyle's back pocket, ready for the next outing. David relaxes in his wheelchair, his clothes rumpled and dusty, hair disheveled with strands of chickweed poking out of it. Lyle lies atop the Log with his hands outstretched, looking as tidy as when he left the house. He's chattering away. He so much enjoys the sound of his own voice.

"And then Sharon Anne says, 'You're the best dancer ever, better than Fred Astaire.' And I say, 'Yeah, yeah, I can shake a leg.' And she goes—"

David interrupts. "And she goes, what about all the stuff you were going to teach me about running?"

Lyle pops up to a sitting position and glares at him. "Hey! I'm tellin' a story, here. She never said that!"

"I know," David shoots back.

"What d'ya think? You think I'm just layin' here blabbin'? Well, I'm not. I'm workin' on it right now!"

"You're working on it? No, you're not. You *are* just laying there blabbing, like you said. First it's Sharon Anne, blah-blah-blah, and then it's blah-blah, Sharon Anne, and then . . ."

Lyle jumps down from the Log.

"All right. All right. You asked for it. Are you listening?"

"Yes!"

Lyle hikes up his pants, high-water style.

"Okay, now do what I'm doin'."

He stands in front of David's wheelchair, stretches his arms out wide and turns his opened palms and face upward, toward the sunlight. David imitates him as best he can.

"Look at the sun with your eyes closed," Lyle instructs him, and David does it.

After a while, David opens his eyes just enough to peek at Lyle, who is standing in exactly the same position.

"How long do we have to do this?" David asks.

Lyle quotes Jack LaLanne. "Listen to me! I promise you if you will just dedicate a few minutes a day you will get results. A few minutes a day. That's all I ask. Are you with me?"

David nods and concentrates. "Yes, I'm with you."

"Okay," Lyle says in a hushed voice. "Now picture yourself running."

After a long silence, Lyle whispers. "Do you feel it?"

"I think so . . . is this really going to work?"

Lyle speaks with hushed reverence. "Shhh. It's already working!"

The boys arrive back at the Dahlke house well before darkness sets in. They hope to find Dennis at home but once they make their way down the ramped sidewalk to the back of the house and into the basement, they discover he's already out for the evening. It's Saturday night, and he is in high school, after all.

They decide Dennis surely won't mind if they borrow some necessary materials from his taxidermy room. Lyle finds alcohol and cotton, and David pops the jar of spiders open just long enough for Lyle to drop in a cotton ball soaked in alcohol. Lyle sets the jar on the coffee table, and they both stare intently at it.

"How long do you think we have to wait?" David asks.

"'Til they stop movin'," Lyle tells him with the confidence of an expert.

They gaze at the jar a while longer, and Lyle gets restless. He glances around the room.

"We're gonna need a box and more cotton, you know, to set 'em on. And pins," he informs David.

"What are the pins for?" David asks.

"You stick pins in 'em. So when we put 'em in our real display, we can stick 'em to the board. But we'll put 'em on cotton now, so they don't get broken."

"Okay," David says, "good thinking. You go out to the garage and get a cigar box off the shelf. There's empty ones in the corner where Dutch hangs out. I'll get some pins from my mom and some more cotton."

"Who's Dutch?" Lyle asks.

"Matt Veale's dog. He's always out there in our garage, well, except when Dennis takes him back over to Matt's house. He lives right next door." David points in the direction of the neighbor's yard. "Except when he lives in our garage, which is usually."

"What's he doin' there?" Lyle's curiosity kicks in.

"He's waiting for Puff."

"The badger? Are you kiddin' me?"

"No, I'm not kidding. Last year, Dennis had Puff's cage out in the backyard . . . under the big elm tree, and she dug a tunnel right through the bottom of the cage, and accidentally came back up over in Matt's yard . . . right inside Dutch's kennel! It freaked Dutch out so bad he crawled into Puff's tunnel and came back up in our yard . . . right in Puff's cage!"

David gets a kick out of the look on Lyle's face, pleased his story is having an impact.

"That is crazy!" Lyle exclaims, always impressed with a good tale. "Is that really true? You can tell me if you're exaggeratin', 'cause I do that sometimes."

"Uh-uh, I'm not. Dennis had to put on his big canvas bee gloves and carry Puff back to her cage and then he had to carry Dutch back over to Matt's house. Dutch is still kind of weird. My dad says he's obsessed. Dennis says he's lost his marbles. He's nice, though. You can pet him."

"He hasn't lost his marbles," Lyle says slowly, at the same time he's figuring it out. "He has a monster *crush* on Puff."

"I don't think so," David shakes his head. "Dogs and badgers really don't—"

"Think about it, David! He's stuck in that kennel all day long and can't get to her and then when he finally does, she wants nothin' to do with him. Mr. Merrick always says, 'Women, can't live with 'em, can't live without 'em.'"

"What does that mean?" David inquires.

"How would I know?" Lyle is out the door before David has a chance to respond.

David's dad is right: Dutch, a purebred German shorthair, *is* obsessed—much the way a dog might become fascinated with a porcupine after getting a nose full of quills, going back time after time for more. Never having fully recovered from the trauma caused when Puff popped up in his kennel, Dutch is left with an insatiable curiosity about the badger, and hangs about the Dahlkes' garage, watching . . . and waiting.

When Lyle enters the dim garage, sure enough, there he is, lying in the corner.

"Hey Dutch," Lyle calls gently, "I know exactly how you feel, buddy."

Dutch thumps his tail, and Lyle gives him a pat on the head and a scruff or two before reaching for the cigar box.

A few minutes later Lyle's back in the basement, glad to see David has collected the pins and cotton. Lyle lifts the jar of spiders and shakes it gently. The spiders don't move. He rolls the jar, making them tumble over each other. They don't react. He shakes the jar harder. Nothing.

"I think they're done," he tells David.

David nods. Lyle removes the lid from the jar and dumps the pile of spiders onto the coffee table.

CHAPTER NINE

RE-ANIMATION

*You gotta be careful if you don't know where
you're going because you might not get there.*

~ YOGI BERRA

Their materials gathered, the boys go quickly to work. David lines the cigar box with cotton, while Lyle snaps open the container of straight pins and inserts one through the back of each spider. He saves the Queen for last, and as he's about to push a pin through her back, David stops him.

"Wait, Lyle!" he says. "Give her the fancy one with the shiny black ball on top."

"Yeah! Good thinkin'!" Lyle firmly inserts the special pin through the back of the black widow.

Using the pins as handles, the boys lift the spiders and arrange them on the bed of cotton in perfectly straight rows. They spread out each hairy leg on each hairy spider to its widest possible span for an extra touch of drama, and then lean back to assess the effect.

"We should fix the legs on those big ones, so they look like they're grabbing something. You know, up in the air, like this." David demonstrates. "Plus, it'll show their fangs!"

"Cool!" Lyle says, and they go back to work, adjusting the legs on the four largest spiders to make it appear as if they're alive and about to pounce on their prey. They work with the intensity and focus of master artists, shaping and positioning each little arachnid, just so. Lastly, they give special attention to the black widow, which they position in the precise center of the display, and then, once again, they assess the results.

"Dang it! That's cool!" Lyle exclaims. "I wanna take this home and show my mom and dad. Do you wanna show it to your folks?"

David shakes his head. "No, they've seen this kind of stuff before. Plenty of times."

Mrs. Hatcher's study materials are spread out in front of her on the kitchen table, and Mr. Hatcher sits across from her, reading the paper. When Lyle charges into the room, her mom-radar instantly detects the cigar box.

"What's in the box?" she asks.

"Don't worry, Mom. Me and David are doin' a science project."

"Partners in crime, huh?"

"Yep. Look, Mom!"

Lyle proudly opens the box to show her the spider display. She catches a glimpse of it and averts her eyes.

"Oh, yuck. That's very nice."

Mr. Hatcher lowers his paper. Seeing what the fuss is about, he shakes his head and goes back to reading.

"Can I take it to school tomorrow?" Lyle asks.

"We'll see. Now, put it away and go outside and play until dinner." Mrs. Hatcher shudders.

Lyle carries the box to his bedroom and glances around for a safe place to store his new treasure. He kneels down and pushes it under his bed. Satisfied it's out of harm's way, he races down the hall, through the kitchen, and out the back door. He doesn't need to be told twice.

Lyle figures he'll find a game in progress at the playground. All the neighborhood kids mingle during the magical time between school and dinner, and almost any time on the weekends. He whistles to Dino and trots off for the school.

Mrs. Hatcher returns to her lesson. She picks up her pencil and goes to work, then puts it down again. Her concentration is broken—and justifiably so, since she's petrified of spiders.

Mrs. Hatcher stands up and stretches. Her husband lowers his newspaper for a second time.

"Had enough for one day?" he asks.

"Just need a break," she replies.

She heads down the stairs to the basement. She enjoys it down here . . . cool and quiet, a pleasant get-away. The room, which divides the length of the basement in half, is empty except for the piano and a half-dozen high-backed wood chairs. The Hatchers hold dance parties and get-togethers here, so Mr. Hatcher covered the walls with dark paneling, to give it a more finished look.

She takes her placc at the piano, and warms up her fingers with a pleasant, lilting version of *The Tennessee Waltz*.

Steve and Linda, attracted by the music, soon interrupt. To them, her playing means one thing, and in no time they're rollerskating on the smooth concrete floor.

Several minutes later, Lyle bounds from the top of the stairs to the bottom in three giant leaps, and sticks the landing hard with both feet. The schoolyard was empty, it turns out, so he's looking for something to do. He rustles up his skates and hurries to attach them to his shoes.

Lyle joins his siblings and before long, being who he is, he can't help but skate faster and faster. Mrs. Hatcher, equally unable to restrain herself, increases her tempo to match the pace of his skating. Steve, a tad reckless and out of control, makes every effort to keep up. Linda simply glides in circles, looking beautiful. She's an expert skater for her age.

Soon, the waltz moves at a faster tempo than any waltz should, and Steve, lacking the finesse to turn at top speed, slams into the wall and pushes off—a desperate but successful way to quickly change direction.

Mrs. Hatcher plays louder, in order to be heard over the sound of Steve's body-slamming and twelve metal wheels on the concrete floor. The louder she plays, the faster Lyle skates. Everything ratchets up, and soon the four of them are in a feedback loop of music and movement which gets louder and louder, faster and faster, by the moment.

Suddenly, out of nowhere, a musical lightning bolt seems to strike Mrs. Hatcher, transforming her into a miniature version of Jerry Lee Lewis, and she lights up with a wall-shaking, key-pounding rendition of *Great Balls of Fire*. Bouncing up and down on the piano bench, she dances while she plays, and her music fills every corner of the room.

Mr. Hatcher charges down the stairs. He arrives smack in the middle of chaos: Steve, repeatedly pounding his body into the wall—Lyle, zooming around the room like a demon possessed—Mrs. Hatcher, banging crazily away at the piano—and Linda, in the middle of it all, skating around like a dancer.

"What in the Sam Hill is going on down here?" he yells.

The music knocks to a halt. Linda executes a graceful quad stop. Lyle flies full-speed through the open door into Linda's bedroom and crash-lands on her bed, as Steve hits the wall again, rocketing backward onto the floor. Steve stares at his dad, and decides to stay exactly where he is.

"Time for a break," Mr. Hatcher orders. "You three go outside and blow the stink off!"

They waste no time doing exactly as he says.

"Good one, Mom!" Lyle fires, as he scampers past his parents up the stairs.

Mr. Hatcher moves to the workbench and takes up a hammer. He taps the nails back into the wall where Steve's incessant impacts loosened the paneling.

"I couldn't even hear myself think with all the racket going on down here," he complains.

"You missed one." His wife points.

Mr. Hatcher pounds in the nail. Frankly, he's glad to have the excuse for it: hammering feels good. "I don't know who's worse, you or the kids," he mutters.

"One of the teachers at school suggested it," she shrugs, improvising a logical-sounding excuse for herself.

"Really?" He lets the hammer drop to his side. "Suggested what?"

"She uses music when the children get out of control, to help settle them down."

"Hmm," Mr. Hatcher starts slowly, his voice full of skepticism, "that may be . . . but I doubt she puts the kids on rollerskates and plays *Great Balls of Fire!*"

"I don't know. I didn't ask for details."

Her husband stares at her, then surrenders to a chuckle. "At least now I know where they get it. Hand me another nail."

He reaches for it, and she pulls it away, out of reach. Hand outstretched, he signals with his fingers for the nail.

His wife steps in.

"It's rock 'n roll, baby," she coos.

She stands on tiptoe, and plants a kiss smack on his lips.

Shortly after midnight, everyone is asleep except Mrs. Hatcher—studying in the kitchen. The house is tranquil: utterly and beautifully silent. She is deep in concentration when a piercing scream erupts from Lyle's bedroom.

"Oh, good grief," she sighs. "What now?"

She hurries to his room and flips on the light. A tornado has hit Lyle's bed. Sheets and blankets are flung to the floor. Lyle dances on the mattress like his pants are on fire, frantically ripping off his pajama top. He hurls it with a cry across the room.

"Lyle! What's wrong?!"

Then she sees them.

They seem to be everywhere: scuttling around the floor, skittering over the bed and up and down the walls, crawling on Lyle's pillow and in his pajamas. They all have pins sticking out of their backs.

Steve and Linda rush to the doorway, freeze for a moment, then Linda emits a loud wail. They whirl and disappear.

"Don't worry. I'll get 'em. It's okay, I can see 'em!" Lyle reassures his mom.

He scurries around the room trying to catch the spiders with his fingers. Mrs. Hatcher—privately horrified but knowing better than to reveal anxiety to children—squishes what she can with a Kleenex, and unceremoniously drops the little corpses into the cigar box. Steve barges back in, armed with a big red plastic baseball bat, and thumps it hard on the floor.

"I'm gonna make mincemeat out of 'em!" he proclaims.

"Mom? How many do you have?" Lyle asks.

She takes inventory. Steve smacks his bat against the wall, narrowly missing one. He takes another whack, squashing the thing flat onto the wall and driving the pin in its back straight into the plaster.

"Who's afraid of a few spiders?" he whoops, waving the bat wildly around his head.

"Steve! Stop it!" Mrs. Hatcher yells. She counts, "Nine, ten . . . there's eleven in here."

"Don't forget this one!" Steve shouts, pointing to the dark spot on the bedroom wall (formerly a spider), anxious to claim his trophy kill.

"Plus the one on the wall," Mrs. Hatcher adds. "Is that it?"

Lyle peers into the box. "No! The Queen's not there!"

"The Queen?"

"The black widow. She's big and shiny with a red hourglass."

"I know what a black widow looks like, for Heaven's sake! Did she have a pin sticking in her back like the rest of them?"

"Yeah, Mom. She had a fancy one with a black ball on top."

"Lovely." Mrs. Hatcher grimaces.

"If you spot her, tell me, 'cause I'm loaded fer bear!" Steve brandishes his plastic bat.

"I'm not going to say it again, Steve! Stop swinging that thing in my face!" Mrs. Hatcher tells him.

After a lengthy search, there's still no sign of the black widow. Mrs. Hatcher leaves the room with the cigar box and returns a few minutes later without it. She makes an announcement.

"All right, everyone. There's nothing to worry about. Now get back to bed!"

"But, Mom, she's a night spider! She hunts and feeds in the dark!"

"To bed!" Mrs. Hatcher yells, a tinge of hysteria in her voice. She's had quite enough for one night.

Five minutes later it is once again quiet in the Hatcher house. Linda is in her bed with the blankets up to her nose. Her eyes are wide open and dart from side to side. Steve sits up on his bed with the covers over his head. The beam from his flashlight shoots about under the blanket. In her bedroom, Mrs. Hatcher climbs into bed beside her husband.

"The whole room was crawling with them," she shivers, snatching the covers up to her chin. "I have never seen so many spiders in one place. Brrrr, I hate spiders!"

"You got 'em all?" Mr. Hatcher asks.

She doesn't respond.

"You did get 'em all. Right?"

"No. Actually, we didn't."

"You gotta be kidding me."

"No, we never found the black widow."

"Where'd it go?"

"I don't know, Ron! I sealed the door to his room with a towel, and I'm going to vacuum every square inch of it first thing tomorrow!"

"That's it? You sealed his room with a towel?"

"I sealed Linda's room and Steve's with a towel, too." She looks over at him. "And ours."

Mr. Hatcher grins. "That's my girl."

She rewards him with a grimace.

They're both quiet for a while.

"I'm going to read," she tells him. "There is no way I can sleep.

"Doesn't look like Captain Courageous here is having any trouble," he comments wryly.

Lyle, sprawled between them under the covers, is already fast asleep.

Sunday, September 26
45 days to Parent Night

Lyle wakes early, with one thing on his mind: finding the cigar box. He crawls from his parents' bed and sneaks out of the room. On his way down the hall, he pokes his head into Linda's bedroom.

"Hey, Linda," he whispers.

There's no answer. He tiptoes up to her bed and whispers something near her ear.

"Mmm," she mumbles, more asleep than awake.

He seems satisfied with the response. He pads into the kitchen, and digs through the contents of the grocery bag under the sink, which serves as the wastebasket.

Empty cereal boxes, banana peels, potato peels and tin cans, all squished together. Crumpled paper. I don't know what that red thing is, it looks squished, too. Lotsa coffee grounds. Gross! That stuff feels like sand off a cat's tongue.

Mom said it would stunt my growth. She should know. She's a shorty-short-short. Coffee smells like stubbly faces and tastes like muddy dirt water.

Lyle smells his fingers, twice, then wipes the coffee grounds onto the edge of the bag. He checks out the rest of the kitchen. No sign of the cigar box. He knows it won't be in his parents' bedroom; his mom wouldn't have been able to sleep if it had been in the same room with her.

The back porch is next. Nothing there, either. He wanders out to the garage and pokes around. Knowing how his mom hates spiders, the garbage can seems a likely place for it. He grins to find a large cement block holding down the garbage can lid. He wrestles the chunk of concrete to the floor and removes the cover. There, resting on top of the trash, is the cigar box.

"Yes!" he exclaims.

He tosses away as much of the Kleenex as possible without losing any of the valuable bug pieces, salvaging everything that looks like it might be a spider or some part of a spider. Clutching the box tightly, he runs into the yard, where Dino waits.

"C'mon!"

CHAPTER TEN

DAY OF REST

If you want to build a ship,
don't herd people together to collect wood . . .
but rather teach them to long
for the endless immensity of the sea.

~ ANTOINE DE SAINT EXUPÉRY

Off they go, full-speed down the street. It's a damp morning, threatening rain, but boy and dog are both glad to be outside, and they take every long-cut they can find, through the vacant lots and the undeveloped sections of pine forest.

Lyle thrills to the fact that this is no ordinary Sunday morning. Normally, he, Linda, and Steve fix their breakfast, put on their best clothes, and walk to Sunday school classes, which are provided for children of parents attending church. Lyle's parents never go to church, but happily send their children to crash the ecclesiastical babysitting service.

It has not escaped Lyle's attention that his parents skip church, or even that they don't belong to any particular religion. When he raised it with Linda, she explained that Sunday school gives them an hour and a half to themselves: a gift of time, as they see it, bestowed by the grace of God.

Today, Lyle thinks, if there is a God, He would want the bug crisis remedied immediately.

Lyle and Dino reach the Dahlke house in no time flat, and David is already up waiting. Lyle hands him the cigar box and moves nervously about the room. He's worried Linda or his mom will find out he ditched church, and call at any minute. David opens the box and stares at the contents in surprise.

"What happened? I thought we were going for the blue ribbon. We can't use these!"

He pokes through the remains with his finger while Dennis, nearby, keeps his amusement to himself.

"I know. I know that! But they all came back to life, and my mom just stomped 'em into the ground! That's all that's left," Lyle agonizes.

"What did you use to kill them?" Dennis interjects, cupping quotation marks in the air around the word "kill."

"Rubbing alcohol," Lyle informs him.

"They didn't come back to life," Dennis laughs. "They just sobered up!"

The boys have no idea what he's talking about and certainly no idea why it's funny. This is a serious matter.

"What d'ya think?" Lyle asks David, taking the box from him.

"What do you mean, what do I think?"

Lyle stops and glares at David. "I mean, what d'ya think?"

"Well, one thing's for sure. We have to find a lot bigger box."

"And next time," Dennis tells them, "you'd better use carbon tetrachloride. Those little buggers are hard to kill."

"You're tellin' me!" Lyle nods.

"We'd better get out there and get started," David says, his spirits coming back. "Forty-five days left to Parent Night."

"You don't have to say that every time," Lyle tells him, suddenly nervous.

"I don't think you'll be doin' any bug huntin' today," Dennis announces. "It's pouring down rain out there. Listen. Check it out."

The boys hold very still. They can hear the sound of the rainstorm—not an aggressive storm that pounds itself out in ten or fifteen minutes, or one of those misty teasers that comes and goes, alternated with brief bursts of sunshine, but the kind that inspires terms like "socked in"—a steady, relentless, drizzling downpour which makes being outside intensely unpleasant.

"We could catch water bugs," Lyle offers hopefully.

Dennis shoots them a sympathetic look and disappears into his taxidermy room. Lyle stands perfectly still for a few seconds, thinking, then abruptly grabs the handles on David's wheelchair and rattles it.

"To the Bubble!" he shouts.

They charge through the laundry room, Lyle making buzzing noises and poking David in the ribs, David responding with involuntary yelps. They blow by Mr. and Mrs. Dahlke, who busily sort through boxes of clothes, household items and toys. David's parents laugh.

"Does he know our son is disabled?" Mr. Dahlke whispers.

"I don't think so," his wife giggles. "And let's not tell him."

David's parents go back to what they were doing. Mrs. Dahlke reaches for a box and trips over Puff, inspiring Mr. Dahlke to improvise a song to the tune of *The Hokey-Pokey*.

"We got a badger and a cat, we got the snakes and a rat, we got a pigeon and a bat, and our dog is way too fat. We got the couch where she sat, and the puppies she begat. Why don't we sell all that?"

"You are so talented, honey," his wife gushes. "But it doesn't change the fact we wouldn't get ten dollars for the entire menagerie, and you know it."

Lyle and David wrestle the wheelchair through the back door and make a break through the rain for the warm steamy interior of the Bubble. They don't slow down until they're zipped inside.

"Are you guys really sellin' all your pets? 'Cause if you are, I wanna buy the badger," Lyle announces, as he sets up for a handstand on the edge of the pool.

"No, my dad's just kidding around. He always makes up songs like that. They're doing a garage sale. It's a fundraiser for the Muscular Dystrophy Association. My mom and dad are the President and Vice-President. Actually, they trade positions every year—I think my mom's President this year. I can't remember."

"What do they use the money for?"

"Trying to find a cure. When I got tested in Salt Lake City, they told my mom it'd take eight years. That was seven years ago. Soooo . . ." David holds up his crossed fingers.

"What? Seven years? And next year is eight? There's no time to waste! We need to get *you* into that pool. NOW!" Lyle instructs, pointing at the water.

"We have to wait for Dennis," David responds, backing his chair away from Lyle.

"I can do it," Lyle insists.

"No, you can't," David argues. "There's a certain way."

Lyle locks the wheels on David's chair.

David protests, "What are you doing? No! Don't do anything. Just wait!"

Lyle plants his hands firmly on the arms of the wheelchair and leans in.

"Listen to me. I know what I'm doing. If you're gonna learn to run, you have to want it. Bad! See the water there? You have to get from here to there and you can't let anything stand in your way. Not anything. You're gonna run, one way or another, and that's how it works!"

Lyle turns away from David, reaching his hands back over his shoulders. "Grab my hands," he orders.

"I need some time to think about this. I'm not sure it's a good idea," David hesitates.

"Just grab 'em!"

David tentatively reaches forward, and grasps Lyle's hands. His weight drags Lyle down into his lap, and he laughs.

"I told you it wouldn't work. Now get off me."

Lyle leans forward and straightens up, clenching David's hands in his. His voice strains with the effort. "You . . . have to . . . want to . . . get to . . . the water."

David hangs from Lyle's back like a gangly human backpack.

"See?" Lyle tells him. "You're walkin'! You're walkin' to the water."

"Lyle. Put me down!"

Lyle ignores him and shuffles to the edge of the pool, David's feet dragging behind him on the concrete. When he reaches the edge—

"Wait! Stop!" David pleads.

—Lyle throws himself forward into the pool, pulling David with him.

Ker-splash!

He lands flat on the water, face down, David still attached to his back. Lyle quickly sinks to the bottom, while David bobs on the surface. When Lyle resurfaces, the boys can't breathe from uncontrolled fits of laughter.

Lyle sucks as much air into his lungs as he can and dives back down. The underwater light throws dancing patterns onto the painted pool walls. He lies on his back on the bottom, holding his breath and enjoying the light show, until he notices the rippling figure of someone standing at the side of the pool. Lyle pops up.

"You were supposed to wait for me! If Mom and Dad knew, you'd be in hot water!" Dennis scolds David.

"It's my fault, Dennis. I'm sorry," Lyle insists.

"Don't do it again. You guys call me when you're ready to get out."

"Okay, Dennis," David says. "Sorry."

Dennis vanishes back into the house. The boys find the encounter sobering, and they calm down considerably. David rolls onto his back. Lyle studies him, to see how he accomplishes the floating thing. David's entire chest is out of the water and so are his feet and knees.

As Lyle struggles to stay afloat, his feet sink first, then his legs, his torso follows, and soon his nose is the only thing sticking out. David lies at the surface, comfortably chatting away. When Lyle tries to respond, he gets a mouthful of water.

"You talk, I'll listen," he gurgles, after almost drowning trying to answer a question.

Before long, Lyle concludes he's never going to be able to float like David. It's a bit of a sore point because even though Lyle loves being in the water, he also has a secret fear of drowning. Trying to stay afloat is exhausting. He prefers sinking to the bottom, where everything's quiet and his lungs are still. Now, he's glad to stop and rest, hanging from the edge of the pool.

"Hey, David, have you ever rollerskated?"

David laughs. "No."

"Well, what I mean is . . . were you ever . . ." Lyle blows bubbles. "I mean, were your legs ever normal?"

"Not really. Not that I can remember, anyway."

"I was wonderin', if there is a God, why doesn't He just fix your legs?"

"If God wanted my legs fixed, they would be fixed. Just like that." David snaps his fingers.

"Yeah, well, why don't you talk to Him about it, then?"

"You're supposed to pray in your happiness, not in your suffering."

"Is that from the Bible?" Lyle asks.

"I don't know if it's in the Bible," David tells him. "But it doesn't matter where you read it. What it means is—"

"I know what it means," Lyle interrupts defensively. "It means you're not sayin' what I think you said."

"What?" David says, completely confused.

"Okay then, say it in plain English!"

"It just means you should thank God for everything you have, and not complain."

Dennis and Jenon enter the Bubble, flirting and laughing, forgetting for a moment they're not alone. Jenon sees them first, and smiles.

"Hey, Lyle, I hope you're all done with the cannonballs for today," she comments, stretching herself out on a lounge chair.

"I'm really sorry about draggin' David into the pool," Lyle hastens.

"We're cool." Dennis says. "Hey! David told me you were visiting your grandma and grandpa at Twin Lakes last weekend."

He lifts David out of the pool and settles him back in his wheelchair.

"Yeah, my grandma Witty is out there with 'em, too. She's almost deaf so we hafta yell. And she's Norwegian, so she can't say her J's."

Lyle shows off his best Norwegian accent, imitating his great-grandmother. "One time she was tellin' me to quit yumpin' on the bed. So I went, I'm not yumping on the bed, I'm jumping on the bed. She goes, I know you're yumpin' on the bed so yust quit with the yumpin'. And I went, Grandma I'm jumping. And she goes, and I yust got done tellin' you to stop yumpin', now—"

Dennis nudges him to a close. "Okay. All right, Lyle. I think we got it. Good story, though."

"You know what else? She calls a joker a yoker," Lyle adds expecting laughter.

No one reacts.

"And, um . . . she always wears a hearing aid when she watches the TV. So this one time I turned the TV way down and did a whistle—like her hearing aid does, like this."

Lyle demonstrates with a high-pitched whistling sound, a good imitation of hearing-aid feedback.

"And she'd adjust her hearing aid and I'd whistle again. It was so funny!" He keeps whistling, and imitates her making the adjustment, mimicking her confusion.

"She kept turnin' up her hearing aid and I kept turnin' down the TV. Then when she got the hearing aid turned all the way up I turned the TV up really loud. You shoulda seen her face!"

He pauses in the telling of his story, to allow himself a well-deserved moment of laughter in celebration of his own comic genius. It's all so hilarious to him he fails to observe no one else laughs. Worse yet, they're all staring at him.

When he finally notices the demeanor of his audience, he switches to a serious expression, and sternly announces, "Boy, I got in trouble for that!"

Dang! I am never, ever tellin' that story ever again!

A bit later, David and Lyle dry off in the basement. Dennis holds their cigar box, turning it over and visually measuring it.

"So you don't think this is going to be big enough, huh? How many bugs are you planning to collect?"

"Every kind there is. Hundreds of 'em," Lyle predicts.

"How many you got so far?"

"We don't really have any yet," Lyle admits.

"I think I've got a box for you. I don't know if it's big enough for hundreds, but it's bigger than this one."

Dennis leaves the room for a while and returns with an enormous shallow wooden box about four feet long.

"Holey smokes! This is perfect!" Lyle exclaims.

"Are you sure you can carry it home by yourself?"

"Hey. It's me," Lyle reassures him.

"I'll set it right here for you," Dennis says, leaning the box against the wall.

He joins Jenon in the taxidermy room and Lyle and David hear her giggle.

"They're making out in there," David declares.

The boys snicker. Lyle puckers up his face, imagining he's kissing Marilyn Monroe. David laughs at him, then immediately turns serious.

"I've been wondering, what's the next step?" David asks.

"Step?"

"You know, for learning to run."

Lyle shakes his head. "I don't know if you're ready for it or not."

"Yes, I am." David insists. "I've been practicing. What is it?"

"You are not ready!"

"I am definitely ready!"

"David, we can't go over it right now. Remember, this is top secret. Not even your family can know."

"I haven't told a soul. I haven't even told Dennis, and I tell him everything."

"Good! Because tomorrow . . . in the library . . ."

Lyle wags his finger at David, a warning about what's coming.

"You're gonna need to be ready. 'Cause this is big."

Lyle gets right up in David's face. "BIG!"

He glances up at the clock.

"Oh, I gotta go. Dinnertime!"

CHAPTER ELEVEN

SCOUT KNIFE

It takes two men to make one brother.

~ ISRAEL ZANGWILL

Monday, September 27
44 days to Parent Night

Lyle and David do their homework at a small study table in the Linwood library. Sharon Anne and Francine read quietly and occasionally whisper to one another at the table behind them, and Mrs. Thompson, the librarian, is at her desk, where she almost always is, checking in books.

Lyle draws a slip of paper from his pocket and lays it on the table, like he's placing a high-stakes bet. He pats it with his open palm a couple of times for emphasis.

"What is it?" David whispers.

"That," Lyle whispers back, "is our Science Day pass."

David's eyes widen. "You got us a Science Day pass? How did you do it?"

Lyle flashes a full-face grin, like a cat with a mouthful of feathers. Science Day is a favorite for all the students, but to get a coveted Science Day pass is the ultimate prize.

When Lyle requested one for himself and David, Miss O'Donnell was hesitant. But Lyle pointed out they had done as she suggested, and had researched the proper methods for collecting dangerous insects. (He stretched the truth, perhaps, but he knows there is a short section in Dennis' entomology book dealing with this very subject, and he's sure David probably read it.) In fact, they *needed* the pass, he told Miss O'Donnell, because collecting the insects on school grounds, at a time when children were present, would clearly be anything but safe. Using her own words against her was risky and he knew it, but it worked.

"We're goin' to the Log on Friday, for bugs," Lyle proclaims.

"Wow . . ." David shakes his head in genuine admiration for his partner's resourcefulness.

"We have to be back to school by two. To show Mrs. Stewart what we got done. That's what Miss O'Donnell said."

Lyle ponders this briefly, suddenly disappointed, as the full weight of this restriction sinks in for the first time.

"But that's okay," he says, brightening. "We'll just have to start really early. And I mean really really early, so you better be ready, David!" He leans in. "And you know what else? When we're out there, you're gonna run, one way or another!"

David's surprise grows. He wasn't expecting anything half this monumental.

"Hey, Lyle," he blurts, "did you hear Jerry Lindgren broke the 5,000-meter record? I'll betcha he knows some stuff!"

Paul saunters by and shoots them a look, dropping to a seat at the table immediately to their right. Lyle eyes him suspiciously.

"You weren't s'posed to tell anybody we're workin' on that!" Lyle whispers to David.

"I didn't," David insists.

"Does Paul know?"

"No!"

"He was lookin' at us!"

David shrugs, completely unconcerned.

"This is exactly what I was talkin' about yesterday. If we're gonna keep workin' on this, we gotta make a pact. And I'm talkin' about a serious one!"

Lyle glances around the room again. No one seems to be paying attention. He digs his Cub Scout knife from his pocket, and slowly opens a blade. His gaze travels from David's face, down to the knife blade, and back over to David. Lyle expects him to react, but he doesn't.

"No, wait," Lyle says, snapping the knife closed.

Dramatically, he opens the largest blade and moves it slowly back and forth so the light glimmers on it.

"That's better. Now, hold out your thumb," he urges in a low voice, eyes darting about for privacy. "Here, give it to me!"

David makes a fist, his thumb sticking out like a hitchhiker's, and Lyle grabs it.

"This is a Blood-Brothers' Pact. Okay? Now once we do this, it means, Scouts' honor, you can't tell anybody ever about me teachin' you to run."

"Gee whiz, Lyle, I already know," David says. "And you can't tell anybody my secret, either."

"That *is* your secret," Lyle informs him. "Now, listen, my dad helped me sharpen this. He says there's nothing more dangerous than a dull knife."

Lyle tightens his grip on David's thumb . . . but hesitates.

"I'm just gonna cut a tiny little bit," he says, stalling. "You don't have to watch if you don't want to."

David watches closely.

"In fact, you probably shouldn't!" Lyle places the knife on David's thumb. "Look away, buddy!" he warns him.

David moves his face even closer and Lyle frowns at him, like the parent of a child who intentionally disobeys.

"Tough guy, huh?"

With a quick push, Lyle jabs a tiny nick in David's thumb and, with effort, squeezes out one drop of blood.

David accepts this without complaint.

"There, that should do it," Lyle nods. "That wasn't so bad, was it?"

"It's your turn," David says eagerly.

"I know. I know that! Hold your horses!"

Lyle puts the knife blade up against his own thumb.

"This is sharper than the dickens!"

David holds up a blood-spotted thumb. "You're tellin' me."

"This takes guts!" Lyle adds.

"You want me to do it?" David offers. "It would probably be a lot easier. Here, let me."

David reaches for the knife and Lyle jerks it away.

"I'm a Lion in the Cub Scouts for cryin' out loud! I think I know what I'm doin'!"

"Okay. I was just asking. Anyway I thought you quit the . . ."

Lyle hyperventilates. Closes his eyes—and slices.

David whips his wheelchair backward and yells, "Holey smokes! You cut half your thumb off!"

Lyle spasmodically flops his hand in the air, an involuntary reaction to the pain, and globs of blood fly from his thumb, some of it speckling his forehead.

David spins his chair toward the girls' table.

"Sharon Anne," he says, more politely than necessary. "Do you by any chance have a Kleenex?"

Sharon Anne locates one and holds it out to David. Francine sees the blood running down Lyle's hand and more of it splattered on his face. She pales, and weaves in her seat. Sharon Anne, noticing her friend is about to pass out, concludes it's time to take action.

"Mrs. Thompson!" she shouts, her hand to her mouth. "Lyle cut his thumb off!"

"Shhhh! No, I didn't! It's not that bad!" Lyle hushes her.

He's desperate to keep the situation from escalating, as so often happens, but it's too late. Mrs. Thompson is already marching in their direction, and in a matter of seconds, she is at the table, holding Lyle's hand for inspection. David hides his own, figuring one bleeding thumb is enough of a problem.

"Keep your hand in the air while I get the first-aid kit. And keep the tissue pressed on there, too. I'll need to wrap it, then we'll get you down to the nurse's station," she tells Lyle, calm and efficient.

The librarian hastens to her desk and locates her first-aid kit, hurries back to Lyle, and wraps his thumb. She presses the clean, white tape into place and snips off the extra with her scissors—just as Miss O'Donnell strides into the room, once again demonstrating her mysterious ability to sense trouble the moment it develops anywhere on school grounds.

"What seems to be the problem?" she asks.

"Lyle's cut himself," Mrs. Thompson explains evenly. "It looks like it's going to require two, if not three, stitches. And he'll probably need a tetanus shot."

"I'm not gonna get lockjaw, am I?" Lyle worries, the pitch of his voice rising.

"Hmm. Not likely," Mrs. Thompson replies.

"I'll take him to the nurse's station and make sure he gets what he needs," Miss O'Donnell says flatly, taking charge. "Come with me, Mr. Hatcher."

Lyle plods behind Miss O'Donnell, out of the library and into the empty hallway. She waits for him to catch up.

"I wanted a chance for you and me to have a talk together, just the two of us," she begins, walking slowly, with Lyle matching her pace. "Trouble seems to follow you, doesn't it, Mr. Hatcher?"

"I guess so," he ruefully admits.

"I wonder if there's a way we could get you to slow down and possibly avoid some of these predicaments. What do you think? Might this be possible?"

"Do you want me to slow down?"

"We've had some difficult days, now, haven't we?"

"Yes, I guess so."

"We're going to need to make sure we don't have any more incidents like this. Does it seem like a good idea to you to open a pocketknife in the library? Or even to bring one to school?"

"Probably not."

"It never is. How do you think we'd manage if we had an entire school full of children playing with knives?"

Lyle thinks about this, and his mind suddenly floods with the imagery.

"That wouldn't be good. That wouldn't be good at all," he agrees.

She continues, suddenly sharp. "No! It would not!"

"Miss O'Donnell? Do I have to go to the boiler room for recess?" He hopes she'll take it as a suggestion. His instincts tell him the boiler room will be less severe than the punishment she has in mind.

"First, we'll have Nurse Baker take care of your thumb. You're lucky she happened to be here the day you decided to do such a foolish thing. When she's finished with you, I want you to report immediately to Mr. Stratton's office!"

"Oh!" Lyle laments.

The two of them arrive at the nurse's station, and Miss O'Donnell stops at the closed door.

"And yes, you *will* be spending recess in the boiler room."

She opens the door. Lyle trudges inside. Miss O'Donnell waits until she sees he's with Nurse Baker, then crosses the hall to her office to place a call to Mrs. Hatcher.

In the principal's structured world, discipline is *not* doled out arbitrarily. She follows a custom-designed set of rules and a special system of punishment. They give her confidence when dealing with unexpected issues, since she instantly knows the correct course of action for any type of problematic behavior.

Her system consists of five levels. The boiler room is level one: minor infractions, one-time errors in judgment, and first offenses. Mr. Stratton handles level two. The hack paddle is always in full view in his office, a constant reminder to would-be transgressors. The hack is reserved for more egregious offenses—anything involving a pocketknife, to mention a random example. Level three requires the parents to meet with Miss O'Donnell and agree on an appropriate punishment, according to the severity of the offense. Level three often pairs with level four, which is suspension, or in more severe cases, level five, expulsion.

As a testament to her system's effectiveness, Miss O'Donnell knew the moment she walked into the library, she had a level-three offense on her hands.

The recess bell rings, and Nurse Baker finishes patching up Lyle's thumb. Lyle wonders if he could get away with skipping the trip to Mr. Stratton's office altogether, thinking perhaps no one would notice. But the moment he steps out of the nurse's office, Mr. Stratton, the gym teacher, is right outside the door, waiting.

Mr. Stratton is an intimidating man. His dark black hair and big thick eyebrows are especially noticeable in his unvarying attire: black framed glasses and a stark, white crew-neck tee-shirt. He's in his late thirties, an ex-athlete who once had the willpower to keep himself in perfect condition, until life made it seem not worth it. Now a belly bulges under his shirt, and serves as a convenient table for the whistle hanging about his thick neck.

Lyle startles to see him there.

"Oh, hi, Mr. Stratton. Are you busy?"

"My office," Mr. Stratton barks, as he turns and strides down the hall. Lyle knows without being told he had better follow.

The hack paddle is oak, the handle sanded smooth for Mr. Stratton's comfort. The paddle board itself is twenty-six inches long, with one-inch holes drilled down its center to reduce wind resistance and increase control.

This is Lyle's first level-two offense. He waits for instructions.

"Grab your ankles."

Lyle bends over, and braces for the blow.

An expert at administering the hack, Mr. Stratton knows just how much pain to inflict without overdoing it. He doesn't want to bruise or damage the little rumps, but he does want to leave an impression on little minds.

Lyle exits Mr. Stratton's office, rubbing his bottom, trying to soothe the stinging ache. David is right there waiting for him, in a show of solidarity. He wheels along next to Lyle.

"Boy, he got me good."

"Did it hurt?" David asks.

"No," Lyle lies.

"I wonder if I'll ever get a hack," David muses.

"I doubt it."

Mr. Merrick sees them coming and accurately reads all the signs. "All right there, rebels. What's goin' on now?"

"What do you mean, Mr. Merrick?" Lyle asks innocently, always anxious to reassure people nothing at all is going on.

"Well, ya got one hand all wrapped up like a mummy and ya got the other one rubbin' your keister. Ya think I don't know what that means?"

"It's nothin'," Lyle insists. "I just accidently cut myself with my Scout knife. Got a hack from Mr. Stratton for it. That's all."

"Ya got a hack for accidentally cuttin' yourself?"

"See, that's what I've been tellin' you, Mr. Merrick. I get in trouble for everything."

"What were ya doin' with your knife out in the first place?"

Lyle doesn't answer. The boys look sheepish.

"Cut your thumb, huh?" Mr. Merrick removes a key from the key chain on his belt. He holds it out to David. "Do me a big favor there, David, and hurry over to my storage closet in the gym. Grab a new bulb for my work lamp. You'll see 'em in there."

David is pleased to have the assignment. As he reaches for the key Mr. Merrick notices the blood on his thumb.

"Okay, Mr. Merrick. I'll be right back."

Once David is out of earshot, Mr. Merrick speaks quietly. "I don't know what ya got goin' on here, but whatever it is I'm thinkin' ya better tell me about it, 'cause doggone it, ya seem to be gettin' yourself in more and more trouble every day."

"But Mr. Merrick, I can't tell you."

"So ya got your blood-brother pact goin', huh?"

Lyle's eyes widen. "How did you know, Mr. Merrick?"

"I wasn't born yesterday. Does this have somethin' to do with all those questions ya been askin' about God?'"

"I already told you, Mr. Merrick, I can't tell you."

"I'm gettin' the feeling you'll be needin' some help on whatever it is you're up to. So come on now, just give me the short version. I'll keep it to myself."

Lyle glances around the room and lowers his voice.

"I'm gonna teach David to run. If he can run again, it means there really is a God. Does that make sense?"

Mr. Merrick exhales heavily. Now he truly wishes he'd kept his mouth shut. "So you've put God on notice, have ya?"

Lyle waits. They hear David at the door.

"Well," Mr. Merrick says, lowering his voice to match Lyle's. "It sounds to me like you're gettin' in way over your head. My advice is ya better be thinkin' things through a whole lot more before ya act. You're way outta your league here. You think about that!"

Lyle nods and goes to work cleaning the furnace filters. His injured thumb, bleeding a little, makes him extremely ineffective at the job, but he works conscientiously just the same.

David wheels into the boiler room with a new lightbulb. He hands it to Mr. Merrick, who notices Lyle struggling with the filters.

"I think you'd better give your thumb a rest," Mr. Merrick finally says, stopping him. "You can finish later this week when you're not bleedin' all over the place. I'll let Miss O'Donnell know."

"No, don't say anything," Lyle tells him. "I can do it!"

"No. Ya got about five minutes of recess left. Now, git!"

Lyle puts down the work, and the boys waste no time getting out to the playground. Lyle spies something on the baseball diamond and streaks to a stop. He stands there, thinking, a faraway glint in his eye.

"Did you catch any more last night?" David asks.

Lyle isn't listening. He's staring.

David bumps him with the chair.

"Hey, you! I was wondering if you caught any more."

Lyle hears him this time. "Heck, yeah."

He rubs his rump again and smiles. The hack makes him feel alive.

"Great! How many?" David asks.

"One."

"One? Only one?"

"Yeah," Lyle counters, holding up two fingers and making his eyes big, still staring out at the ball diamond. "But it's crazy bug number two! It's a giant silk moth, big as a catcher's mitt—"

"We definitely need another trip to the Log," David sighs.

Lyle doesn't answer. He's focused on the diamond, and now David sees why. Sharon Anne and her friends huddle around home plate, chatting and laughing.

Lyle speaks as if in a trance. "Right now I've got a different plan. It's called The-Sharon-Anne-Meets-Lyle-and-Falls-in-Love-with-Lyle-and-Marries-Lyle-Who-Is-Big-and-Tall-Plan."

"Big and tall? Are you kidding me?"

"This is a good one. See, what I'll do is I'll railroad you right into 'em like you're outta control. And then, at the last minute,

I'll stop your chair and save the day. Yeah! What d'ya think about that?"

"I don't like this plan at all. I'll look like a big corn-dog doofus!"

"No, you won't. C'mon, David!"

"No way, José! Forget it."

"Doggone it, David! I was really countin' on you! C'mon!"

The boys reach the top of the small incline above the diamond where they have a perfect view of the girls.

"In case you hadn't noticed, I'm in a wheelchair. Can you slow down for just a minute?"

Lyle, embarrassed at being insensitive and getting caught, tries to turn it around on David, hoping to get himself off the hook.

"Yeah, David. I can't believe you were thinkin' we'd just *do* it. It's a new plan, for Pete's sake! You can't be so impatient all the time. You haven't even got the picture in your mind yet. This could take days or even weeks of careful planning. This time I hope you can wait!" he rambles.

The two boys stare at each other as if it's a showdown.

"Well, can you?" Lyle says, demanding an answer.

"Wait? Of course I can wait." David says. "You don't need to tell me that."

"What d'ya think?" Lyle asks him. "Sharon has freckles on her nose. I like that. How 'bout you?" He gazes at her in near-adoration. The gleam in his eye ignites his pilot light.

"Freckles? I've never really—"

"I like freckles!"

All burners are in full-blaze.

"You know when's the best time to get goin' on something, right? It's not Christmas! It's not New Years! It's now! N-O-W!"

"No, Lyle! Wait! Are you crazy? We're waiting, right?"

Lyle aims David's chair toward home plate, carefully lining up his shot. Without hesitation, he rockets the chair down the hill, directly toward the group of girls who are wholly unaware of what's coming.

"All systems go!" he shouts. "*Blast . . . off!*"

CHAPTER TWELVE

GIRL

Put your hand on a hot stove for a minute,
and it seems like an hour.
Sit with a pretty girl for an hour,
and it seems like a minute. That's relativity.

~ ALBERT EINSTEIN

David yells, "Look out! I can't stop! No brakes!" His chair hurtles down the hill.

"Don't panic! I've got him!" Lyle shouts.

The girls look up and see Lyle, careening David's wheelchair directly at them while pretending he's trying to stop it. None of them are fooled by the ruse, but they all fly out of the way just the same—all of them except Sharon Anne. Only at the last second does she try to escape, just as the wheelchair bumps into her, and she plops into David's lap with a squeal. Lyle straightens and wipes his brow.

"Whoa! Good thing I grabbed this heavy chair before someone got seriously hurt."

Francine, having led the charge to safety, whips around and yells, "You're a stupid jerk, Lyle Hatcher! Do your parents beat you with an idiot stick?"

"They must! It's the only possible explanation," Colleen adds.

"Come on, Shay," Marla says to Sharon Anne. "Let's go."

Colleen sticks out her tongue at Lyle. The girls laugh and flounce away, but Sharon Anne remains comfortably situated in David's lap.

"Are you all right?" David asks her.

"David," she says, her face close to his. "You have the most incredible blue eyes I've ever seen."

David blinks slowly. "Really? You think so?"

Sharon Anne nods. Then she springs up and chases after her friends.

"See you later, David!"

David waves, even though her back is to him and she can't see it.

"'Bye, Sharon Anne."

The moment fades. He turns to Lyle.

"She's so nice."

"Yeah . . . so nice," Lyle echoes in dream-like agreement.

As the boys make their way toward the classroom, there is something different in their manner—a new confidence, visible even on David, in the way he throws his hands from the wheels as he pushes along. Lyle's light step is all but a swagger. These are young men in the making.

"D'ya think it worked?" Lyle asks his friend.

"Yes," David responds in a warm, satisfied voice. "It definitely worked."

Miss O'Donnell, who stands inside the fourth-grade classroom gazing out the window, moves her mouth in one unspoken word.

"Un . . . be . . . lievable!"

Witnessing Lyle wield David's wheelchair as a means of dangerous self-entertainment, worries her far more than anything he has done in the past. She has never had a child seriously injured at her school, but she has a nagging premonition that's exactly where this is headed.

She weighs the option of calling their parents and informing them she's canceling the Science Day pass. She decides against it, for David's sake, but hopes it won't be a decision she regrets.

That afternoon, while David waits for Dennis to help him with his therapies, he sets up his Webco reel-to-reel on the worktable. Singing is his hobby, and he uses the recorder to practice.

He retrieves a new three-inch reel of tape from his drawer and easily threads the machine. He pushes "Record," takes a deep breath, and sings the first verse of The Beatles' new hit, *Girl,* in his full voice. He hits "Stop" and rewinds the tape. As he listens to playback, he's annoyed with the result, especially the last line, where he can hear some missed notes. He practices several more times.

Now, the lyrics remind him of Sharon Anne, or perhaps he was already thinking of her. Slowly, knowing he can't help it, he wheels to the doorway of the taxidermy room, peeks in and spies, as Dennis shares a kiss with his girlfriend. Absorbed in each other, the couple is oblivious to all else. After only a brief moment, David hurries back over to his worktable. He barely gets there before Dennis and Jenon barge in on him, smiling.

"Who was that singing in here? Paul McCartney?" Jenon asks Dennis, loud enough for David to hear.

"No," David says, "That was me."

"You sure? Because I could have sworn it was one of the Fab Four." She winks. "See you later, David. Peace."

She flashes a V with her fingers, then turns and bounds up the stairs.

"Time to get to work," Dennis announces.

"Let's not do my therapy today," David murmurs. "I'm in the middle of this project I'm working on."

"What are you doing there?"

"Practicing my singing. I really wanna learn this song."

"Hey. Somethin' eatin' at you, Champ?"

"Thinking about some things, that's all."

David's voice has an edge to it Dennis hasn't heard before, a surprisingly serious contrast to the lighthearted banter of their trek home from school. Indeed, it seems to carry a new strength. Dennis is pretty sure he knows where it's coming from; he also knows he can probe. He and David talk about things neither would discuss with anyone else in the family.

"Are you sure nothing's wrong?" Dennis presses.

"Yeah, I'm sure."

"What have you been thinkin' about, exactly?" Dennis inquires casually, pretending he's busy straightening items on the shelves.

"You know, you don't have to take care of me all the time. I'm just fine on my own."

Dennis waits.

"I just thought," David adds, eyes traveling to the stairs where Jenon disappeared a moment ago, "maybe you'd like to go do something else for a change."

A serious expression crosses his older brother's face.

"You know, it's funny, because there's something I've been wanting to talk to you about. Something I've been worried about, lately."

Dennis sits down next to David.

"What?" David asks. He's curious.

"I know it won't be long before you have a girlfriend."

David stifles a smile, not wanting Dennis to know how much it pleases him to hear this.

"And the thing is . . . I mean . . . well, to tell you the truth, I'm worried when it happens you won't have time for your big brother anymore."

David grins.

"For your information, a girl at school told me I had the most incredible blue eyes she'd ever seen," he blurts out.

"No way!"

"Yeah, she did," David insists. "I met her at the backstop. Here, smell my arm."

Dennis obliges. "Oooo, Tabu."

"Here." David leaves his arm under Dennis' nose. "Smell it again."

Dennis obliges a second time. "Yep, still there."

"Dennis?" David says, hesitantly. "What do you think my chances are of maybe . . . you know . . . getting a kiss? Not today or anything like that, but you know . . ."

Dennis pretends to be deep in thought, as David trails off and waits.

"Girls are a mystery," Dennis finally says. "But to be honest with you, I think kissing might be overrated—way overrated. In fact, it's slimy and it tastes sorta like silly putty. I could take it or leave it, no problem."

"Take it or leave it?"

"Yep. Take it or leave it."

"Really?" David is enormously disappointed to hear this.

Dennis gives his brother a push and steps back. "No, I'm just teasin' you!"

"Come on, Dennis!"

"Okay, let's get serious." Dennis cracks his knuckles.

"All right, kissing. First? Your heart starts pounding like a jackhammer . . . and you can't breathe."

Almost without thought, David sucks in a deep breath.

"Second? Once her lips touch yours . . . you can't think."

David's mouth involuntarily squeezes into a slight pucker.

"And third?" Dennis says, enjoying the effect this is having on his brother. "All of a sudden . . . you . . . can't . . . move!"

He holds up a finger to make it clear he isn't finished yet. "And I swear . . ." Dennis pauses, swallows, takes a deep breath. ". . . You totally, positively, baby-baby-oh-baby, *don't want to*. Ever."

David gasps, "I . . . I can't breathe . . . just thinking about it."

Dennis explodes with laughter.

"You should see the look on your face, little brother. It looks like you're gonna fall right outta your chair!"

David straightens his back and relaxes his face, laughing at himself.

"Look, Mr. Incredible Blue Eyes, you're only in the fourth grade. Don't be in such a hurry to grow up. Heck, I didn't get my first real kiss 'til I was a junior in high school. It'll happen when the time is right, okay? Now, let's get your therapy over and done with, so we can go for a swim!"

CHAPTER THIRTEEN

SCIENCE DAY PASS

*You can outdistance that which is running after you
but not what is running inside you.*

~ RWANDAN PROVERB

Friday, October 1 – Science Day
40 days to Parent Night

Today is October first, which means one thing: Science Day has finally arrived! Lyle leaps out of bed, determined to get to David's house as quickly as possible. He finds David in the basement, hard at work on a painting. Lyle leans over his shoulder with interest while David puts the finishing touches on Jupiter.

"What's with you and the planets?" Lyle quizzes.

"Someday, when I die," David tells him, "I'll be able to fly from planet to planet, and visit all of 'em."

"Dyin'? Who's thinkin' about dyin'?" Lyle scoffs. "There's blue sky out there and we're wastin' it! *So let's fly!*"

"Okay. You don't have to yell. Let me go find my sweater."

"You don't need a sweater. It's gonna be a cooker."

Lyle's wearing shorts. The morning chill doesn't bother him in the least, most likely because he's constantly moving.

"Well, I have to take one, anyway," David informs him.

"Hurry up!"

"Mom!" David shouts. "Where's my sweater?"

David wheels off on his sweater search and Lyle plops down in front of the television to wait. It's shortly after eight, and *The Jack LaLanne Show* is on.

"At first you'll think it's impossible, but believe me, if you just use the willpower that we talked about yesterday and ask the Good Physician above for guidance and to give you the willpower to go ahead and do it, then I don't care what your problem is, you can make yourself whole. You can be reborn again if you do something with it. Please don't get discouraged. Promise me. That's all I ask."

"Ready?" David asks, pushing back into the room with his sweater on.

Outside, the boys are greeted enthusiastically by Dino. Despite the bright sun, it's a chilly autumn morning, and last night's light freeze renders the maple, elm and oak trees a brilliant kaleidoscope of color.

"Hey! Guess what? My dad gave me a dollar so we could get a couple small Slurpees," David announces.

"I'm not s'posed to have Slurpees. They make me hyper."

"Okay," David says, dropping it. "Did you bring the jars?"

Lyle jiggles his backpack so David can hear the sweet music of mason jars clinking against one another.

"It's more like they make me crazy!" Lyle isn't ready, quite yet, to ditch the Slurpee possibility.

"You mean crazier," David clarifies. "Hey, I told my mom not to pack me a lunch because you always have enough for four people. She thought it was funny. And I remembered to bring the bug book."

"I get *the feel* . . . *ing*. You know what that means!" Lyle drums like a crazy man right up in David's face.

"Are you still talking about it? Okay. I got it! No Slurpees!"

Lyle picks up a rock and chucks it at a telephone pole. The rock misses the pole by at least ten feet and bounds across the paved road. David winces as the projectile bounces and spins toward the beautifully waxed and polished Corvette in the Robinsons' driveway. It veers to the left and misses the car by no more than a few inches.

"Close one!" David whistles.

"Wait a minute," Lyle says. "You know what? For a dollar . . ." His fingers draw numbers in the air, calculating, and then he announces triumphantly, "We can get two humongous Slurpees. The giant size! What d'ya think of that?"

"Dad said two *small* Slurpees. S-M-A-L-L. Small. And you already said you can't have 'em anyway."

"I know. I know that, but I was just sayin' for a dollar— Hey!" Lyle exclaims, interrupting himself, "Let's go to the 7-Eleven down at the Y."

"The Y? It's way too far."

"Not if we're goin' to . . ."

Lyle gets up close to David and then shouts at him.

". . . *the fish hatchery*!"

"No! We're supposed to go to the Log, not the fish hatchery. It says so right on our Science Day pass. Do you know what would happen if Miss O'Donnell—"

"Look, this is our last chance to get to the fish hatchery this year. Besides, it'd be against Mother Nature if we didn't."

"Against Mother Nature?"

"That's right!"

"We're supposed to go to the Log, Lyle. We need to collect bugs. You know how many days we have until Parent Night? Forty! That's all! We need to go to the Log!"

"Okay, I gotta tell you, then. I was savin' it, but we *have to* go to the fish hatchery. I was savin' it for a surprise! Because that's where we're gonna catch a robber fly, and a blue darner dragonfly, and all of the water bugs!"

"But Lyle, it says on our—"

"Look!" he tells David. "We only have 'til two o'clock and that's not a lotta time. Hang on, and I'm gonna explain it on the way."

Lyle whips David's chair around in the direction of the fish hatchery, and they're off. It takes them about a half an hour to reach the fork in the road known as the Y. It gives Lyle plenty of time to talk.

He explains to David, in his own unique way, how Miss O'Donnell has never collected bugs, and so she has no way of knowing how bug collecting is affected by such things as the weather conditions, and the time of day, and the time of year and a host of other uncontrollable factors. Consequently, she would never give them permission to go to both the Log and the fish hatchery, because she could never be convinced it was necessary, because she really doesn't know anything about it. So they just have to take care of it themselves, since they are, after all, the experts, and as any expert will testify, you can never predict in advance where it is you need to go to collect bugs.

It's not clear whether Lyle's impeccable logic finally convinces David, or if he just gets tired of listening. But they're already at the 7-Eleven—halfway to the fish hatchery— by the time Lyle sputters to a close. David gives in.

The 7-Eleven is a welcome sight. They buzz into the store and moments later emerge, each of them carrying an enormous Slurpee. They attempt a toast, but the slippery-wet cups slide off each other and Slurpee sloshes all over the sidewalk, much to Dino's satisfaction. They try it a few more times, laughing, manage to almost connect, and figure it's close enough.

David has some of the syrupy red ice spilled on him by now, but Lyle is as spotless as when he left the house. Dino is in charge of clean-up, and they wait for him to finish before they continue on their journey.

As they mosey along, David suddenly slams his Slurpee between his knees and grabs the side of his head, screaming in agony. Lyle practically drops his on the ground, and grabs onto his friend.

"What's wrong, what's wrong?!"

David holds his head down, squeezing tightly at the temples. He turns his head sideways and squints at Lyle with one eye completely closed, his face contorted in pain.

"Oh-man-oh-man, it's killing me!"

"What?! What's wrong?" Lyle presses, glancing around for help.

"Brain freeze!"

"Brain freeze?" Lyle shoves David away. "Dang it, David. You scared me."

David holds his palm over his eye and continues to agonize.

"Oh. I forgot. That's something you will never ever, ever, ever know about."

David gestures for Lyle to come closer. Lyle puts his face up next to him and David whispers, clearly enunciating each syllable.

"Be . . . cause . . . you . . . don't . . . have . . . a . . . brain."

Lyle grabs David's chair and tilts it backwards.

"Whoa, whoa—I don't know if I can hold you!" He drops the chair repeatedly, letting it fall farther each time. "Whoa! That time I almost totally missed!" Then he does let go, and lets the chair drop all the way to the ground, catching it only at the last second. "I really wanna stop, but I *can't* stop, 'cause I don't have a brain!"

"All right," David screams. "All right, you do have a brain! You have a big brain. The biggest brain in the world! In fact, you're a genius! Put me back!"

Lyle sets David upright and David wheels himself forward a few yards, then spins the chair around, facing Lyle. He holds up a hand with his fingers crossed.

"The biggest pea-brain, that is," David adds, waving his crossed fingers in the air. "Yeah! King's X!"

Lyle, ramping up, slams down the rest of his Slurpee. He picks up a rock and hurtles it at a tree, missing of course, by five or six feet. He grabs the back of David's chair, yelling "Onward!", and they take off down Waikiki Road at high speed.

When they arrive at the fish hatchery, Lyle parks the chair and immediately digs through their lunch sack. He borrows a slice of bread from one of the sandwiches, and tosses pieces of it into the fish pool. Hundreds of hungry fish attack the food in a splashing fury.

"Did I tell you Dennis took me fishing up at Douglas Creek?" David asks.

Lyle approaches a full-blown Slurpee hype-out, moving around a lot more and a lot faster than usual. He tries to flip over a large rock, grunting and groaning at the effort, but he can't even budge it.

"Yeah," David continues, "He shot a chucker and two doves with his .22. We roasted 'em and fried up some trout in a skillet, with bacon grease. I love bacon grease. Oooh, yeah."

Lyle finds a heavy stick and tries to jam it under the rock, by repeatedly jabbing at it.

"Are you listening to me?" David asks him.

"You like bacon grease. Who doesn't? My mom cooks eggs in it. Crusty bacon eggs. Yeah!"

Lyle manages to pry the rock loose and roll it over.

"What are you doing?" David asks.

"Lookin' for somethin'."

"What?"

"This!"

Lyle grabs a huge night crawler and holds it up.

"Fish love these. What'd you guys fish with?"

"Corn," David replies. "We caught five brookies on corn. Some people use maggots. Not us. Maggots give me the creeps. If you think about it, though, it doesn't make sense for fish to like corn. There's no corn in a creek. Fish've never even seen corn."

Lyle lies down on the edge of the pool, takes a deep breath, and drops his face into the water. He opens his eyes wide and immediately yanks his head out, shouting a warning.

"Shark-infested waters!"

He grabs another breath of air, and plunges his head back under, dangling the worm very close to his face. The fish swarm around him.

David continues talking, not really noticing that Lyle's head, and therefore his ears, happen to be under water.

"Grasshoppers make sense, though. So do crickets and flies. Spinners work, too. Mepps, mostly. We use 'em on the Little Spokane, red and white, not the silver ones. And worms. You know, you can't beat a can of worms, no way. But—Lyle? Lyle? Hey! What are you doing?"

Unbeknownst to David, a school of large fish is attacking the crawler in Lyle's hand, in a flurry of scales and tails and churning water—right in front of Lyle's face. The worm rapidly vanishes, devoured by the fish. Lyle hauls his head out of the water, his face dripping wet. He's excited and yelling.

"Wow. Did you see that? I stuck my head under the water and the fish ate the night crawler right outta my hand! They were swarmin' me! It was a piranha attack!"

"You're not supposed to stick your head in there. Read the sign! And they feed 'em pellets. Not night crawlers."

"Well, they might feed 'em pellets, but what they really like is night crawlers."

"What about corn?" David asks him.

"What *about* corn?"

"That's what I've been saying. Why do fish eat corn?"

"Fish *don't* eat corn. Are you nuts?"

David rolls his eyes and says to himself, "We caught 'em all on corn. That's all I know."

Suddenly, Lyle grabs a jar from his backpack and takes off.

"Where're you going?!" David yells after him.

"Dragonfly!" Lyle cries, looking back—pointing forward—all the while running.

Lyle chases around the fish ponds, into the woods, across the dirt road and back, up the hillside and down. Sometimes David can see the dragonfly he's chasing, and sometimes he can't. A few times, Lyle slips out of sight and then reappears somewhere else. It goes on for close to fifteen minutes and David begins to wonder if he'll ever stop. And then suddenly, he does.

Lyle has the jar in one hand and the lid in the other and he's inching forward, ready to pounce. The dragonfly takes flight, and Lyle takes off after it again. Then an amazing thing happens. The dragonfly, darting in low to the ground, grabs a robber fly out of the air, and Lyle brings the jar down over the top of *both*. He lets out a shriek.

"Got 'em! Got 'em both!!! We got 'em!"

He hurries back over to David with the capture and proudly puts it up in his face.

"A dragonfly and a robber fly! Those are impossible to catch and we got 'em both! We are soooo lucky! Quick, get me another jar!"

A half-hour later, they've collected several dragonflies, some spiders, and a jar full of what Lyle calls "water bugs." They stow their new treasures in the backpack. Lyle gets behind the wheelchair and pushes, and they jostle back up the dirt road, eager to get to the Log. It's a long journey, nearly five miles, and the entire trek is uphill.

When they finally arrive, Lyle plops himself down on the ground and dives into the lunch sack. David unbuckles from the chair, glad of any chance to be free from his straps. They eat until there is nothing left, and then Lyle leaps to his feet.

"Work time," he announces.

He grabs a jar and flies across the field, leaping haphazardly, flipping rocks, kicking open rotten branches, turning over logs, and doing anything else it takes to find a bug. David lifts a small crowbar from the backpack. He pries some bark from the Log and grabs a beetle as it tries to scurry away. He slips it into the jar and replaces the lid. Both boys focus on capturing insects for the next hour or so. When Lyle returns, he finds David sitting with his arms spread wide and his palms open—eyes closed, face turned up toward the sun.

"Good one, David!" Lyle praises him.

"Yeah, I'm picturing it in my head, like you said," David replies. "I'm going to run one way or another. That is what you said."

There's a long silence.

"So, what's the next step?" David opens his eyes and stares straight at Lyle.

Another silence. David waits, not budging a muscle, scarcely blinking. Lyle can see he'd better deliver.

"Okay," Lyle announces. "Here it is. And it's a doozey! Now, listen! I don't want you to get discouraged, or anything to get in your way. At first you'll think it's impossible, but believe me if you just ask the Good Physician above for guidance and to give you the willpower to—"

"Wait a minute. What did you say?" David sits straight up in his chair.

"Huh?"

"What did you say, right then, about the Good Physician above?"

Lyle's lips move as he runs through the lines in his head.

"Oh! Oh, yeah. What I said was, just ask the Good Physician above for guidance and to give you the willpower to go ahead and do it, then I don't care what your problem is, you can make yourself whole. You can be reborn again! What d'ya think about that?"

"Wait a second. Wait just a doggone second. I've heard that before! It's Jack LaLanne! This whole thing is Jack LaLanne!"

Lyle rolls his eyes around, waiting for the perfect explanation to drop out of the sky. It doesn't.

"Yeah?" he finally says, lamely.

For a long and awkward moment, David waits for his explanation, while Lyle tries to think of a way to save face.

"Okay. That does it!" Lyle declares emphatically, reclaiming his control of the situation. "Reach for the sky, partner."

"What?" David asks.

"You heard me!" Lyle imitates John Wayne, talking through his teeth. He pistol-draws with his fingers and repeats, "I said, stick 'em up!"

Even now a good sport, David raises his hands in the air, laughing and shaking his head. In a flash, Lyle spins around to face away from David, reaches back over his shoulders, grabs David's wrists, and heaves him up out of the chair.

"No! Not this again!" David groans, hanging from Lyle's back.

He struggles to wrest his hands free, but Lyle holds him with a grip of steel.

"This didn't work last time we tried it!" David complains.

Lyle ignores his friend's protests and staggers away from the chair, dragging him along.

"Okay, now walk!" he orders David. "Try to do it! I've got you. Come on, try!"

Dino bounces along beside them, barking encouragement. Lyle moves his legs even faster.

"See? You're startin' to run!"

"No! I'm not! I can't breathe! Lyle! I can't breathe."

But David is laughing—which, along with the awkward positioning, blocks his air. Lyle hoists him up higher and picks up the pace even more. He scuffles over to the Log, and circles around it, ignoring David's protests. They start to move at a pretty good clip.

"Back to the barn! Hang on!" Lyle shouts.

Lyle breaks into a full run.

David suddenly finds air and pulls it into his lungs.

He whispers—"Faster."

David can't believe the feeling, the air against his face. His legs hang free, and there's a long-forgotten wind beneath them. He takes another deep breath, and speaks louder.

"Faster, Lyle!"

This time Lyle hears him.

"Faster! Go faster!" David yells, clearer now. "Come on, faster!"

"You wanna run?" Lyle yells back, determined. "Let's run!"

Lyle shuts out the world, shuts out the weight of David on his back and the heaviness in his own legs. Focusing intently, he throws every shred of energy he can summon into the last twenty yards. If boyhood is a time when your feet never touch the ground, then this, without question, is one of those times. For a suspended moment, running with David on his back becomes easy . . . almost effortless . . . as if they are about to fly!

David lets out a whoop of exhilaration. He can feel the rush on his cheeks and the smooth motion of a runner's stride. They collapse by the wheelchair, both of them exhausted, and they lie on their backs, staring up at the clear blue sky.

"Man-oh-man, we were really bookin'," David says.

Lyle sits up and finds his badly dented canteen in the backpack. He takes a swig, and passes it to David.

David falls back on the ground to watch the clouds, but Lyle, suddenly, feels a peculiar anxiety—one he shouldn't feel, not after that moment—a gut sensation telling him they need to get back to the school, or at the very least leave the Log. He scans their surroundings. Something is not right.

Lyle crams the canteen in the backpack.

"We'd better get goin'. It's gettin' late, and we're s'posed to be back at school by two."

"Are you kidding me? Are you sick or something?"

"Are you sick or something?" Lyle shoots back.

"No," David laughs. "I'm not. I'm just saying . . ."

Lyle starts transferring their jars into the backpack.

"C'mon, we gotta go!" he tells David.

Because of the urgency in Lyle's voice, David doesn't question him, and a nervousness rises in his own chest. The boys quickly load their materials and Lyle helps David strap into the wheelchair. David has one of the jars in his hand and he holds it close to his face.

"Check out the color of this moth." His voice is tentative. "It's amazing. Red and brown and—"

"If it's not blue, I can't see it. I'm colorblind. Blue's my favorite color anyway. The rest are all mush. It's why animals can't hide from me. My Mom says it's a gift I got from a recessive gene. Dang it! I left one of the jars over in the trees. Hang on." Lyle hesitates. Then, in an uncharacteristic move, he instructs the dog, "Dino, stay!"

Dino sits, obediently.

Lyle careens around the Log and back over to the treeline. He leaps over the shallow drainage ditch and turns along the gravel road bordering the meadow. He charges into the bushes and through the underbrush, and finally locates the jar he'd stashed earlier.

Lyle hears a dull *POP!* He feels a sharp sting on the back of his leg, and lets out a small yelp of surprise, craning his neck around to look. There's a red mark about the size of a nickel, on the skin right below his shorts. Another *POP!* He feels the pain again, this time in his calf.

Two older boys emerge from the woods. The tall one carries a BB gun. Lyle has never seen either of them before. Wayne, stocky and threatening, strides up to Lyle and grabs him roughly.

"How'd it feel, punk?" Mick, the boy with the BB gun, snarls.

"You shot me! My dad's right around the corner," Lyle throws back.

"You're lyin'," Wayne snaps.

"Hold him down!" Mick orders, his face creased into a smirk. He has a sinister meanness about him, as if he feeds on this sort of activity.

Wayne tries to wrestle Lyle to the ground, but Lyle fights like a wild banshee.

"Can't you hold him down?"

"Shoot the little runt!" Wayne yells, locked in a struggle with Lyle.

Mick steps up close and fires directly into Lyle's legs. He pumps the gun and fires several more times, placing the barrel within inches of Lyle's skin.

Wayne furiously pins Lyle down, and neither of them notice the boy in the wheelchair headed in their direction. David Dahlke is steaming mad. Dino, conflicted, runs back and forth, yearning to charge ahead, but told to stay with David. David doesn't wait. He wheels his chair right over the edge of the drainage ditch and slams into Mick's heels. Mick screams and grabs the back of his ankles, falling to the ground.

CHAPTER FOURTEEN

DILEMMA

*In any moment of decision
the best thing you can do is the right thing,
the next best thing is the wrong thing,
and the worst thing you can do is nothing.*

~ TEDDY ROOSEVELT

"Stop it! Leave him alone! What's wrong with you?!" David cries out at them, his voice shaking with emotion.

Dino goes crazy, tearing in circles and barking. Mick swallows the pain and leaps back to his feet, enraged. A car approaches on the meadow road, and everything changes when its wheels crunch the gravel. Wayne grabs the gun from Mick.

"Let's get out of here!" he yells.

The teenagers scramble up the steep hill leading to Five Mile Prairie. Lyle, in a state of absolute fury, scoops up the first object he can get his hands on—anything will do, as long as it's heavy—and flings it with all his strength at the escaping thugs.

The dirt-clod rockets straight toward its target, missing every tree in its path, and strikes Mick squarely in the back of the head. It hits with force, dead-on, in a thick and satisfying explosion of black dust, like the detonation of a small bomb. Mick lets out a yell as it pitches him forward, knocking him flat on the ground. He's down for a few seconds, but recovers and sprints up the slope, holding the back of his head with one hand. He and Wayne vanish into the maze of basalt outcroppings covering the hillside.

"Did you see that? I nailed him! Yeah!" Lyle shouts, ecstatic.

The car brakes to a stop, and the driver's side window rolls down. A man leans his head out.

"What's going on here? You kids okay?" he inquires, concerned.

"They shot him with a BB gun!" David cries. His words echo with distress.

"You boys need a ride? I could get you to some first aid."

"We're okay," Lyle reassures him.

"You sure? I don't mind giving a ride." The driver sounds reluctant to leave.

"Thank you, sir, but we're okay," David seconds, trying to control the shakiness in his voice. He can scarcely hear his own words, his heart pounds so loud in his ears.

The driver hesitates, then nods, and the car glides slowly away.

David sways from side to side in his chair, slapping his legs, even more upset now than before. "Look at that! Why did they do it? Why?!" he demands, staring at the BBs in Lyle's legs.

"It's okay. It only stings a little," Lyle says, trying to calm him and make him feel better.

"But you weren't doing anything! You were just standing there!"

"Hey, don't worry. They're gone now."

Lyle brushes two of the BBs from his calf, and scrapes off three others, which didn't penetrate the skin.

"See?" he tells David, "They come right off."

Lyle positions his leg so David can't see the BB that's deeply embedded there.

"I don't feel good, Lyle. Let's go home," David tells him.

"Sure, buddy. C'mon."

Lyle gets behind the chair and pushes, and they start back up the road.

"My legs don't hurt. So don't worry about it," Lyle impresses upon him. "It only hurt when they were doin' it."

He grabs a stick, and swings it above his head. "Hey, David, let's tell Dennis! We'll go back and pound those guys!"

David doesn't respond. Lyle tosses the stick away. They're silent for a while, and they move along slowly. After about a mile, Lyle stops and checks his calf.

"God, this is startin' to hurt!"

"Say 'gosh'," David tells him.

"What'd you say?"

"It's better not to say 'God' unless you're talking to God or talking about God," David explains, diplomatic even when exhausted.

It takes Lyle a moment to process this. He had no idea there were rules when it came to referencing God.

"Hey, David," he finally says. "I need you to do me a favor."

"Okay. What is it?"

"Next time you talk to God . . . I mean, can you ask Him somethin' for me?"

"What do you want me to ask Him?" David says.

"I want you to ask if you'll ever run again." Lyle pauses. "Could you do that?"

There's a lengthy period of silence. Lyle begins to wonder if he asked the wrong question.

Finally, David nods. "I did ask God about it," he says quietly.

"You what?! I've been buggin' you and buggin' you all this time, and workin' on a runnin' plan, and you didn't even tell me?"

David doesn't reply. The pace of the conversation makes Lyle squirm, but he forces himself to be patient. He waits.

"I didn't think you'd believe me. I asked Him if I would run—you know, no wheelchair, no braces, just like everybody else. I asked Him if I would ever run that way."

Lyle stops. He's afraid to ask, afraid maybe God has blown his cover, but he gets up the courage to form the question.

"What did He say?"

David lifts his head and his eyes meet Lyle's.

"He told me I would, with you!" he says, pointing.

Lyle is shocked. His voice is a solemn whisper, intensely genuine.

"With me? God told you that?"

David nods, emphatic.

"That'll be great! You and me, running? We'll fly!"

The way Lyle sees it, this is important to David, and David is his friend, and whether Lyle believes it or not, he backs his friend. Right now, he'd fight a pack of wolves for him.

The boys continue up the road, too tired to talk. David can no longer hold his head up. He's dusty, disheveled, sore and depleted; he wishes for nothing except to be at home in his bed. They cross Country Homes Boulevard, and a police car cruises up in front of them and stops.

Officer Jenkins climbs out. "Hi, boys," he says pleasantly. "Some reason you're not in school?"

He's been out searching for them, following a report phoned in to the Police Department. It takes him one good look to see that these kids are in trouble. He immediately switches to business.

"Come on. Let's get you boys home."

A few minutes later, the police car noses into the Dahlkes' driveway. Mrs. Dahlke rushes from the house, and hurries to the car.

"No problems, Mrs. Dahlke," Officer Jenkins hastens to reassure her. "Just a couple of very tired boys."

David's mother exhales, visibly relieved.

"Thank you so much for bringing them back, Jim. I'll make sure Lyle gets home okay. We don't want to use up any more of your time."

Mrs. Dahlke and Officer Jenkins get both boys and the wheelchair into the house. She thanks him again, and the officer leaves.

David's head droops and he can barely keep his eyes open.

"I'll give your mom a ring," Mrs. Dahlke tells Lyle, "and let her know you're all right. The school might call, we don't want her to worry."

"Thank you, Mrs. Dahlke. Wait—what time is it?"

She eyes the clock. "It's two thirty."

"Oh." Lyle knew they never stood a chance of making their deadline. "I'd better get goin'."

Lyle heads to the door. He pauses by the wheelchair.

"Great day. Huh, David?" he whispers.

David smiles, "The best."

Officer Jenkins' next stop is Linwood Elementary. He finds Miss O'Donnell alone in her office, and tells her upfront how David and Lyle had shown him their Science Day pass, eliminating any concerns this might be a visit about truancy. He then tells her of a report he received regarding an altercation on the gravel road below Five Mile, involving some kids with a BB gun and a boy in a wheelchair.

"I thought you should know, since the boys were technically out there on school time," he tells her.

Miss O'Donnell thanks Officer Jenkins for his trouble, and for taking the time to bring this to her attention. She keeps him there longer than necessary, probing for every detail. She isn't sure why she does this. Perhaps it's because she enjoys the presence of another authority figure; she usually has to deal with these problems on her own. Perhaps it's because she's attracted to this tall strong man in a uniform; she doesn't get much male attention. But one thing is certain: she is gathering evidence to deal with a mounting problem—and the mounting problem is Lyle.

When Officer Jenkins leaves, she sits heavily in her chair. Up until now, she lacked certainty about what she would do with Lyle. Now, she knows how to proceed. It hasn't been an easy decision to reach, and she dreads the conversation with Mrs. Hatcher.

She reaches for the phone, but as she does, she imagines what must be happening at the Hatcher and Dahlke households.

She decides that it can wait a few hours.

At home, Lyle launches into his explanation. "We were out at the Log collectin' bugs and these guys came along and started shootin' at us. *Bam! Bam!* BBs flyin' every which way. And I was fightin' 'em off and startin' to wear 'em out, but they finally got me on the ground. And they kept on shootin' me fulla BBs. They musta hit me at least a hundred times.

"And David kept dodgin' the bullets and came slammin' right smack into 'em, screamin' and yellin' and they prob'ly thought there was ten of him, and they took off runnin' for the hills. I clocked one of 'em with a huge dirt clod, smack on the melon!"

Lyle's dad paces the room, severely upset. "Those little sons a' guns. I'm going to track them down and beat them within an inch of their lives. Who were those boys, son? Are they from around here? Did you recognize any of them? I want to know who did this!"

Mrs. Hatcher sits on the edge of Lyle's bed, examining Lyle's injuries as he lies on his stomach.

"Ow, Mom! Ow!" Lyle cries out.

"I'd like to go find them right now!" Mr. Hatcher rants.

"I'm ready right now, Dad! They haven't seen the lasta me! I was just gettin' started! Ow, Mom, that really hurts!"

"Hold still. The more you move, the longer it takes. Ron, you're not helping things. Go call the kids in for dinner."

Mr. Hatcher storms out, and his wife concentrates on the task of removing the BB from Lyle's leg.

Steve charges into the room.

"Mom, you want some help?" he asks, working his way in, as close as he can. "How're you gonna get that out? Want me to go get some pliers?"

"No! What I want you to do is go set the table."

"Mom," Steve whines. "I know how to fix it! Come on, Mom, please?"

"No. Now, go!"

Steve drags out of the room.

"Good Lord, this is deep. Hold still!" Lyle's mom watches his eyes. "And don't you start tearing up on me, now. Tears are for hurts of the heart."

"It's not about that, Mom. It's about David. I need to help him."

"I'm listening."

"Mom, he didn't look good today. I *gotta* help him."

"I don't know if that's possible, honey. Sometimes being a good friend is everything you can do."

"I don't think so. Not this time, Mom!"

Mrs. Hatcher finally gets the BB removed from his leg. She holds it up for him to see. He reaches out and takes it from her.

"I am definitely savin' this!" he whoops.

"Fine," Mrs. Hatcher tells him, "but right now, it's time for dinner."

After he consumes an enormous amount of food at the table, Lyle heads back to his room. A little later, Mrs. Hatcher checks on him.

"Are you okay, honey?" she asks, poking her head in the door.

He lies on his bed, gaze fixed on the ceiling, a serious look on his face.

"I'm thinkin'," he tells her.

"A penny for your thoughts."

Lyle lowers his voice. "I already told you, Mom."

"Well, tell me again, then."

"I need to figure out a way to help David fix his legs, a real way. It's gotta be somethin' that'll work."

Mrs. Hatcher comes into the room and sits down on the bed. She matches his subdued tone.

"We discussed this before, Lyle. Some things are just meant to be. We do the best we can, and that's all we can do."

"No, Mom. Mr. and Mrs. Dahlke are raisin' money for muscular dystrophy. The more money they have, the faster they can find a cure. That's what David said. Last year he could walk, and now he's in a wheelchair. He's gettin' worse all the time. So I need a way to get money."

"You can collect pop bottles and cans," she suggests helpfully. "Or you could pull weeds for Mrs. Dewitt."

"That's like twenty-five cents. This is gonna take a lot more money than that."

Lyle has a peculiar expression on his face. It's not the first time she's seen it, and she knows very well what it means. He'll obsess over this, and he'll stay locked onto it until he finds an answer.

The phone rings in the kitchen, and a moment later they hear Linda call out, "Mom! Phone!"

"I'm sure you'll think of something," she whispers to encourage him, and hurries to the kitchen to take the phone call.

It's a brief conversation requiring only three terse responses from her: "When would be convenient? . . . Tuesday morning would be fine . . . All right then, thank you for the call."

She replaces the receiver.

"Who was it?" her husband wants to know.

"Miss O'Donnell."

"Trouble at school again?"

"No, nothing serious, I'm sure."

He lets it go. If she says it's nothing serious, it's good enough for him. Besides, Mr. Hatcher reassures himself, Lyle couldn't very well be in trouble with Miss O'Donnell, since he wasn't even at school today.

Tuesday, October 5
36 days to Parent Night

Mrs. Hatcher sits in the principal's office, hands in her lap, by all appearances attentive and respectful. She has been forced to sit through these lectures before, and she never accords them much weight. She allows Miss O'Donnell to say what she needs to, then tells her, in all earnestness, "I'll take care of it." As a child, she spent more than her own share of time at the principal's, which unquestionably taints her perspective.

Miss O'Donnell's presumptions about Mrs. Hatcher's son, in the frankest of terms, annoy her. She knows more about Lyle's behavior than anyone else ever can or will. Granted, he requires more maintenance than her two other children, but Mrs. Hatcher knows there is nothing inherently wrong with Lyle. She simply must see to his needs: a carefully controlled diet, liberal quantities of discipline, frequent and aggressive exercise, and a sufficient amount of sleep. When it comes to the lecture on all she's *not* doing, Mrs. Hatcher politely pretends to listen.

"What you need to be aware of is things have reached a critical juncture," Miss O'Donnell begins. "You already know about Lyle's disorderly conduct in dance class, making fun of Mrs. Maxfield, and his disobedience running on the sidewalk and knocking me to the ground."

Miss O'Donnell sits erect and calm. She takes an unhurried breath, and continues. "We had his reckless behavior on the playground with the black widow spider, the pocketknife incident in the library—which traumatized several other students, believe me; I received a number of calls from parents. And, as I reported to you on the phone last week, I saw him push David Dahlke's wheelchair into a group of children on the playground, actually hitting one of them with the chair. Then, of course, there was the incident with Sandra Murphy's dress."

The phrase "Sandra Murphy's dress" pierces Mrs. Hatcher's inattentive fog, and instantly she finds herself concerned.

"I did not hear about the dress."

Miss O'Donnell shakes her head, dismissing it.

"We have far more important things to discuss this morning. Lyle and David had a Science Day pass to work in the field below Five Mile, and were to report back here by two o'clock which they failed to do. Officer Jenkins came by instead, and informed me there was an incident involving a BB gun reported to the Police Department, and he had to locate the boys and take them home. I assume you're already aware of all this."

Boys will be boys, Mrs. Hatcher thinks to herself, nodding for Miss O'Donnell's benefit.

"The point I want to make today is, I strongly suggest you call your family doctor."

Mrs. Hatcher startles. "Why? Is Lyle sick?"

Miss O'Donnell looks Mrs. Hatcher in the eye. "I want you to ask your doctor about a pill that is available."

A sick feeling creeps into the pit of Mrs. Hatcher's stomach.

"A pill?" she manages.

"Yes," the principal continues. "I've spoken with several doctors about this. They've been using it in other schools around the country, and it's been a very successful way to mainstream some of these children. Very successful."

Miss O'Donnell pauses.

Mrs. Hatcher chooses to remain silent.

"According to the doctors with whom I've spoken," Miss O'Donnell proceeds, "Lyle displays many symptoms of the condition they call 'MBD'."

"What does it stand for?" Mrs. Hatcher asks in a monotone, not sure she even wants to know.

"Minimal Brain Dysfunction," Miss O'Donnell tells her.

"Miss O'Donnell, you can't possibly believe—"

The principal raises her hand and stops her.

"I know it sounds extreme, Mrs. Hatcher, but it's just a technical term and it's really not what it sounds like at all. This drug they're using can help with Lyle's memory problems, and his concentration, and the constant need to be moving around.

"The doctor explained to me these things are caused by problems with the nervous system. His impulse functions are impaired. This pill can fix them. Basically, it will calm him down and make it possible for him to focus on what he's doing. It will also make it far less likely he'll engage in his typically reckless, I should say dangerous, behavior. You know, he's not the only one who might get hurt by these antics.

"Naturally, this would all be done very discreetly, and no one else needs to know about it—except, of course, Mrs. Stewart."

Mrs. Hatcher feels a rage rise within her. Her lips tighten in a grim line, and she lets the awkward silence hang in the air.

Miss O'Donnell plainly sees she isn't getting the desired reaction. Unruffled, she keeps her tone even. "I was aware, when I called, you might not be as enthused about this solution as I am . . . and I want to offer an alternative. The point is we have to do something."

She searches Mrs. Hatcher's expression. Seeing no yield, she goes on.

"The other option is to place Lyle in a Special Education program at the Guild School. But—," she hastens before Mrs. Hatcher can speak, "—if he is to remain here, in my school, I will need a note from your doctor stating this problem has been properly dealt with."

Mrs. Hatcher's rage turns to desperation; she feels trapped. Her feet dig into her shoes, her muscles tight.

"That's not right," she objects quietly, containing herself with every effort. "He gets good grades in school. Why would Special Ed even be an issue?"

"It's a behavioral concern, and it affects the other students. He's disruptive. I should say, extremely disruptive. The two options I have presented are the only ones I can offer. Of course, the choice is yours. But I'll need an answer by the end of the week. I can't continue to risk the safety of the other children."

The two women sit in silence, their eyes locked.

CHAPTER FIFTEEN

THE PILL

*A dose of adversity is often as needed
as a dose of medicine.*

~ PROVERB

At home, Mrs. Hatcher dwells on her discussion with Miss O'Donnell for the remainder of the afternoon. She loathes the idea of giving Lyle a drug—she's never heard of such a thing, and what's more, she likes him the way he is.

Pacing back and forth by the door, she wishes her husband would come home. Suddenly, she stops. Ron is sure to ask questions, and she doesn't have answers, other than the feed from Miss O'Donnell.

She crosses quickly to the phone, calls Doctor Lyon and relays her conversation with the principal.

"Is there really a pill like this for children?" she asks.

"Yes, there is," he informs her. "It's been around a while, although I've personally done very little with it."

"Do you know of anyone using it?"

"Yes. I've heard it recommended on the basis it's a better choice for overly active and difficult-to-manage children than the long road of juvenile delinquency."

There's a pause. Mrs. Hatcher is too shocked to speak.

"Which some people think awaits them," he hurriedly adds.

"He's not a criminal, Dr. Lyon," Mrs. Hatcher replies. "He's not going to become a criminal, and he's not going down the road to juvenile delinquency."

"Of course not, Mrs. Hatcher. I wasn't implying anything of the sort. He's only ten. But at the same time, it doesn't sound as if the principal of your school has left you any alternative, unless you're willing to move him into a Special Education program."

"I am not going to do that."

"Why don't we try the drug? We could give it a week and if there are any difficulties, you could just let me know. This might not be the enormous problem you're imagining."

Silence.

"Mrs. Hatcher? Are you—?"

"Let me talk it over with my husband. I'll call you back if we decide to set up an appointment." Before he can respond, she hangs up.

Pacing again, Mrs. Hatcher can't think. She hears Lyle coming home from school, and he's still an entire block away. He invariably whistles, talks loudly to Dino, or lets loose with shouts of exuberance. She never knows what those are about, but she can always hear them as he approaches the house.

Lyle barges into the kitchen. "Hey, Mom, did you make any oatmeal raisin cookies?"

"No—," she reaches out an arm and stops him mid-run, "but I had a visit with Miss O'Donnell today. She mentioned a story I hadn't heard yet, about Sandra Murphy's dress."

Lyle doesn't seem too concerned. "She started it," he insists, opening the refrigerator and absently staring inside.

"Close that!"

Lyle shuts the refrigerator and almost slams his thumb in the door. Mrs. Hatcher winces.

"And just how did she start it?"

"She was makin' fun of me."

"What exactly did she say?"

Lyle imitates Sandra's tone of voice, exaggerating it and adding a disdainful twist.

"Nice . . . hair . . . cut."

Mrs. Hatcher shakes her head. "Well, Lyle, maybe it was a compliment. Maybe she likes you."

"Yuck, Mom. She meant my head looked like a block of cheese. That's what she meant. So I told her, 'Hey, I like it that way.' And she said, 'Oh, good. I hope you do because nobody else does.' And I said, 'You think anybody else likes this?' and I flipped up her dress with my ruler. And she said, 'If you do that again, I'm gonna tell,' and I said, 'No, you won't,' and she said 'Oh yeah, I will,' and I said, 'Oh no, you won't,' and she said 'Oh yeah, I definitely will,' and I said—"

"Lyle," Mrs. Hatcher cuts him short, "For Pete's sake!"

"Mom! I'm tellin' a story. So I said . . . dang it! Now I forgot where I was."

Mrs. Hatcher sighs heavily. "You said, 'No, you won't,' and she said, 'Oh yeah, I definitely will.'"

"Right! Thanks, Mom. And so I flipped up her dress with my ruler again, and she squealed on me. Can I have a snack?"

"Lyle, we're talking here, so stay focused," Mrs. Hatcher says sternly. "And you know that behavior is not going to be tolerated. Why would you do such a thing?"

"She was buggin' me."

"Well, I hope it was worth it," Mrs. Hatcher tells him. "Because you're going to bed right after dinner. No ice cream for a week."

Lyle already knows how the No-Ice-Cream-for-Lyle scenario plays out. He's been through it many times.

After dinner, she'll make a big deal about gettin' bowls for everybody and slicin' up bananas and gettin' out the jar of chocolate and the jam and askin' everybody, "What kind of ice cream do you want?

What do you want on top? Does anybody want butterscotch? We have Rocky Road."

She knows what she's doin' and I know because she knows. Then she'll dish everybody a big bowl and fix it just right, exactly the way they want it, and I'll have to watch.

I always say, "That doesn't bother me."

And she always says, "I know. That's fine."

Dang it! That whole thing with Sandra Murphy was so long ago I barely remember it. Why is Miss O'Donnell talkin' about that now? What'd I ever do to her?

The front door opens, breaking through Lyle's thoughts. His dad's grin fills the doorway. He gets home from work at the same time every day, four o'clock, and Lyle runs to him and gives him a ferocious bear hug. With Lyle scarcely four feet tall and Mr. Hatcher six foot two, this amounts to Lyle squeezing his hips.

Mr. Hatcher prepares to engage him in their daily wrestling match, but Mrs. Hatcher shakes her head, ever so slightly, no. Instead, he musses Lyle's hair and they trade a little small talk.

Lyle loves the icy-cold odor of ice cream freezers on Mr. Hatcher's clothes. He gives his dad another big hip-hug, then turns and darts out the door.

Mr. Hatcher kisses his wife. After a long day away from his family, he hates to come home to a situation that calls for emotional distance—or worse, punishment—and he knows Mrs. Hatcher knows it. Yet they always maintain solidarity before the children, and neither has ever abused it. So when she quietly tells him, "There's something we need to talk about," he knows, indeed, there is.

Mr. Hatcher listens calmly while his wife explains. He occasionally ventures a question, but keeps a lid on the rising frustration and uncertainty. He is fully aware that Lyle gets in trouble too often, and there are times, although he never outwardly shows or admits it, that Lyle's screeching voice and the constant buzz of frantic activity very nearly drive him to the breaking point.

Mrs. Hatcher regards her husband sympathetically. They both know the source of Lyle's energy. Mrs. Hatcher sings while she cooks and dances doing housework. She exercises hard with Jack LaLanne nearly every weekday morning. She takes spontaneous treks through the woods with Lyle, just to view a huge wasp, or something trapped under a mason jar. She understands and shares her son's high-paced journey through a day—and so when Miss O'Donnell stresses medication, it's as if she, too, should have been fixed.

Mr. Hatcher treads carefully. "What did Dr. Lyon say about it? Are *we* doing something wrong? I mean, is this how they do it nowadays?"

"He said he's heard of it. I guess he's read about it, too."

"Is there anybody else in the school taking it?"

"I don't know, Ron. Miss O'Donnell said it's all confidential."

The phone rings. Mrs. Hatcher answers it. "Hello?"

She recognizes the voice of Connie, their neighbor across the street, and shoots a grim look at her husband. When she hangs up, she tugs on her sweater.

"He's stuck in a tree," she says simply.

When they get to Connie's yard, she's waiting. Arms folded, feet doing a nervous shuffle, she repeatedly glances down at the street and then back up at the tree.

"Right up there," she says, pointing.

Mr. Hatcher peers up at the towering Ponderosa pine, close to seventy feet high. He can't see any sign of Lyle. He glances back at Connie, puzzled.

"Are you sure—"

"Dad, Dad! I'm stuck!" The sound of Lyle's voice, much smaller than usual, comes from somewhere high above.

"He's hanging from the top," Connie offers helpfully. "The *very* top."

Mr. and Mrs. Hatcher step back out into the street to get a better view. From there they see Lyle, clinging to the tip of the tree. The breeze is gusty up there, and his weight—slight as it is—bends the treetop, causing it to swing back and forth.

"Dad. I can't get down!" he cries in desperation.

Connie's nervousness escalates. "Do you want me to call the Fire Department?"

"No! He got himself up there, he can get himself down," Mr. Hatcher responds gruffly. He turns his attention to Lyle and his voice rings out, audible to every neighbor on the block. "You get down from there, right now!"

"I'm stuck, Dad," Lyle calls back.

"Grab the bigger branches. And get down here! Take it one step at a time! Come on, now!"

It's a nail-biter, no question. Mrs. Hatcher is terrified for her son, but she knows if anyone can get him down, Ron can.

"Honey," she says, taking his arm, "tell him to be careful."

"Let me handle this," he says, his eyes locked onto Lyle.

Lyle gets stuck again as he searches blindly with his foot for a solid branch.

"Dad!"

"You're fine! Move your foot a little to the left! That's it!"

Lyle's foot touches the next branch. His fingers tremble as he reaches for a good handhold. For the last fifteen feet the giant tree has no branches, and he is forced to lower himself like a raccoon, slicing his fingers and arms on the razor-sharp bark.

"Dad!" he pleads, looking down.

The ground looks a long way off.

Mr. Hatcher stands close to the trunk, stretching his arms to their limit, straining to catch his son. He gets a grip on

Lyle's tennis shoe and Lyle, feeling the security of his father's touch, falls into his arms.

Mrs. Hatcher rips into him. "Do you have any idea how easy it would have been to fall out of there and break your neck? What were you doing up there in the first place?"

"All the guys said nobody could ever climb that tree. Besides, I could see David's house from the top! Can you believe it?"

"Where are all these guys now?" Mr. Hatcher grills him.

"I think they went home. Hey, Mom, what's for dinner?"

"Let me see your hands," demands Mrs. Hatcher.

He holds out his arms, and she checks out the dozens of cuts and slices. "I don't feel sorry for you one bit!" she snaps.

"I showed those guys!"

Mr. Hatcher grips Lyle's shoulders and pivots him toward the house. "Well, good for you. I hope it was worth it because now you're going straight to bed without dinner."

"Dad!"

"Go!"

Lyle bolts for home.

Mr. Hatcher gazes at his wife. He's at a loss.

"I'd already told him he was going to bed right after dinner, and he's lost his ice cream privileges for a week . . ." she muses.

He puts his arm around her, and they cross the street.

"It seems we have a decision to make," Mr. Hatcher says quietly.

Friday, October 8
33 days to Parent Night

Miss O'Donnell is alone, working, listening to her radio. When she glances up at the large window in her office, she sees Lyle trudge through the main door. She sets aside her work, knowing immediately there is something different about him. Lyle's movements are slow and steady. She feels a surge of relief as he opens the door and steps into her office, completely calm.

"Good morning, Mr. Hatcher," she ventures.

"'Morning, Miss O'Donnell."

Lyle digs into his pocket and produces a folded piece of paper. He holds out the note. She takes it, unfolds it, and reads:

> *Lyle is taking the medication as prescribed by Dr. Lyon. If there are any problems or difficulties, please call me and send him home.*
>
> *Sincerely,*
>
> *Mrs. Hatcher*

"Thank you, Lyle. You may go to your classroom now," she tells him.

Lyle dutifully plods out the door.

In class he sits quietly. To Mrs. Stewart's great relief, he keeps his eyes to the front of the room while she's teaching, and appears to do his assignments when given. His disruptions have always caused her anxiety, as she's not an experienced teacher. The constant discipline of a child has never been within her comfort zone.

Gradually, however, her relief gives way to a new anxiety, a different anxiety. Mrs. Stewart finds herself unable to stop watching him out of the corner of her eye, as though she expects something to happen at any moment. Only at the end of the day—and only with Lyle out of sight—is she finally able to relax.

After school, David wheels himself, and Lyle ambles along beside him. Dino waits in the usual spot, but Lyle either forgets to call him or doesn't feel like doing it. The dog trots up to meet the boys, without the customary invitation.

"Hey, Lyle," David says excitedly, "are you ready for the Log on Sunday?"

"Yeah," Lyle responds.

"I think we're doing pretty well. We only need a couple more butterflies, a garden spider and a recluse, and well, a bunch more dragonflies would be nice, but you'll have to catch those, and the rest of the grasshoppers and then the beetles. Except the water beetles. We got enough of those at the fish hatchery. Hey, do you like the new Beatles song?"

"What one?"

"*Yesterday*. They play it about a hundred times a day on the radio."

"They're okay. I don't see what the big deal is. I like the Beach Boys and Elvis way better."

They arrive at the Dahlke house and Dino charges ahead into the backyard, expecting them to follow.

"Are you gonna stay and swim?"

"No, I gotta go home. I'll see you tomorrow."

"Okay, see you later, Lyle."

Lyle doesn't really have to go home. But he's tired and subdued and therefore embarrassed. Without his high energy and dizzying level of activity, he just doesn't feel like himself. He continues down the street, and eventually Dino—who waited in the Dahlkes' backyard—figures out they aren't stopping there today, and breaks at a clip to catch up with him.

When they reach the corner of Avon Street, Lyle plops down on the curb. He picks up a long brown pine needle from the gutter and pokes at the tiny red ants, busy doing their work along the street.

The school bus rumbles past and Lyle waves at his classmates. He sees Sharon Anne, sitting next to her friend Francine. He's almost sure Francine glares at him. One thing's for sure: she doesn't wave.

I wonder why Francine doesn't like me. I can't think of anything I ever did to her. She acts like she likes everybody else. I'll just make sure I don't ever

> *talk to her or look at her, if that's what she wants.*
> *Maybe I drove Francine crazy. Mom said I was drivin'*
> *people crazy. Did buggin' the kids on the bus count?*
> *They look like they're havin' fun. Maybe I can start*
> *takin' the bus again. That'd be cool.*
>
> *Boy, I'm hungry. Please please please, no liver and*
> *onions.*

He stands up and walks the half-block to his house, thinking about dinner the entire way.

O n Saturday morning, Lyle and David hang out in Mrs. Dahlke's zinnia patch. David figured out a way he could catch butterflies, using Dennis' net, and Dennis showed the boys how to freeze the delicate creatures so as not to damage their wings. The results exceed even fourth-grade-boy expectations. So far, they have several perfect specimens, including a tiger swallowtail, a painted lady, a checkerspot, a mourning cloak, several white cabbage butterflies, and an orange tip.

Oddly, it's David who's patiently catching them, while Lyle mostly watches, occasionally probing for further information about God. The Sunday school classes don't interest him, but David's claim to one-on-One contact is a subject he cannot leave alone. Whether or not the God connection exists, David sure is having luck catching butterflies.

While David works, he reminds Lyle of how little time remains to complete their collection, how big the box Dennis gave them is, and how many bugs it will take to fill it. His chatter stems not so much from concern about their deadline as from Lyle's atypical silences, which make David strangely uncomfortable.

Another development also strikes David as peculiar. Lyle isn't going after the tough or crazy catches. Last Thursday, when they came up with the zinnia garden idea, they spotted the monarch, rare in this area, and Lyle pursued it around the neighborhood, scaling fences and cutting through yards, eventually chasing it up the Five Mile cliffs. By the time he returned with the butterfly in hand, it was almost an hour later, and David had nearly given up on him.

Today, Lyle seems content to do nothing but watch.

On Sunday, a heavy, slushy rain falls. By evening, Mount Spokane is completely capped with a clean white layer of snow, and even the lower-lying hills above Liberty Lake show a light skiff of it. The weather forces Lyle and David to postpone their trip to the Log, and Lyle spends the day playing Monopoly with Steve.

Mrs. Hatcher observes her boys—Steve, bouncing on his knees, jumping eagerly and diving in over the board, and Lyle, quiet, focused on the move at hand. She makes a concerted effort to keep Lyle occupied, but later in the afternoon she finds him asleep in the backyard, his head resting on Dino.

Monday, October 11
30 days to Parent Night

For the first Monday in memory, Mrs. Hatcher doesn't hear Lyle when he comes home from school: no whistling, no loud talking to Dino, no outbursts. He doesn't even slam the door as he slips into the house, and goes directly to his bedroom. When she checks on him later, he's face down on his bed, asleep.

Mr. Hatcher comes home, and Lyle isn't there with his hip-hug. His dad doesn't think anything of it, imagining Lyle is probably at a friend's house or outside playing. But when dinnertime rolls around, he notices his wife slowly ease open Lyle's door, peer in, then softly close it.

"Lyle's in there?" he asks, surprised.

She nods.

"Is he sick?"

She shakes her head.

After dinner she checks on him again. He's now underneath the blankets, fully clothed, feet sticking out, still wearing his tennis shoes from school. Mrs. Hatcher unties his shoes and removes them, and tucks his feet under the covers.

In the middle of the night noises carry from the kitchen, and when she investigates, she finds Lyle standing in front of the open refrigerator, munching on a carrot, reaching for an apple.

"Lyle, what on earth are you doing?"

"I'm hungry, Mom!"

"That's what you get, Mr. Sleepyhead. Sit down, and I'll make you something to eat."

He doesn't move.

"And don't stand there with the refrigerator door open."

Lyle closes the refrigerator and looks up at his mother.

"You guys ate without me?"

"We didn't eat without you. You were out like a light. Do you want a grilled cheese sandwich?"

"That sounds great."

He gets situated at the table and finishes the apple and the carrot while he waits. Mrs. Hatcher brings the plate of food, and sits down with him.

"How are you feeling?"

"Fine."

"Everything okay at school?"

"Yeah. Mrs. Stewart said I was behaving very well in class and she was proud of me, something like that."

"Good for you!"

He's pleased to see she's pleased.

"Mom, this is tasty," he smiles.

Tuesday, October 12
29 days to Parent Night

Lyle attends Mrs. Maxfield's dance class, along with the rest of his classmates, as they do every Tuesday morning. The dance teacher's position is unique, in that once a week she can observe Lyle on the outskirts of control, and encourage it. Dance is a time to let it all go, and Lyle does just that.

Mrs. Maxfield delights in how his raw, uninhibited enthusiasm for moving to music is infectious and spreads to the others, particularly the less confident children, the shy ones. But today, to anyone viewing the class for the first time, her free-spirited pupil would go unnoticed. As the children file out, headed back to class, Mrs. Maxfield takes him aside.

"Are you feeling sick today, Lyle? You're awfully quiet."

"No, I'm okay. I take a pill now 'cause I was drivin' people crazy." He smiles for her benefit. "Thank you, Mrs. Maxfield," he adds politely.

A threatening glow squeezes into Lyle's room, creeping toward the bed from the corner near the ceiling, casting a ghostly light down the wall and onto the floor. Lyle wants to tell it to go away, but his mouth has been sealed by some sinister force. He fights against it, struggling to cry out.

The ominous light steals in his direction, steadily growing larger and more forceful. Its pulsations render Lyle sick with fear, and the fear makes him breathe harder and faster, tightening his chest and throat.

The thing reaches for him. His heart pounds and he snatches quick breaths of air.

No! No, go away. Get out! I can't breathe. I can't get air. Help! Stop it! Go away!

Horror surges through him in jolts of electric shock, and when he's sure he is lost, he hears his father's voice drift through the room. Lyle takes hold of the words, a tangible thing, and clutches them tightly—a momentary lifeline.

"You have to face your fears. You have to fight back."

Lyle holds his hands up and away from himself, straining against the frightening energy. It vibrates more intensely now and emits a low, unearthly, fluttering noise. He can feel it reaching for him, as it pushes against his hands, forcing him down onto the bed.

Suddenly, he's out on the street. His parents lie side by side, asleep next to the curb, and an enormous black car rolls slowly in their direction. Moving like molten lava, it slides forward, and he knows it will crush them if he can't stop it. He pushes with all of his strength against the weight of the car but the vehicle presses him backwards. He hears tennis shoes skidding on the pavement—his shoes—crunching and grinding, into the gravel and sand.

He tries to scream at his parents, warn them, wake them, but he's unable to open his mouth. He makes as much noise as he can through his clamped jaw and lips, but his parents don't move. The monstrous car grows heavier and blacker and more forceful.

Lyle cannot hold it; he is powerless to stop it. He tries one last time to scream.

CHAPTER SIXTEEN

SELF

The greatest danger, that of losing one's own self,
may pass off quietly, as if it were nothing;
every other loss . . . is sure to be noticed.

~ SOREN KIERKEGAARD

This time, a scream does come, and it is a scream to God for help. Lyle shoots straight up in bed with a yell, dripping wet with perspiration. The light to his room snaps on, and Mr. Hatcher fills the doorway.

"Lyle? Wake up!" he orders firmly.

Lyle, wild-eyed and drenched, still partially clutched in the horror of the dream, stares at his dad.

"There was something in the corner up there! And then a huge car was going to run over you and Mom."

"It was just a dream, son. It's over now."

He sits down next to Lyle on the bed.

"Is Mom okay?" Lyle asks, shaken and anxious.

"Mom's in the kitchen studying," his dad reassures him. He rubs Lyle's back, helping him relax. "Hey, I'll tell you what. How about we take a scooter ride down by the fish hatchery tomorrow when I get home from work . . . how's that sound?"

Lyle nods. Mr. Hatcher notices something, and reaches out and wiggles the headboard. It's crooked.

"What happened to your bed?"

"I don't know, Dad."

He gets down on the floor and checks beneath the bed. The screws have been stripped from the metal frame, and barely hold it in place.

"I'm gonna need to fix it. I'll be right back," he declares.

Mr. Hatcher heads into the kitchen where his wife is studying. She glances up, and the expression on his face tells her everything.

"Another nightmare?" she asks.

He opens the tool drawer and rifles through it.

"He said it was a light up in the corner. And a car was going to run over us, you and me. I guess it was pretty spooky."

"Did you wake him up?"

"No. He was already awake when I turned on the light. I heard him scream."

Mr. Hatcher picks through the items in the tool drawer, thoughtlessly, aimlessly. He's forgotten what he's searching for, consumed by a problem he's unable to fix. For all his size and heart, this isn't a door he can rip open or force closed. He wishes he could battle his son's demons. He wishes he could make them go away, these very real monsters in the closet.

"Ron, what are you looking for?" his wife asks quietly.

"Where do all those screwdrivers disappear to?" He bangs around, rough and frustrated.

She gets up from the table and calmly moves to the drawer, picks up the screwdriver, and hands it to him.

"What are you fixing at this hour?"

"His bed is coming apart. Must've done it in his sleep, pushing against the headboard—stripped the screws right out."

"Do you have to do this right now?"

Mr. Hatcher closes the kitchen drawer too loudly.

"Yes, I do. He needs me to fix it."

Wednesday, October 13
28 days to Parent Night

By afternoon, the weather clears and the boys are finally back at the Log, prepared to continue their bug collecting. Lyle wanted to wait until the weekend, saying they wouldn't have enough time today with the sun going down so early now. He was also thinking about the scooter ride his dad promised, but David insisted they needed to make progress on the project, and Lyle finally agreed.

Lyle goes to work scanning under rocks and limbs in the tall grass, and David peels some of the bark from the Log. Several beetles take flight.

"Lyle! Bark beetles!"

Lyle doesn't look up.

"It's okay. Once they take off, you really can't catch 'em. It's too late. Let 'em go!"

Disappointed, David readies a jar in his other hand as he peels away another piece of bark. This time he traps a bark beetle in the jar before it takes off. He grins over at Lyle. Lyle hasn't moved, except to sit up, working within his arms' reach.

Moments later Lyle announces, "I think we got enough. Let's head home. It's gonna be dark soon anyway."

David thinks he's joking.

"I'll take these home and freeze 'em," Lyle says, and he packs the jars into the backpack.

Just then, an emerald dragonfly zooms past, alerting them with its characteristic whirring sound. Quickly, David fishes a jar from the pack and hands it to Lyle, never taking his eyes off the bright green insect. Lyle, equally entranced, stands with the jar in his hand, watching the dragonfly dart around the Log then zip across the field.

"Quick, Lyle! It's getting away."

Lyle turns to David. "Hey, remember the blue darner I caught right when it grabbed the robber fly? That was so cool. I saw him grab the fly outta the air and I knew right then—"

"I know, I know, I was there," David cuts in, distressed at the possibility the emerald dragonfly won't be in their collection. They've never missed an opportunity, no matter how slim the chance of success. David desperately wants to climb out of the chair and chase it down himself, which, of course, is impossible.

For the first time in their friendship, he feels inadequate.

He feels crippled.

When David arrives home, he and Dennis start right on his therapy. First, David loosens up his muscles with a swim. Then, while still in the pool, Dennis holds David's legs between his own, and lifts under his arms, pulling up on his shoulders. The stretch helps counteract the twist in David's spine, which draws his body downward to the left. He regularly wears a brace under his shirt, and must constantly lift and straighten himself, doing what he can to hold his back erect. The moment he relaxes, the twist in his spine once again forces him into the leftward lean.

Therapy, Dennis figures, as does Dena, is at least *something* they can do for a brother who fights an incessant daily battle against his own body.

Later, inside the house, Dena and Mrs. Dahlke take over. David is unusually silent as they unstrap him from the wheelchair and help him to stand. Once he's on his feet, Dena provides him with support.

"Mom?" David says, as he toils away from his wheelchair, one labored step at a time. "I think there's something wrong with Lyle."

"Do you mean he's sick?"

"No. It's not that."

Dena kneels on the floor in front of her brother and helps him lift his feet with each step.

"When we were catching bugs he seemed really tired, or something. He was just sitting there."

"Come on, David," Dena interjects. "Lift these puppies."

"We all have off-days," Mrs. Dahlke comments.

"Off-days? Are you kidding me, Mom? He's usually flying all over the place. And he never lets anything get away without at least trying! Last week he chased a butterfly all over Five Mile Prairie. He was gone so long I thought he forgot about me. And today he didn't chase anything. Not one thing! Not even when we saw an emerald dragonfly, and it's a crazy bug—super-crazy!"

"Lift," Dena reminds him.

"And hey, he's almost stopped talking," David adds, trying to lift his foot higher.

"He is a talker," Mrs. Dahlke nods.

After a moment of silence, Mrs. Dahlke stops and looks into her son's eyes. "David," she broaches gently, "Lyle's probably been put on something to slow him down a bit."

"Why?"

"Sometimes the school requires it, honey."

Mrs. Dahlke has her own opinions on the subject, due to her years teaching kindergarten and swimming to hundreds of neighborhood children. But she prefers her children form their own thoughts, so she doesn't elaborate, and they finish the walk in silence.

When they finally reach the wheelchair, David plops into it, exhausted. Dena and Mrs. Dahlke let him rest a few minutes while Dena sets up the portable therapy table.

They help David onto the table, and he settles on his back. His mother and sister work his legs, folding them to his chest and then extending them, while David is deep in thought.

Thursday, October 14
27 days to Parent Night

The next morning, on his way to school, Lyle treads along the curb-top, balancing like a tightrope acrobat. All of his books and homework, including the ones he usually forgets, are tucked neatly under his arm.

Dino, half a block ahead, turns to wait and wags his tail hopefully. Suddenly, Lyle stops, and gazes up the street, squinting into the sunlight. Dino turns, too, to see what Lyle is seeing. Four blocks away, Mr. Dahlke and David have arrived at the crosswalk on their way to the school.

Dino gets excited, dances a little dog dance, and lets loose with a bark to notify Lyle it's time for the ready-set-go they both love: time for the race to begin! Lyle ignores him and resumes his curb-walk. He is determined to balance all the way to school without falling . . . so far, so good.

I'm glad Miss O'Donnell isn't watchin' me anymore. That's good. And she quit buggin' my mom. That's really good. I guess I am better. Everybody says so. "You're doing so well" . . . "You're so quiet" . . . "Do you want something to eat?" Dang it, I forgot my lunch again.

I wish people would quit askin' if I'm okay. I'm okay. Okay? Why don't they give pills to Stanley? He was shootin' spit wads yesterday. I know . . . why don't they give a buncha pills to those guys who shot me with the BB gun? Then they'd lose all their power and somebody could shoot them in the legs over and over and over. How about that?!

I guess I'll talk to Sharon Anne's friend, Francine. Linda said maybe she thinks I don't like her. I don't really care, but Mom said to make it right.

I wish people would leave me alone.

Lyle slips off the curb.

"Dang it!"

He steps back up and continues where he left off, moving along the curb, one careful step at a time. Dino trots back and stays close to him all the way to the school.

Once in class, things are quiet. David sneaks glances at his friend. Lyle concentrates on his work, and never once speaks out of turn to the boy in the wheelchair beside him.

David raises his hand.

"Yes, David?" Mrs. Stewart says, glancing up.

"May I go to the restroom?"

"Do you need someone to go with you?"

"No, thanks."

She nods, and he wheels himself out the door and into the empty hall. He rolls right past the restroom without slowing, and when he reaches the main entrance to the school, navigates himself into the principal's office. Miss O'Donnell looks up, surprised.

"David? Why aren't you in class?"

"Miss O'Donnell, I need your help. There's something wrong with Lyle."

Miss O'Donnell sets down her work. "Come with me. We need to get you back to class."

"But I need to talk to you, Miss O'Donnell."

"You can talk to me on the way back to class," she says sternly. She helps David through the doorway and back out into the hall. "Now, what seems to be the problem?"

David thinks for a moment before answering.

"Miss O'Donnell? Sometimes kids ask me stuff like, did you fall off a horse? Or did you get hit by a car? They want to know why I'm in a wheelchair. But you know it's none of those things. It's just one day the doctor told me there'd be no more running. And then, they told me there'd be no more walking. It's not like I—"

Miss O'Donnell breaks in, uncomfortable with the direction of the conversation. "David, I'm sorry this has happened to you. I truly am, but—"

"No, no, no, what I mean is, there's nothing anybody could do about me. But with Lyle it's different."

The principal's spine stiffens.

"You know, David," she advises him curtly, "I have to find the best way to protect everyone in this school. Do you understand?"

"But he just sits there and doesn't do anything," David protests.

"This is simply not true, David. I've been closely following Lyle's progress. He's behaving in class and he's staying out of trouble. I have no idea why you're upset about this."

They arrive at the classroom and Miss O'Donnell opens the door for him. He wheels through and then angles back.

"Because Miss O'Donnell . . . I can't catch a dragonfly."

They gaze at each other. She has no idea what he means, and he doesn't know any other way to express it. Finally, Miss O'Donnell closes the door, without saying a word.

When Mr. Hatcher gets home from work, again Lyle is not there to greet him. What surprises Mr. Hatcher, as he absorbs the absence of his welcoming committee of one, is that it isn't just the bear hugs he misses. It's everything about Lyle, even the things he normally finds irritating.

Later, in the stillness of night while the entire family sleeps, Mr. Hatcher is awakened by a noise. At first it sounds like water running, the shower perhaps, or maybe the washing machine filling. As he comes fully awake, however, he checks to his left and finds his wife asleep. He climbs out of bed and follows the sound.

The house is completely dark except for an eerie bluish glow emanating from the living room, bouncing into the kitchen and hallway. As Mr. Hatcher enters, he sees Lyle in his pajamas, seated on the floor, staring at the television set. There's nothing on at this hour, except the broadcast test patterns and the steady sound of static, but Lyle watches with intensity, as if it were a riveting episode of *The Twilight Zone*.

"Son, why aren't you in bed?"

No response.

"Lyle?"

Still nothing.

"Lyle!" Mr. Hatcher barks loudly.

Lyle gazes up at his dad. "Hi, Dad."

Mr. Hatcher calls out to his wife. "Hazel, you'd better come in here!"

Seconds later, she hurries into the room, shuffling and bleary-eyed . . . until she sees Lyle.

"Lyle?" she cries. "What are you doing?"

"Nothin'."

"What's wrong with him? Is he asleep?" Mr. Hatcher asks.

She helps Lyle to his feet. "Lyle. Come on back to bed." She accompanies him back to his room.

"This is a bunch of malarkey," Mr. Hatcher grumbles. He switches off the television. "Malarkey!"

He wanders into the kitchen, and then back into the living room. He paces, and even that frustrates him. The house is too small to allow a man of his size to pace effectively.

His wife flips on the kitchen light and picks up the bottle of pills from the counter. She unscrews the cap and dumps the pills into the sink. As she reaches for the faucet, he stops her.

"If you do that, then what?"

She slams the pill bottle down on the counter.

"I don't know, but I'm worried sick about this!"

"Isn't he behaving himself at school? No notes, no calls, no hacks, no Miss O'Donnell?"

"Yes, but it doesn't seem right to me. He's not the same, and I—"

"Won't that put us right back where we started?"

"It's the way he is. He doesn't need to be fixed!"

"Let's talk to another doctor."

"What if he says the same thing? Then we're worse off than if we hadn't."

They listen to the silence of the night. The only sounds are the hum of the refrigerator and the faint rise and fall of Steve snoring.

"I *hate* this feeling, like we're being held hostage," Mrs. Hatcher says. "We could put him in the Catholic school down the block."

"St. Thomas More? That's great. Those nuns'll have a field day with him." He pauses. "Maybe we should move."

"We can't move! The checkbook is empty. And you're already working extra shifts."

"We could borrow enough for the down. Maybe you could put off graduating for another year or two."

"Well, if we're selling the house, let's sell the car, too. There. There's our money. How about that?"

"Fine!"

They fall into silence.

Mr. Hatcher turns and leaves the room, and Mrs. Hatcher picks up the pills, one by one from the bottom of the sink, and drops them back into the bottle.

She lies awake all night.

Friday, October 15
26 days to Parent Night

The recess bell rings. Lyle ambles out to the sidewalk and stands there, blinking in the bright October sunlight. Content for the moment, he watches the activity on the playground.

Mr. Merrick leans against the boiler room wall and takes it all in. It's been clear to him for days that the boy's frenetic adventures have given way to something calmer, and he's sure he knows why. It bothers him more than anything that has happened the entire time he's worked at Linwood.

"This is bull! Absolute bull!" he mutters under his breath.

He steps into the boiler room and slams the door behind, kicking the garbage can, sending it flying. In the small room the din is deafening as the aluminum container smacks and bounces on the metal pipes and concrete walls. It lands on its side, a huge dent showing, and rocks back and forth, clanging an off-beat rhythm. Mr. Merrick stares at it for a while, then reaches for his pipe. He knows better than to lose his temper. It does not serve him well.

The janitor's views are simplistic, black-and-white, old school. He doesn't trust authority, or respect it, and this includes clergy, government, and doctors. In his world, Lyle's medication is no different than a street drug, and doctors who prescribe drugs to children are no different than pushers in Haight-Ashbury.

Strategically, he keeps his opinions to himself. Not only does this leave them untested, but it also allows him to keep his day job. Miss O'Donnell would surely find his thinking radical, disruptive and wrong, although knowing this does not distress him in the least.

After recess, as the children file in and take their seats, David searches the room.

"Hey, Mike. Have you seen Lyle?"

"No, I thought he was with you."

"He was out there during recess," Colleen offers helpfully. "I saw him."

"Yeah, he was out by the Slickery Tree when we were playing Crack the Whip," Johnny recollects.

"Just standin' there," Mike adds.

"I think he was gettin' ready to climb it," Johnny nods. "Everybody knows you can't get up the Slickery Tree."

David wheels himself to the window and checks along the street, where the tall Ponderosas line the edge of the school property, and his eyes go straight to the largest. The "Slickery Tree" (so named because repeated attempts to climb it have worn away the roughness from its bark) towers over the playground, and the small crumpled pile at its base seems even smaller in its shade. David spins in his chair and is almost instantly to the door, struggling with it.

"Open this door!" he shouts.

"What is it, David?" Mrs. Stewart asks, rushing to the window. She sees Lyle, and turns to the child nearest her. "Go, get Miss O'Donnell! Quickly!"

CHAPTER SEVENTEEN

SECOND CHANCE

*The greatest and most impossible problems of life
are all in a certain sense insoluble.
They can only be outgrown.*

~ CARL JUNG

David rocks back and forth, as he fights to get through the doorway. His wheel catches on the frame and in his agitation he can't get it free. Mrs. Stewart squeezes around him.

Mr. Merrick, exiting the boiler room for a smoke, spies Lyle under the tree. He drops his pipe and tears across the playground. Mrs. Stewart, relieved to see him, stops and waits near the end of the sidewalk, trying to catch her breath.

When Mr. Merrick reaches the tree, he drops to his knees beside Lyle. He can see that the boy is breathing.

"Lyle?" he urges, careful to stay calm.

Getting no response, he gently shakes him. Lyle opens his eyes and tilts his head to look at the janitor.

"Hey, Mr. Merrick."

"What happened?" Mr. Merrick's voice is kind.

Lyle has to think for a moment. "I . . . I guess I fell asleep . . . please don't tell anybody, Mr. Merrick."

"No problem, Sparky," Mr. Merrick reassures him, helping the boy to his feet. The two of them walk slowly across the playground, back toward the school.

In the classroom, the children crowd around the window.

"What's he doin' out there?" Billy asks.

"Obviously he is sleeping," Melvin Schmeck says. Melvin pays more attention to what's going on than people realize.

"He's sort of a spaz, isn't he?" Francine whispers to Sharon Anne.

Sharon Anne ignores her friend. She's concerned for Lyle, but right now mostly for David, and she hurries over and helps him get his chair through the doorway. She pushes him to the sidewalk's edge, where Miss O'Donnell, already arrived at the side exit, stops her.

"You two wait right there," she orders.

Sharon Anne stands protectively close to the wheelchair.

"Is he all right?" David asks Sharon Anne.

"I don't know."

She puts her hand on his shoulder to comfort him.

Mr. Merrick and Lyle reach the spot where Miss O'Donnell and Mrs. Stewart wait. The principal takes Lyle's chin in her hand.

"Lyle, look at me," she instructs, her voice less stern than usual.

He stares into her eyes.

"How do you feel?"

"Fine, Miss O'Donnell. I'm sorry. Am I in trouble?"

"No, you're not in trouble. Mrs. Stewart will take you to my office. I'll be there in a few minutes."

"I need to go with him," David announces.

"David, I will take care of this," Miss O'Donnell replies.

David doesn't budge.

"Sharon Anne," commands Miss O'Donnell, "help David back to class, please. Go on! Both of you!"

Sharon Anne obediently wheels David in the direction of the classroom.

"Just a minute!" Mr. Merrick interjects.

David, almost to the school with Sharon Anne, brakes the chair when he hears Mr. Merrick's voice. He angles around, a look of determination on his face.

"Come on, David," Sharon Anne whispers urgently. She tugs on the chair, but David holds it in place with his hands on the wheels.

"No! I want to hear this," he insists.

Mrs. Maxfield, who has been standing in the doorway of the fifth-grade classroom, joins the group on the sidewalk.

"What are you doin' to that boy?" Mr. Merrick growls at Miss O'Donnell.

"This is none of your affair!"

He points an angry finger.

"It is not right! And you know it!"

A hand on his arm silences him. Mrs. Maxfield holds it there a moment, as she addresses the principal. "We need to put a stop to this, Miss O'Donnell. I understand the reasoning behind it, but it doesn't seem to be working for Lyle."

Miss O'Donnell seethes at the challenge to her authority.

The dance teacher doesn't falter. "There's not a thing wrong with the youngster. Not a thing, and he needs to be taken off the medication."

Miss O'Donnell whips her head and catches David and Sharon Anne eavesdropping by the classroom. She thrusts her finger in the direction of the door, and they hurry into the school.

"We'll discuss this later," she says to Mrs. Maxfield, overtly ignoring Mr. Merrick.

She spins, and retraces her steps to her office. Once inside, she places a call to Mrs. Hatcher, to inform her of the occurrence on the playground.

Mrs. Hatcher arrives at the school a few minutes later and rushes Lyle to the Paulsen Medical Building to see Dr. Lyon. She explains everything she's observed about Lyle's reaction to the drug, positive and negative: Mrs. Stewart's glowing reports about his behavior, his ravenous hunger for the first few days but almost complete loss of appetite for the remainder of the week, the erratic sleeping patterns, and the nightmares.

Dr. Lyon listens closely—more to the desperation in her voice than to the content of what she is saying. When she's finished, he writes a note to Miss O'Donnell stating that he's discontinuing Lyle's medication, as he no longer considers it a viable option for him.

Relieved at this development but anxious about where it might lead, Mrs. Hatcher drops Lyle at home and drives directly to Linwood.

Once seated in Miss O'Donnell's office, she uses every tool in her repertoire to achieve what she knows she must. She compliments Miss O'Donnell on her efforts, readily admits things need to change, and assures her that she and Mr. Hatcher will see to it Lyle is no longer a problem at school. She holds out the doctor's note as if in apology.

To Mrs. Hatcher's amazement, Miss O'Donnell folds away the note without reading it . . . and agrees to give Lyle another chance.

When David gets home in the afternoon, he can't wait to tell his mom about the day's events. He races through the words, energized by his discovery: the course of events can be changed through other people's efforts, in this case, even his own.

He's so talkative and animated, and moves around so much, that his mother and sister have difficulty with his therapy. Finally, Mrs. Dahlke has to beseech him to quiet down awhile.

"Okay, Mom, I was just saying," David explains, borrowing one of Lyle's favorite lines.

"Oh, you were just saying, were you?" Dena challenges him with a grin. "Well, try just saying this. 'I want a proper cup of coffee from a proper copper coffee pot.'"

"Easy," David says, convinced for the moment he can do anything. "I wanna proper cup of coffee from a proffer coffer coffer poff."

They all explode into laughter. Dena helps David onto the therapy table, still laughing, and Mrs. Dahlke turns her efforts to his Achilles tendon. Massaging the ankle into relaxation, she cups David's heel in the palm of her hand and braces her forearm against the bottom of his foot. She lifts the heel while pushing her arm forward, stretching his toes toward his shin. They laugh a little more, chat a little more, and she's just about finished, when she hears a sharp, abrupt *snap*—and feels something break and separate in her hand.

David screams.

White-hot pain shoots through his ankle and lower leg. His foot dangles as though disconnected, and it lies on his shin, loosely flopping there. He cries out again, in agony.

Mrs. Dahlke wails, and runs to the opposite end of the room, terrified at what she has done. She drops to her knees at the davenport, sobbing and praying. Dena grabs David's foot and tries to move it back in place. It feels loose and unattached in her hand.

"Mom, we have to get him to the hospital! Quick!"

Mrs. Dahlke doesn't respond. She's praying so hard she doesn't hear or see anything else in the room, as if she is deep in a trance. Dena races upstairs to the phone and dials the therapist's number.

"John! I think Mother has broken David's heel cord. Can you come?"

"I'll be right there," he assures her.

Dena hurries down the stairs, and hovers near David, comforting him.

In a matter of moments, John lets himself in and trots down the basement stairs.

Dena sees him coming—and at the same time, a look of peace comes over David's face, and she feels him relax under her hands.

"Mom, I'm okay," David calls out to Mrs. Dahlke, "I'm okay."

John hurries forward and examines David's ankle. He tests it with care, moving it around and applying pressure. Dena watches, her heart in her throat.

"You didn't do anything to this," he reports, relieved. "It's fine. Really."

Dena's mouth drops. "But we—"

"There's no way this tendon could have snapped, and spontaneously repaired," John explains patiently.

"But his foot was flopping against his shin . . . like it had broken off!" Dena objects.

"Dena . . . I have no idea what happened, but it couldn't have detached or broken, or he would be in a great deal of pain even now. You can see for yourself. There's nothing wrong with it."

"You don't have to believe me, I know what I saw," Dena insists, lowering her voice.

"Sometimes in a traumatic situation our senses deceive us. You can't always trust what you see in the middle of an emergency," he explains, trying not to sound condescending, though not very well succeeding.

Dena doesn't respond, but she crosses her arms and shakes her head, stubbornly unconvinced. She knows John will never believe her, and she bites her tongue as he again reassures her and hastens to make a quick exit.

"Hysterical women," he mutters to himself, pushing aside the fact he knows better. The Dahlke women are not hysterical, nor are they prone to exaggeration. And then there was Mrs. Dahlke . . . on her knees the whole time he was there, frozen and quiet, even after the episode was over.

He gets in his car, and starts the ignition. *Something strange happened back there*, he thinks. *I have no idea what, but it happened.*

Inside, everyone recovers. David resettles in his wheelchair, testing his ankle, rotating it and adding pressure.

"It's fine," he concludes. "Are you okay, Mom?"

Mrs. Dahlke is unable to get up from her knees. Dena puts her arms around her mother, and helps her to her feet. She turns her and lowers her onto the couch, and Mrs. Dahlke sinks there, feeling nothing but an immense, overwhelming fatigue.

Sunday, October 17
24 days to Parent Night

L yle dumps a basket of paper into the burning barrel, and strikes a wooden match against the rusted metal surface. He drops the match onto the papers, and when the fire takes hold, he drags the screen over the top of the barrel. The smoke drifts up into his face and he moves away, remembering one of his favorite lines he likes to say at Scout camp.

Smoke follows beauty and me.

He tries to laugh, but he doesn't feel like it. The burning-barrel is rusty and dented, and peeling from the hundreds of small fires it has contained over the years. Lyle kicks the side, and sends ash and grit floating into the air. The flame noisily engulfs the paper, and the crackling sparks play tiddlywinks on the cover screen.

Linda passes by the window and sees him standing by the barrel. She wanders outside to check on him.

"Hey, whatcha doin'?"

"Thinkin'."

"What're you thinking about?"

"I'm thinkin' I don't want to go to school tomorrow."

They both gaze absently at the barrel, even though the flames have died away.

"I know your week was worse than mine. But I had a rough week, too," Linda shares.

"What happened?"

"I was wearing my green wrap-around dress. You know the one I'm talking about?"

Lyle tries to picture it, but since green is not among the colors he can distinguish, none of her dresses come to mind.

"You know, the one with the fringe around the bottom?"

"Oh yeah, I like that dress."

"I used to like it, but I guess it makes me look like the Jolly Green Giant."

"Who said that?" he demands to know, puffing up like a little bulldog. He feels his heartbeat rev up. Nobody messes with his sister.

"One of the teachers," she replies, with an even, matter-of-fact tone.

"Did you tell Mom?"

"Yes."

"What did she say?"

Linda makes him wait a little while, knowing the pause will give impact to her answer.

"She told me to rise above it."

"Rise above it? That's all she said, 'Rise above it'?"

"Yep. Come on, dinner's ready," Linda tells him.

They head back to the house, side by side. Lyle wants to make her feel better.

"You know, people don't know. 'Cause if they did, they'd know . . . uh," Lyle stumbles and goes on, ". . . that you are smart, and pretty . . . and brave, and um . . ."

He trails off, looking up at her.

"What's for dinner?" he asks.

She smiles and puts her arm around his shoulders.

"Fried chicken, mashed potatoes, biscuits and homemade jam," she relates.

"Fried chicken," Lyle says, with a tone of deep gratitude. "That sounds so good. I'm starvin'."

Linda lets loose with a bit of singing, even though she's indisputably challenged as a vocalist. She sings the Jolly Green Giant ad they've both heard a hundred times on television. Lyle, not the greatest singer either, joins her in the chorus.

Monday, October 18
23 days to Parent Night

Lyle climbs out of bed with a feeling of dread about going to school. He can't believe he fell asleep on the playground where everyone could see, and he knows the other kids will be talking. What's more, Mrs. Stewart has been so proud of him this week, and now he's afraid he'll disappoint her. He resolves to try very hard not to get in trouble.

He stalls for a while, watching *The Jack LaLanne Show*. Jack walks across the room on his hands then springs to his feet and delivers a fast-paced challenge to his viewers.

> *"Listen, my friends, do you feel like you just can't get anywhere 'cause you've got such bad luck? You've got those people out there that are always working against you? Maybe your boss, or your spouse, or some other person you have to deal with?*
>
> *"Well, listen to me. Are you listening?*
>
> *"It's not them. It's you! Only you can change it. And I've told you this before. You have to change it now! Not tomorrow. If you wait 'til tomorrow there'll just be another excuse!"*

Lyle is glued to the television. Mrs. Hatcher's breaks in.

"Lyle, I am not writing a note!"

Eyes on the TV as long as possible, he grabs his lunch sack and backs out the door. Then he spins, leaps off the porch, and runs across the lawn to the backyard fence separating the

Hatchers' yard from the alleyway, opting for a shortcut through the alley.

There was a hard freeze last night, and a heavy layer of frost covers the upper edge of the wooden fence. As Lyle scales it and clears the top, he slips on the slick surface. His pant cuff catches on the wooden slat and he falls, swinging sideways until he hangs upside down, dangling in the air on the alley side of the fence.

Confident he can get himself out of this predicament, he gets to work trying to free himself. He struggles and strains and grunts with the effort, trying every maneuver he can devise. Nothing works.

Dino, waiting in the front yard, senses Lyle used the back door today. The dog ambles down the alley, searching, and when he arrives at the scene, he stands there, mouth open, tongue hanging, eyes on Lyle.

"Dino. Good boy. Go get help!" Lyle urges. He witnessed Timmy doing this with great success on *Lassie* just yesterday.

Dino sidles up, closer to Lyle, and sits.

"Dino! Go!" Lyle urges him. Dino wiggles a little, then lies down in the tall grass to wait. This dog is definitely not Lassie. Lyle takes an enormous breath.

"MAAAHHHMM!" he bellows.

CHAPTER EIGHTEEN

INSPIRATION

I know you believe you understand what you think I said,
but I am not sure you realize that what you heard
is not what I meant.

~ ANONYMOUS

The back door to the house swings open. Lyle, from his inverted position, squints through the cracks between the fence boards as Mrs. Hatcher steps out onto the porch. She scans the yard, expecting to see him there.

"Lyle?" she calls out. "Where are you?"

"Over here, Mom!" he yells. "I'm hangin' from the fence!"

Lyle has a good view—through a knothole—of her crossing the yard upside-down. She grabs a bucket from under the faucet, flips it over, and climbs on top, barely high enough to peer over at him.

"Oh, for Heaven's sake! What are you doing?"

"I'm not doin' anything, Mom. I'm stuck," he informs her.

Mrs. Hatcher reaches over the fence. "Grab my hand," she instructs.

Lyle has to do a hanging sit-up to reach for her, but even then they barely manage to touch fingers. When he attempts it a second time, they manage to wiggle the tips of their fingers together. They start to laugh, and the more they try, the harder they laugh. Mrs. Hatcher laughs so hard she loses her balance and falls off her bucket onto the lawn.

Lyle, now completely weak from the ordeal, hangs from the fence like a wet pair of long-johns. Mrs. Hatcher climbs back onto the bucket and sets about trying to pry the stubborn blue jeans from the fence board.

"Come on, Mom!" Lyle encourages her. "You can do it!"

When she finally succeeds, still laughing, he falls onto his hands with his legs extended directly above him in the air. He inadvertently palms a few steps before he falls to the ground. He leaps to his feet, grinning up at his mom, barely able to see her eyes above the fence line.

"Mom, did you see that?"

Before she can answer, he turns and runs.

"Hey! Get back here!" she shouts. "You're going to need a note. You're late!"

Mrs. Hatcher is anything but mad.

M r. Merrick whistles to the rhythm of his mop as he cleans the front entrance for the second time today. Lyle bursts through the door at full throttle and leaps over the mop bucket.

"You're late!"

"It's okay!" Lyle relays as he darts past. "I have a note!"

Lyle hurtles down the hallway, rounds the corner and disappears. Mr. Merrick chuckles, glad to see he's back to his old self.

Within seconds, Lyle reappears, slipping and sliding on the wet floor.

"Careful, Sparky! I just mopped there."

"Hey, Mr. Merrick? I got 'n idea, to raise money, you know, for David Dahlke."

The janitor wrings out his mop. "For David Dahlke? What's he need money for?"

"Research. On muscular dystrophy, so they can find a cure. See, that's how I can help him run."

"So you've fine-tuned your plan, have ya? Are ya leavin' God outta the mix, now?"

"No, He's still in the mix. This is all part of it, Mr. Merrick. I'm gonna walk across the gym on my hands and everybody's gonna pay me a quarter to do it. On Parent Night."

Mr. Merrick leans on his mop handle. "Listen, I know you two are thicker than thieves, and I'm glad to hear you got a way to help him. But do you really think everybody'll just pony up a quarter?"

"Pony up a quarter?" This is a new phrase to Lyle.

"Can you even walk on your hands?"

"Almost. I was practicin' this morning in the backyard." Lyle bends over and flattens his palms on the floor. "I can already do this."

He kicks his feet into the air, and takes about a step and a half on his hands. He falls over sideways and curls into a ball. Mr. Merrick is amused. Lyle springs back to his feet, expecting accolades. Instead, Mr. Merrick is staring at a spot on the floor where Lyle's hand had been a moment before. He whips a scraper from his back pocket and expertly scoops up a small gooey brown spot from the tile.

Mr. Merrick smells it. "Pitch?"

Lyle sniffs his own hand.

"It's from the fence, Mr. Merrick," he says, grinning.

Mr. Merrick hands him the mop. "Here, hold this."

Surprisingly limber for a man his age, Mr. Merrick reaches down and lifts himself into a handstand, straining but in control. Once he finds a balance point, he holds the position with ease.

"Head up . . . arch . . . your back . . . legs . . . straight," Mr. Merrick puffs, between intakes of air. His face is already bright red. He hasn't tried this in a very long time.

"Wow! Mr. Merrick, you're strong."

Mr. Merrick lands back on his feet.

"State wrestling champ, 1930," he boasts, checking to make sure his shirt's tucked in. "Nothin' better'n wrestlin' to build up those arms."

"Mr. Merrick, you just gave me a great idea. Thanks!"

Lyle thrusts the mop back in his hands.

"Can you believe this day? No, you can't," he proclaims.

He points at Mr. Merrick and grins before he turns and runs, vanishing almost instantly around the corner.

The janitor stares after where Lyle disappeared.

"Lord, hide the women and children," he chuckles.

Lyle slips into the classroom as quietly as possible and takes his seat. He keeps his eyes on Mrs. Stewart as she talks and writes the lessons on the chalkboard. He's learned the importance of pretending to pay attention. But his mind races with more important things: the brilliance of his new plan and his excitement over how everything he needs is coming together so perfectly.

He sniffs the pitch on his hand, taking in the odor of piney resin. It brings a smile to his face; it smells like his grandma's hope chest.

>Grandma's told me a thousand times, "Things always work out." I caught my jeans on the fence. That was lucky. I was gonna wear my cords and they don't have a cuff! My mom was laughing and laughing and that made me laugh. I got my power back.
>
>So far I have not seen Miss O'Donnell. Not once. Even if I did I would say, "Good morning Miss O'Donnell. I like your shoes."
>
>Sharon Anne is sure cute. I wonder if I'll be a good kisser! What a lucky day!

The recess bell rings, and Lyle wastes no time getting outside. He gazes around, as if searching for something or someone, and then hotfoots it up to Mark Ellings, a thirteen-year-old who happens to be the biggest kid out there. Lyle positions himself squarely in front of Mark.

"You wanna wrestle me?" Lyle challenges.

Mark is large, even for his age, no question, but he's not a bully and never has been. Nor is he particularly interested in fighting, not even for sport. He's more of a checkers player.

"Are you talking to me?" Mark asks, certain he isn't.

"Yeah. Do you wanna wrestle me?"

"No. I . . . I don't."

"C'mon! Wrestle me!" Lyle encourages him, almost begging.

Mark glances around. A few kids gather and more are on their way. This looks like trouble.

"No! Pick on someone your own size!" Mark deflects, good-naturedly.

He turns his back to Lyle and walks away. Lyle hesitates, then takes a running leap onto Mark's back. The kids go crazy, screaming and cheering and closing in a circle around them.

In no time, everyone on the playground converges for the show. Mark throws Lyle to the side by heaving with his back, catches him under one arm, drops him to the ground, and holds him there.

Lyle struggles, but there's nothing he can do against the strength of the larger boy.

"Satisfied?" Mark asks.

Miss O'Donnell's whistle pierces the air as she strides up and parts the sea of children.

"You better not have gotten me in trouble," Mark warns, climbing to his feet and brushing himself off.

"I'm sorry, Miss O'Donnell," Mark offers. "Right out of nowhere, he jumped on my back."

"Who started this?" the principal demands to know, suspicious eyes parsing the crowd.

Before any of the others can respond, Lyle holds his hand in the air and announces, "I did, Miss O'Donnell. I started it!"

The faintest glimmer of surprise flashes across her face. She takes a tight hold on Lyle's shoulder and marches him all the way to her office without releasing her grip. She doesn't let go until the door closes behind them and he's placed firmly in the visitor's chair.

"What were you and Mark fighting about?" she inquires, keeping her anger under control.

"Oh, no, no, Miss O'Donnell. Me and Mark weren't fighting. We weren't mad at each other or anything like that. I know the rules about fighting. No fighting! I know that. And I wasn't!"

Miss O'Donnell shakes her head in disbelief. Now, she understands the confession.

"It certainly looked like fighting to me," she replies brusquely.

"No. It wasn't anything like that. It was training, Miss O'Donnell. I have to wrestle every day, to make myself super-strong. See, I need to walk across the gym on my hands on Parent Night to raise money for muscular dystrophy, so I have to get stronger, and Mr. Merrick said there's nothing that'll make you stronger than—"

"Stop! Stop right there." Miss O'Donnell raises her hands, palms out, like a double stop sign. "I do not want to hear one more word from you. Not one. There's no fighting allowed on school grounds and you know it!"

"But Miss O'Donnell, that's what I was tryin' to tell you—"

Miss O'Donnell snaps her fingers loudly. She points at Lyle with a flick of her wrist and then up at the clock the same way.

"That is not what this conversation is about," she scolds him, "and you've got ten seconds to make a choice. I can call your parents right now and they can deal with this, or you can take a trip down the hall to Mr. Stratton's office, and you already know what that means! It's your decision. If you leave it up to me, it'll be both."

Lyle gawks at her, afraid to speak, but also realizing he's trapped.

"Five seconds left," she tells him, her pointer finger aimed dramatically at the clock.

"Mr. Stratton," he squeaks, defeated.

"Well, come along then," she tells him, "and when you're done with Mr. Stratton, I want you back in here. Immediately."

Miss O'Donnell delivers Lyle to the gym teacher's office, ushers him in, then proceeds down the hall to the boiler room. When she opens the door, Mr. Merrick, surprised, switches off his turntable, extinguishing the final crescendo of a soaring aria.

"What an unexpected pleasure," he comments wryly.

"What's this about training Lyle Hatcher to walk across the gym on his hands?" she demands, her own hands squarely on her hips.

"Well, now I'm thinkin' maybe I put the wrong idea in his head. If you want me to, I'll straighten this out," he offers.

"I suggest you do. I don't appreciate you undermining my authority this way," she rebukes him.

"I thought you might want to give him a chance to do a good thing. He could surprise you."

Mr. Merrick lights his pipe and takes a puff or two on it.

Miss O'Donnell waves her hand in front of her face. "I cannot stand the smell of that smoke."

He politely puts out the pipe.

"He's a handful," Mr. Merrick observes. "No doubt about it."

Mr. Merrick digs out his pack of Sen-Sen and shakes a few into his hand. He offers one to Miss O'Donnell. She brushes them off in refusal, barely disguising the revulsion on her face.

"You know," Mr. Merrick comments, "if you could make this work, the rest of the year might go a lot smoother."

"I beg your pardon! I'm not making deals with fourth-grade children. Have you no understanding of disciplinary boundaries?"

"Maybe I worded it wrong, but whatever you wanna call it. It'd keep him busy, give him somethin' to focus on. It might end up keepin' him outta your office, for starters, outta Mr. Stratton's office, and outta the boiler room for a while. I'd think that'd be somethin' you'd want."

"I'll tell you what I want," she responds coldly. "I want you to stop encouraging this kind of behavior. We saw on the playground this morning where it leads."

She notes the detachment on his face. "There's something you need to realize, Mr. Merrick. This is not a school for special children. We don't make those accommodations, for the simple reason it could jeopardize the safety of all the other children, exactly as we've seen over the last few weeks. I'm sticking my neck out for him, just by allowing him to remain here, in my school. He'll show up on time, he'll do his homework, and he'll stay out of trouble, or he'll be expelled. You're not doing him any favors by encouraging him in this direction, do you understand me?"

"Perfectly," Mr. Merrick says, reloading his pipe.

Miss O'Donnell takes it as a signal to leave, and she does. Down the hall, Lyle exits Mr. Stratton's office, rubbing his backside. Without hesitation, he heads for her office, as he was told to do.

Seated once more across from the principal, Lyle launches into his plan to walk across the gym on Parent Night. Having come up with the idea only a couple of hours earlier, he hasn't had time to refine the details and logistics, so his presentation is less than compelling.

Miss O'Donnell allows him to ramble until he's finished, listening politely for the duration. Despite her vehement response to Mr. Merrick only a few minutes earlier, his words did have an impact, and she redoubles her effort to be fair-minded. If she could read Lyle's mind, however, she would realize he feels pressured by her patient attention, which renders his delivery even less effective.

Lyle trails off to a rickety finish. His last word, naturally, is "um."

"Lyle," Miss O'Donnell says in very firm voice, "first of all, there's a time and place for everything, and Parent Night is not where we raise money for charitable causes. That is the reason we have the March of Dimes campaign every spring. Secondly, it is Mrs. Thompson, not I, who handles the organization of Parent Night, and I'm not going to bother her with this. Do you understand me? It's a *grandiose* idea . . . *grandiose*." She exaggerates the word twice with a head-shudder for emphasis. "And frankly," she continues, "it's the last thing on my agenda, and so I don't want to hear another word about it. Are we clear?"

Lyle nods.

"*Here's* what you need to do. Are you listening to me?"

Another nod.

Miss O'Donnell counts the requirements on her fingers, one at a time, as she says them. "What you need to do is . . . finish your science project and do a good job on it . . . *and* behave yourself, and get your schoolwork done . . . *and* focus on not creating any more disruptions on the school grounds for the rest of the year." She pauses. "Do you understand me?"

Lyle nods again, agreeable and excited. He does understand her. He understands perfectly.

After school, the old routine is back in place. David and Lyle arrive at the crosswalk and David plugs his ears while Lyle hollers for Dino, who immediately comes running and joins them.

Lyle has a paddleball which Mr. Stratton gave him from the Lost and Found, thinking it might help keep him busy. He received it with specific instructions to use it only outside the building and never within ten feet of other children. He's mastered it pretty well, paddleballing like crazy while David talks, already violating the ten-foot rule.

"Hey! Watch it!"

"Sorry," Lyle hastens, meaning it. "Hey! Listen to this. I got a plan."

"Oh, no. Is it better than the Lyle-Falls-in-Love-with-Sharon-Anne-Who-Is-Big-and-Tall Plan?"

"That's an old plan, David, and for your information it was called The-Sharon-Anne-Meets-Lyle-Who-Is—"

"Okay, okay, okay, okay. What's the new plan?"

"This is good. Are you with me? Okay. I'm gonna walk all the way across the gym floor on my hands and everybody's gonna pony up a quarter and we're gonna give the money to muscular dystrophy research, what d'ya think of that?"

David dodges a paddle shot. "Wait a minute! All the way from one end of the gym to the other? Nobody can do that!"

"They said the same thing about the peg climb, didn't they?" Lyle argues. "And I did that, easy."

"But walking that far on your hands. Is that even possible?"

"Heck yeah, it's possible. I saw Jack LaLanne do it."

David shakes his head. "Well, I'll tell you one thing. Jack LaLanne never had to get Miss O'Donnell's permission. She'll never let you do it. Never in a million years. Never!"

"Then listen to this, Mr. Know-it-all." Lyle stills his paddleball and gets in really close. He puts his eyes right level with David's so he won't miss a single word.

"I already asked her . . . and she said YES."

David's eyes bug wide. "No way," he shakes his head, deciding on a technique he learned from Lyle. "Tell me her exact words."

Lyle imitates Miss O'Donnell's precise delivery including the headshakes.

"She said . . . it's a *grandiose* idea . . . *and* we have to finish our science project first . . . *and* we have to talk to Mrs. Thompson about it 'cause she's in charge of Parent Night, not Miss O'Donnell."

Lyle counts the three points on his hand exactly as the principal had done.

David quickly gets into the spirit of things. "I've almost got all the labels finished. Only eleven more to go, and we're there," he apprises, thinking fast.

"Cool!" Lyle says. "Just tell me when and I'll come get 'em." He starts to trot off toward home.

"Day after tomorrow. Aren't you staying to swim?" David asks, disappointed.

"Nah, I can't. My mom told me to come straight home 'cause my grandpa's at a golfin' tournament and so my grandma's comin' over for dinner. See you tomorrow, though!"

Lyle takes off running, with Dino chasing.

"Hey!" David calls after him. "Don't forget about the field trip tomorrow. And don't forget your permission slip!"

Lyle spins and waves.

"Adios!" David yells, even though Lyle is already out of earshot.

Yes, David thinks. *This is going to be the biggest Parent Night ever!*

Tuesday, October 19
22 days to Parent Night

L yle explodes into the house, this time with a praying mantis clinging to his finger. He rushes up to his mom and lifts the insect right in her face, oblivious to the fact that she's knee-deep in a load of laundry, *and* in the middle of preparing dinner.

"Hey, Mom," he says. "I caught it in the field behind the McDonald's!"

"Oh! Wow! Okay. I've never seen a praying mantis before. Isn't it something? So . . . big."

Mrs. Hatcher examines it closely and the mantis engages her in a staring contest, easily winning.

"How's my bug-collecting grandson?" Grandma Hatcher chimes from the kitchen table, where she's playing cribbage with Lyle's dad. She leans back as Lyle sidles over to catch one of her smoky kisses.

"Okay, that thing's kinda creepy," Mrs. Hatcher gestures to the mantis. "Why don't you take it outside now and come back and get washed up for dinner? It's almost time to eat."

"I'm keepin' it, Mom, for our bug collection."

He's already out the door.

"Fine," she calls after him.

Mrs. Hatcher goes back to the clothes washing. On the radio, Nat King Cole croons Walkin' My Baby Back Home, and she sings lightly with the chorus, swaying to the music as she works.

She empties Lyle's pockets and finds a toy telescope, a few pennies, a couple of plastic toys, and a tightly folded piece of paper. She takes a peek through the telescope, and startles to see a photo of Marilyn Monroe posing poolside in a swimming suit. She has to check it again to make sure she saw what she thought she saw. She grabs Lyle as he tries to dart past her.

"What's this?" she quizzes, holding it out.

"I found that!" Lyle says, grabbing for it.

"Well, now it's mine," she tells him, moving it out of his reach. "And what about these?" In her hand are the little plastic toys. Lyle peruses them as though he's never seen them before.

"Those are . . . nothin'," he tells her.

"Something from a box of Cracker Jacks, perhaps? Where did you get money for Cracker Jacks?"

"I didn't eat 'em. They were somebody else's. I told 'em I can't eat Cracker Jacks."

Mrs. Hatcher gives him the look.

"Okay, maybe one," he admits, holding up one finger.

Mrs. Hatcher swats away a fly while she unfolds the piece of paper she found in his pocket. It's tightly creased into a tiny square, so it takes a while.

"And this?"

"It's a permission slip. You need to sign it."

"Permission for what?"

"We're goin' to Strick's Donuts."

"Strick's Donuts?" she repeats in astonishment.

"Yeah. It's the factory, Mom! Isn't that great?"

Mrs. Hatcher stares at her son. He smiles back, eyes wide, no doubt envisioning a vat full of sugar.

"It's something, all right," she acknowledges. "It sounds to me like a recipe for disaster."

CHAPTER NINETEEN

THE TROOPS

To do great, important tasks,
two things are necessary:
a plan and not quite enough time.

~ ANONYMOUS

Besieged with Lyle's pleas, Mrs. Hatcher sticks the permission slip under a magnet on the refrigerator and brushes the fly away again.

"But Mom, everybody's goin'! And David needs me there. Mom! Please?"

"We'll see," she concludes. "It's time for dinner. And Lyle, get that thing. It's driving me crazy."

She rolls up a section of the *Spokesman* and hands it to Lyle. He stands very still, with the newspaper hanging in his left hand, and tracks the fly as it buzzes around the room. All of a sudden, he grabs it out of the air with his right hand, flattening it in his fist.

"Got him!"

Lyle proudly displays the squished fly in his hand.

"For Heaven's sake, that's what the newspaper was for. Now go wash your hands."

A few minutes later the family sits around the dining room table, sharing their meal. With a quirky cock of his head, Steve signals Lyle to pass him the salt. Lyle nods his head back at Steve to ask if it's the salt or the pepper he wants. This quickly develops into a head-sign-language-only conversation. No one at the table pays any attention. When Steve finally gets the salt, he dumps generous quantities of it onto his food and casually announces, "I wanna try smokin'."

"What!?" Mr. Hatcher exclaims, smacking his fork down on the table.

"I wanna smoke."

"Why on earth would you want to start smoking?" Grandma Hatcher asks. "It's a terrible habit. Terrible!"

"You smoke all the time and I wanna try it. It's so cool when you blow it out your nose."

"Steve! You are not going to smoke!" his mom states with finality.

Steve resumes eating. He silently asks Lyle to pass the potatoes, like a baseball coach signaling a batter. The wordless requests escalate into a wordless conversation, which escalates into wordless joke-telling, until all the head-bobbing and weaving starts to irritate their dad.

"Knock it off. If you want the milk, then ask for it," he commands with a frown.

"He didn't want the milk, Dad, he was asking for—"

"Lyle!" Mrs. Hatcher stops him.

"Would you please pass the milk?" Steve pipes meekly.

The family eats in silence for a few minutes, until Lyle interjects. "Grandma? How come Grandpa doesn't believe in God?"

Everyone stops eating. Slowly, all eyes shift to Grandma.

The clock on the wall seems louder with each stroke. Mr. Hatcher puts his fork down again. He realizes he's going to have to handle this one.

"What did you say?" he stalls.

"How come Grandpa doesn't believe in God?"

"Is that what he told you? Is that exactly what he said?"

"I think that's what he said."

"I don't think you heard him right."

"He doesn't go to church, does he?"

Grandma Hatcher clears her throat. She dabs at her lips, taking her time, and then folds the napkin in her lap. Everyone waits respectfully.

"Your grandpa went to church with me once. He was so handsome with his white shirt and tie. He even bought a sport coat for the occasion. I was very proud of him and I wanted to show him off, so we sat in the front row. The minister's sermon happened to be about how people don't need to dress up for church, and your grandpa thought he was talking about us. I guess he was embarrassed.

"Ever since then he's always said, 'You don't need to go to church to talk to God. You could be in a closet, and He'll hear you.'"

Steve imitates his grandfather's way of speaking. "You could be in a darn-blasted closet, and He'll sure as tootin' hear ya."

The boys come unglued. Steve laughs so hard he chokes on a pea, and believes he's in danger of dying. He waves his fork wildly and points to his throat, certain his face is turning blue. His parents seem unconcerned.

"That's enough. Eat your dinner," Mrs. Hatcher orders.

Grandma Hatcher leans in close to Steve.

"After dinner, you and I will have a little conversation about smoking!" Grandma Hatcher tells him. "Just the two of us."

She pats his hand. This more than satisfies Steve, and Steve's parents seem strangely content with the arrangement as well.

Later, after the dishes have been washed and put away and everyone has settled into evening activities, Lyle retreats to his bedroom to organize his dead insects. He tries out various combinations and arrangements in the display box, and then stands back to see how it's working.

He's aiming for a specific result, and he'll know when he gets it. It's a bit slow-going because he's very careful when handling dead bugs, having already learned a few lessons on how easy it is to damage them. Some have dried to the point that antennae, legs or other delicate parts could easily break off and render them unusable. Normally, he would simply go out and find more, but the hard freeze late Sunday all but eliminated this as an option.

In the kitchen, Steve perches on a stool as if it were His Majesty's throne, and can barely contain his excitement. Grandma Hatcher stands next to him and touches a cigarette to the flame of her lighter.

"So you think you want to smoke?" she inhales, sounding indifferent.

"Yes. Yes, I do," Steve responds, enthusiastic, eager to be a good student.

"I think that's a wonderful idea. How about we get started right now?"

She hands him the newly lit cigarette, and he hurriedly takes it from her. "Is it good?" he asks, expectant, but also a bit nervous.

"Sure," she tells him, "it's super. It tastes great. You're going to love it. And when you get done with that one you can have the whole pack."

She sets the package of cigarettes on the counter, within her grandson's reach, so it's ready for him as soon as he's ready for it.

Steve puffs a few times, not inhaling. He blows little cloud formations, feeling all grown up, watching his mom out of the corner of his eye.

"I'm smoking," he announces proudly.

He puffs away like a pro, but it doesn't take long before it isn't enough to satisfy him.

"Grandma? How do you make those smoke rings?"

"Smoke rings, huh? You'll need to learn to blow it through your nose first. Watch closely, now. Are you watching?"

Steve nods. He feels like he's making very good progress, and he's quite impressed with himself.

"First, blow all the air out of your lungs."

She demonstrates, exaggerating for effect, and places the cigarette near her lips.

"Next, take a very deep breath and suck it all in. Deep."

She takes a long draw on the cigarette and blows the smoke out through her nose.

"Then, out your nose it goes," she adds, as though it was the most natural thing in the world.

"That is so cool, Grandma. I wanna try it." He raises his voice. "Hey, Mom! Watch this."

Steve empties his lungs, wraps his lips around the cigarette, and confidently sucks in a deep drag. His eyeballs bulge, his face turns bright red, and he collapses into a fit of violent coughing. He leaps off the stool and scrambles for the bathroom.

Lyle hears the noise and emerges from his room. He pokes his head into the bathroom and checks out his brother, who's retching into the toilet. Lyle wonders if maybe he'll choke up a lung, and in a panic runs to the kitchen.

"Grandma! What's wrong with Steve?"

"Nothing," she calms him. "Nothing at all. He thought he wanted to learn to smoke."

Relieved, Lyle plops himself down in a nearby chair.

"Grandma, what does *'grandiose'* mean?" Lyle uses Miss O'Donnell's headshake as he says it.

"Where's your dictionary?"

Lyle leaves the room and returns with a *Webster's Collegiate Dictionary*. He lifts it up onto the table.

"It's not mine, it's Linda's," he tells her.

Grandma Hatcher smiles, and helps him locate the word "grandiose."

"See here?" she says. "It means 'magnificent, noble, or brilliant.' I'll use it twice in a sentence for you. 'Steve thought it would be a *grandiose* idea to learn to smoke, and it turned out he was wrong! What a *grandiose* discovery for Steve.'"

"Cool!" Lyle responds, happy with the detailed definition. "Thanks, Grandma." He plops a kiss on her cheek and rushes off to check on Steve before heading back to his bedroom to practice his handstand technique.

Wednesday, October 20
21 days to Parent Night

Lyle scampers to the boiler room in search of Mr. Merrick and finds him doing some repair work on the boiler.

"I practiced all night long," Lyle relates proudly.

Mr. Merrick narrows his brows. "Have you cleared this with Miss O'Donnell?"

"Yeah, yeah. I told her all about it! Right after I got my hack. I'm talkin' about my last hack. Not the one I got for—"

The janitor interrupts with a glower.

"I'm just sayin'. I went straight to her office and explained the whole thing. She knows all about it."

"What'd she have to say?" Mr. Merrick grills him, surprised.

"She said it was a magnificent and noble idea. That's what she said. She told me to talk to Mrs. Thompson about it, since she's in charge of Parent Night, not Miss O'Donnell."

"What was the deal?" Mr. Merrick asks.

"The deal?"

"I'm askin' you what it is you have to do in exchange for her lettin' you do this."

"Oh, yeah! Here's the deal." Lyle once again enjoys the principal's theatrical method of counting a list of spoken points with the fingers. "She told me we have to . . . finish our science project and do a good job on it . . . *and* I have to behave myself and get my schoolwork done . . . *and* not get in any trouble on school grounds for the rest of the year."

"Well, now," Mr. Merrick comments, "that's a pretty tall order. So you're serious about this, huh?"

"Yes, Mr. Merrick. Super-serious!"

"Then I guess you'd better start gatherin' the troops."

"Troops?"

"You'll be needin' people to help ya out."

"Help with what? I'm the one doin' it."

"What do you *think* you might need help with?" Mr. Merrick asks, trying to steer him in the right direction.

Lyle's wheels are spinning now.

"Hmm," he says thoughtfully, "I guess I'll need somebody to help collect the quarters . . . and it'd be cool to have a drum roll like they do on TV, and someone to protect all the money."

"All the money?" Mr. Merrick nods, holding in his laughter. "If it's money you're after, you'll be needin' to tell everybody ya know. The more people who come to see it, the more quarters you'll be collectin'. Now, be a man of your word and go after that Science Fair."

"I will, Mr. Merrick."

"And ya can't go out there half-cocked," Mr. Merrick adds. "I'll help ya, but ya have to take this serious and do your part. I want to see ya in here during recess for your training. Now, let's get to work."

Mr. Merrick hands him a box of dirty erasers. Lyle hands them back.

"I'm not in trouble, I just came to talk to you," Lyle says, and out he goes, glad to be free.

Mr. Merrick is speechless.

In the cafeteria during lunch hour, Lyle spreads the news about his plan, going from one table to the next with David rolling along beside him.

"Hey, guys, I'm gonna walk across the gym on my hands to raise money for muscular dystrophy."

The announcement delivered to a table of kids results in a mix of responses.

"Cool."   "Far-out!"   "Idiot!"   "That's hairy."

"Keeno."   "Heavy."   "Neat."

"Good luck!"   "In your dreams, man!"

They move on to the next table and Lyle repeats the message, eliciting a similar range of responses.

After they finish telling all the students, they approach the lunch ladies, who know Lyle well. He's always extremely polite to the lunch ladies. After all, they control the food. They dote on both boys now, listening closely to their story and providing oohs and ahs in all the right places. Heaping plates of extra food reinforce their praise for the undertaking.

"You boys will need your strength," they say.

During recess, Lyle goes straight to the boiler room to train under Mr. Merrick's supervision, as agreed.

"How many push-ups can you do?" Mr. Merrick asks.

"Fifty."

"You need to do a hundred. For starters. How many chin-ups?"

"Haven't been doing those," Lyle admits.

"Oookaaaay," Mr. Merrick whistles skeptically. "We'd better get to work."

Mr. Merrick puts Lyle through a hefty workout, then sends him out on the playground for five minutes of real recess time. When Lyle hits the field, he immediately organizes a game of Crack the Whip, and not the regular version of it.

"Girls and momma's boys not allowed!" Lyle announces, and the game begins.

The object of the game, according to Lyle, is to whip the person on the end of the human chain with such timing and force that they let go and fly into a large and conveniently located mud patch. The outdoor conditions are perfect for the game, and Lyle himself is a master. One after another they take the fall, while David sits nearby, whooping and hollering and directing. By the time the bell rings, all of the boys are wet and dirty except for David and Lyle.

Mrs. Stewart is furious when they trudge in from recess, clothes muddied, faces and hands streaked, and muck all over their shoes. She sends them to the restroom to clean up, and upon their return, extracts all the information she needs from the first few coming through the door. When the entire class is seated, she makes a pronouncement.

"I am so disappointed with you boys. You know better than to do what you did out there. And just look at you! I am absolutely furious with all of you!

"I've decided only the girls will take the field trip tomorrow. The boys will *stay*—," she raises her voice to be heard over the groans, "—and have a two-hour study hall with Mrs. Thompson in the library!"

There is not a sound as her gaze travels the room. Her eyes come to rest on the boy in the wheelchair.

"Except for David. He will be allowed to go."

The boys' complaint is long, loud, and heartfelt. Mrs. Stewart has to aggressively raise her hands to stop it. "You brought this on yourselves," she declares.

Lyle is not prepared to give up on this field trip so easily. He sneaks a devilish grin at David, and politely raises his hand. Mrs. Stewart, wary, asks what he wants.

"Why does David get to go?" he inquires.

"David was not a part of it," she enlightens him.

Lyle has a habit of noticing people's quirks, and what he's noticed about Mrs. Stewart is that she's never tough on David. He's confident there's zero risk she'll punish David, and she will never keep him from the field trip. So . . . if he can just convince her David is as guilty as the rest of them . . .

"David was the whipmaster. He sat there yellin', 'Crack 'em, crack 'em good!'" Lyle tells her, stealing another glance at his friend. "So why should he get to go? That's not fair."

The other boys murmur their agreement. A chorus of "That's not fair!"s crops up, shaking Mrs. Stewart's tenuous grip on the class.

At the moment, David feels like he's getting the best of both worlds. Mrs. Stewart wants to give him special immunity, and the boys want him to be included in the punishment. It's great to be popular. He reacts by shrugging innocently.

At a loss, Mrs. Stewart waits for David to defend himself. When he doesn't, she's forced to assume that what Lyle is saying is true. She stomps around in front of the class a while longer, then finally acquiesces, precisely as Lyle had figured she would.

"All right, then, I'm going to overlook it *this time*. You can go. But this will be the only time you get away with something like this, and I mean it."

A cheer erupts from the boys in the class.

"Quiet!" Mrs. Stewart snaps, unhappy.

Everyone sticks to their best behavior for the entire rest of the day. After school, David and Lyle pay a visit to the library.

"Hi, boys," Mrs. Thompson greets them. "What can I help you with today?" She delights when children come to see her. Cheerful and optimistic, she doesn't have a dishonest bone in her body, and consequently never suspects it of anyone else. In the case of Lyle and David, this means she isn't one to check facts.

Lyle takes the lead. "Miss O'Donnell said you were in charge of the program for Parent Night. She said she doesn't want to hear any more about it."

Mrs. Thompson laughs. "She never likes to be bothered with Parent Night, so yes, I take care of it. If you boys want to sign up for one of the demonstrations, you need to have Mrs. Stewart turn the form in to me."

"We aren't doing one of the regular events. This is different, Mrs. Thompson," David explains.

The librarian registers surprise.

David produces a neat piece of paper. "This is our written proposal," he says proudly. Last night, Dena helped him write it, explaining that this is what's needed "when you want to make an impression."

Mrs. Thompson conceals her astonishment, and peruses the single sheet of paper. The proposal consists of a few sentences describing what Lyle will be attempting to achieve, and a paragraph outlining his workouts with Mr. Merrick. It even includes some fourth-grade-level financial projections for the money they expect to raise.

"Well, boys, this looks quite professional," Mrs. Thompson intones, very clearly impressed.

Lyle and David blow out of the school very pleased with themselves, and enthused about their new enterprise.

Lyle pats David on the shoulder.

"Nice job, partner," he tells him.

"Yeah," David says. He feels good about the future—very good, indeed.

CHAPTER TWENTY

BLUE SPRINKLES

*It is in periods of apparent disaster . . .
that the greatest improvement
in human character has been effected.*

~ SIR ARCHIBALD ALISON

Thursday, October 21
20 days to Parent Night

For Lyle, this day is monumental. It's life-changing. There will not be a day to rival this one for a very long time. It's not just that it's a day involving a field trip— this is a field trip to Strick's Donuts.

As Lyle says, it's the factory.

He leaps out of bed and heads straight to the refrigerator, but not for food, not this time. The rest of the family is there, eating breakfast. He reaches up and yanks the permission slip off the refrigerator door. The decorative magnet flips into the air, and he catches it mid-flight and snaps it back in place.

"Mom! I need you to sign this!"

"What about 'Good morning'?" Mrs. Hatcher corrects him.

"Good morning," Lyle tosses out to everyone in general and no one in particular. "Can you sign it, Mom. Please?"

"Your dad and I talked about it, and we don't think a donut shop, of all places—"

"A shop! It's not a shop, Mom! It's the factory! And David needs me. I have to go," he pleads. "Besides, I haven't been in any trouble in forever."

Mrs. Hatcher sighs in resignation, takes the note from Lyle, signs it and tucks it into his pocket, along with a dollar bill.

"Here's some money for hot lunch. I checked the menu, it's beef stroganoff, green beans, and peaches."

She holds a large red apple so close to his face it makes his eyes cross and he has to pull his head away to focus. She gives it a little shake for emphasis, and hands it to him. Taking Lyle's cheeks tightly in her hands, she squashes his lips into a fish pucker.

"Okay. I signed it. But I don't need to tell you . . . are you listening? No donuts! You know the rules. That's why I gave you that big apple."

"Okay, Mom. But is it snappy? It has to be snappy."

"Yes. I picked it out just for you, Mr. Snappy. Now, go!"

She gives him a kiss on the forehead and pushes him out the door. Lyle pauses on the porch to give the apple a shine on his pant leg and tuck it into his jacket pocket.

He and Dino race to Monroe Street and then head north to the school. Lyle spots Mr. Dahlke and David at the crosswalk, and he takes off, sprinting in their direction.

"C'mon, boy!"

When they arrive at the school, flushed and out of breath, the long yellow school bus is parked in front. Students mill about the door, lining up and climbing aboard. Lyle finds David and waits near his chair.

Ben Holmberg, the driver, clambers down from his bus and squeezes through the children. In his mid-twenties, all sorts of cool with his cowboy hat and drawl, Ben is a magnet for kids.

"Hi, Mr. Holmberg," the boys greet him as he approaches.

"Mornin', boys," Ben grins, tipping his hat and exaggerating his Texas heritage, striding around bowl-legged for their amusement.

David tips his own hat to Ben—his favorite green aviator cap—and feels grown-up for doing it. Lyle jumps ahead of them, clearing a path.

"Outta the way," he orders, nudging the other kids aside. "David's comin' through."

Ben readies David to be carted onto the bus, and David organizes help with the wheelchair. "Hey, Mike," he calls out. "Will you guys load my chair?"

"You got it, David Dee," Mike shouts back.

Lyle clears the last step onto the bus, and there's Terry, comfortably settled in the front seat.

"You're gonna have to move," Lyle advises, matter-of-fact.

"Why do I have to move?"

"That's David's place, that's why!"

"Huh, that's funny," Terry fires back, looking around the seat area, checking the back, sides, and bottom of the bench. "I don't see his name on it."

"You don't?" Lyle blusters, instantly getting worked up over it. He holds the back of his hand directly in Terry's face, fingers spread wide open. Closing his fingers one at a time, he spells it out for Terry.

"D - A - V - I - D!"

When he finishes he holds a tightly clenched fist, inches from Terry's nose. Terry slaps the fist away and kicks him hard in the side of the shin.

"That didn't hurt," Lyle says, not reacting to the pain.

"Didn't hurt, huh?" Terry kicks him again, harder. "How 'bout that?"

"Ow," Lyle says. "Kickin' like a girl. Makes you feel like a man, kickin' like a girl?"

Lyle knows this isn't going to end well for him, but he's already up to his eyeballs. Terry stands up, grabs him in a headlock and bears down hard, scratching his eyebrows. Lyle pushes away and snap-kicks him in the leg. Terry winces at the impact, but it only makes him madder.

"How'd that feel?" Lyle taunts.

Ben's voice booms, as he steps into view carrying David.

"What's goin' on here?"

"He has to move! That's David's spot!" Lyle exclaims.

"I can sit somewhere else," David offers, not wanting any trouble on his account.

Ben glares at Terry. "You! Plant yourself in another seat! Now!"

Terry stomps to the back of the bus, shooting a black look over his shoulder at Lyle. "This ain't over, you stupid punk. You're mincemeat!"

Ben sets David in his usual location, the front row seat by the aisle. "Both of you, simmer down," he orders, glancing sternly in Lyle's direction.

Lyle climbs over David and plops himself down on the inside seat. He stares out the window at David's green aviator cap on the seat of the empty wheelchair, and it sends an odd shiver down his spine. His eyes lock onto it until Mike and Johnny swoop in, fold the wheelchair, and drag it onto the bus.

Lyle keeps his face glued to the window, angry and frowning, deep in thought as the door clanks shut and the bus rattles up to the intersection at Monroe Street. David nudges him.

"Are you all right?"

"Yeah."

"What do you think he meant by 'This isn't over'?" David wonders.

Lyle gazes at the floor of the bus and talks out of the side of his mouth, so no one except David can hear what he's saying or see that he's even talking.

"He didn't say, 'This *isn't* over.' What he said was, 'This *ain't* over!'"

"What's the difference?" David asks.

"The difference is, he's gonna pound me into the ground and pulverize me. That's the difference."

"You mean you're going to fight him?"

Lyle eyes David without answering.

"Well—," David begins.

"Don't say it!

"Don't say what?"

"Don't say, 'Fight-eth not for it be-eth not good' or 'Loveth he who want-eth to slay-eth thee dead,' or any of that other stuff. I'm not in the mood to hear it because right now I'm thinkin' about how I'm gonna get slaughtered. Thanks a lot for sayin' nothin'."

"Like what? What was I supposed to say?"

"I don't know, anything, anything. Shoot, you coulda spit on him."

"I wouldn't do that."

"I know."

"What's that supposed to mean?" David asks. "I didn't have anything to do with that."

"It means they have a vaccine for polio, that's what. Why can't they find a cure for you?" Lyle challenges, getting down to what's really on his mind.

David maintains his calm. "Everything is exactly how it's supposed to be and I already know—"

Lyle cuts him off. "Sometimes you have to fight. Mr. Merrick says, 'Never let fear in until after the fight.' So why don't you fight?"

"Fight? Me? Are you joking?"

Lyle wants to smile, but he can't. "You know what I mean!"

"Now you're mad at me, aren't you?" David asks.

"Don't you ever wanna just scream and yell?"

"What good would it do?"

"My mom says a good screaming session can be therapeutic."

David pats his shirt pocket and yells, "Hey! Hey! Hey! What's this?!"

Ben turns and shakes his head at Lyle, a threatening expression on his face.

"It wasn't me!" Lyle says, trying to defend himself. "Dang it, it wasn't me!"

David slowly and dramatically draws a dollar bill from his pocket, an inch at a time, like a magician doing a trick.

"Looks like hot chocolate for me and Sharon Anne. She loves hot chocolate, you know."

Lyle panics, suddenly realizing he has utterly neglected his pursuit of Sharon Anne. She's still his one true heartthrob; a guy just gets busy with other things.

"Yeah, she likes to drink hot chocolate and gaze into my incredible blue eyes."

"C'mon, are you kiddin' me?" Lyle despairs, his face falling.

David laughs. "Gotcha!"

"Holey smokes, David. You scared me. Talkin' about Sharon Anne and your blue eyes, and hot chocolate," Lyle says, heaving a big sigh of relief. "For a minute there, I thought you were serious."

David smiles to himself.

The bus rattles through the north-side neighborhood, soon reaching the top of the Monroe Street Hill. The road begins its downward slope with a graceful curve to the right (known to the neighborhood kids as the "Big Turn"), and then swings back to the left and straightens. At the bottom of the hill, Lyle watches as Strick's Donut Factory comes into view like the Eighth Wonder of the World. Ben parks the bus and the children file out. Mrs. Stewart and Mrs. Maxfield direct them into the front area of the donut shop where their guide, Tony, is waiting.

Tony grins and keeps his voice loud to command their attention. "Hey kids. How're we all doin' this mornin'?"

The room resonates with a chorus of enthusiastic "Good"s and "Fine"s as the children answer him.

"Now, I want you to take a look out the big window," he continues. "You can see the Monroe Street Hill from here."

The kids rush to the window and crowd in, jostling for a view. Lyle wriggles his way upstream through the throng to get over to the pastry display cases.

"Before this road was paved," Tony continues, "it was used as a sledding hill in the wintertime."

Those words, as expected, elicit excited reactions from the group. From the window of the donut shop, the incline appears steep and long, and the thought of sledding from the top to the bottom is exhilarating. Even Lyle turns to look, but he can't see out the window. He's the shortest one in the room and everyone else stands in front of him. He goes back to studying pastries.

"Now, over here," Tony crosses the room, "Grace and the gang are making every type of donut ever invented—plus a few of their own creations."

The workers behind the counter wave to the children as they crowd the display cases, mesmerized by the irresistible attraction of fresh pastries. Now, Lyle is in the front row. He forms blinders with his hands on both sides of his head, and leans into the slanted glass of the display.

"We've been making donuts since your parents were born. We have apricot tarts, bear claws, cheese Danish, chocolate éclairs, cinnamon rolls, cream puffs, apple turnovers, maple bars, apple fritters, cake donuts, sugar donuts, chocolate-covered donuts, they're all there. See for yourselves—and remember . . ." He scans the faces of his enrapt audience and adds, ". . . it's a great way to bribe a teacher!"

Tony gets a well-deserved laugh from the adults in his audience. The children, however, are far too busy for subtle humor, as they try to locate all of the options he mentioned, eagerly discussing among themselves which of them they want to try.

Lyle isn't even listening to Tony. His eyes fall captive, as Grace sets three fresh donuts on the counter and waves her hand over them, sending a rain of blue sprinkles like sparkling fireworks drifting down over the donuts. Lyle has never seen anything so beautiful as that deep, rich shade of blue, and his stomach calls out to him, begging. Grace balances the tray with one hand while opening the case with the other, and she deftly inserts the donuts into the display.

"Are those blue sprinkles?" Lyle asks, not changing his position, his gaze fixed glassily upon them.

"Yes, sweetheart," Grace says. "Would you like one?"

Lyle knows this is absolutely not, in any way, shape or form, allowed. He promised his mom he wouldn't have a donut, but somehow the blue sprinkles make it seem like fate, like they were intended for him by some unknown force even greater than his mother. He checks to his right. He sees no interference. He cranes even farther to his right, to survey behind him. The coast is clear, so he swings to his left, and his head snaps back in surprise.

Right in front of his eyes, mere inches away, is a menacing, black, .45 caliber pistol in a polished black leather holster. Lyle's gaze travels slowly upward until he focuses on the profile of Officer Jenkins.

"Grace?" the policeman says, "I'll take those. The ones there, with the blue sprinkles."

Officer Jenkins winks at Grace, who lifts the donuts from the tray and hands them over with a smile. Lyle is in a state of total despair. Just then, Officer Jenkins, donuts in hand, turns around . . . and does a most amazing thing.

Officer Jenkins holds out a donut to Lyle, nodding for him to take it.

The blue-sprinkled wonder hangs in front of his eyes, a symphonic overture of flavor, texture, and color, flawlessly shaped with a perfectly round center, nothing more and nothing less than irresistible. Lyle is overcome with gratitude, realizing instantly it would be wrong to refuse, to disrespect the law in that way. What would his mom say? "The law is the law" is what she'd say. He reaches up and gently accepts the gift from Officer Jenkins' hand.

"Thank you, sir," Lyle says, with reverence.

David grabs Lyle's arm from behind, almost roughly, startling him into nearly dropping his donut.

"Hey, you're not supposed to eat those!" he reprimands.

Lyle holds out the donut for David's examination, rotating it slowly in the air, so he can appreciate its beauty from every possible angle.

"Look," Lyle explains, "they're blue. Blue sprinkles. Did you know blue is the only color I can see?"

"Yeah, yeah, yeah. Blue, blue, blue. Who cares? You're not supposed to eat donuts. And you know it."

"What's the big deal? It's just one."

Lyle eats it as quickly as possible, insurance against the possibility he might lose the debate. He doesn't allow a mouthful of pastry to get in the way of critical conversation.

"You're dot godda dell eddy body, are you?"

"No. I'm not your mother."

David takes tiny bites from his pastry. He's scarcely touched it.

"Whad's thad?"

"It's an apple fritter," David replies. "I can't eat it. It's too hard to swallow."

David wheels himself over to the waste basket and is about to plunk the fritter into the garbage when Lyle rushes in and stops him.

"No, no. Don't do that. There are people starving in China," he exclaims, the urgency in his voice clearly conveying the dire nature of this global emergency. He holds out his hand, prepared to save the world with one selfless gesture.

"Fine. It's your funeral," David replies, handing it to him.

Lyle takes a huge bite of the fritter.

"Addy way, id's jus' like eadin' an abble, righd?" Lyle says, for his own benefit.

He swallows hard a couple of times and then he gulps down the rest of it.

A few minutes later, the class files out of the donut shop, stretching and blinking in the sunshine. Lyle and David wander into the wide open space of the parking lot. Lyle flexes his hands, his palms itching. He clenches his toes and grits his teeth. Suddenly, he grabs the back of David's chair and whips it around, pushing it into the street.

"Hey, David," he shouts, "Let's go sledding."

"Far out!" David exclaims.

David reaches for the wheels to help move the chair along.

"Yeah, booster rockets," Lyle encourages him.

They zip around the corner of the building and onto the sidewalk leading up the hill. There's little chance of getting caught, since all the others are gathering around the school bus, in the parking lot behind the donut shop. No one can see them. They start up the hill.

Lyle pushes as hard as he can, and David helps with both hands on the wheels. They gain elevation quickly, and in no time they have worked their way up the entire straight stretch. When they reach the Big Turn, Lyle stops.

"How 'bout right here?"

"Let's go all the way to the wall!" David insists, pointing to the retaining wall on the left, farther up the Big Turn.

"You're the boss!"

Lyle goes back to work, jogging him up the hill again, and David continues to do what he can to help, breathing hard and sweating from the exertion. There is no traffic this time of day, and they are now far enough away from the donut shop that everything seems quiet. The only sounds are David's heavy breathing, the wheels of the chair turning, and Lyle's shoes slipping in loose gravel.

"How's this?" Lyle asks, spinning the chair sideways on the hill so David has a view to the bottom.

"Holey Mackerel!" David exclaims. "This might be too far."

"No way, it's perfect!"

Lyle faces the chair down the hill and hops on the back, bracing his feet firmly against the frame and clinging tightly to the handles.

"Let's fly!" he shouts.

CHAPTER TWENTY-ONE

THE MONSTER

*Whoever fights monsters should see to it
that in the process he doesn't become a monster.*

~ FRIEDRICH NIETZSCHE

The wheelchair starts a slow roll down the steep incline.
"Maybe we should've gone higher up," David comments, a bit disappointed at the crawl. He has come to expect at least a small rush of adrenaline from any adventure Lyle devises.

"Yeah," Lyle agrees.

But the chair quickly gains momentum, and in no time it moves at an exhilarating clip. The boys lift their faces to the wind and shout at the freedom and delight of it. They throw back their heads like riders on a roller coaster, and revel in a sensation of the world flying by. And then, they both realize it at the same time: the world *is* flying by. They are going far too fast.

Lyle lets out a whoop and nudges David with his forearm.

"Okay, Captain! Pull the brakes! Slow and easy, now."

David reaches forward, wrapping his hands around the levers. The climb up the hill tired him and he doesn't have the strength to yank them back. He tries, over and over again, in vain.

"Brakes! Brakes!" Lyle shouts at him.

They are now speeding down the hill at a frightening pace, and both are beginning to panic.

"I can't do it!" David cries desperately. Gravel spits up behind the tires, and the chair rattles and shakes.

"David!" Lyle yells. "Pull the brakes!"

David throws himself forward and tries, with all the strength he has, to yank the brakes back.

"I can't!" he screams, terrified. "I can't do it!"

The chair's course is now erratic and out of control. The front wheels wobble precariously, shaking the chair so hard the boys can feel their skin bouncing. The vibrations make it difficult to see clearly.

David screams again, "Help me, Lyle!"

Lyle lunges forward, reaching for the brakes, but his body is too short. He stretches and strains as far as he dares—any more and he will fall—but his arms are still inches from the handles.

Realizing he'll never reach them, he tries to slow the chair by dragging his feet, but they rocket too fast and the friction of the pavement claws at his shoe, threatening to tear him from the chair, leaving David to fend for himself. Lyle's mind floods with a horrifying realization—they are not going to stop, and what happens now is completely beyond their control.

He reaches his arms around his friend, enfolding him, wanting desperately to protect him from what he knows is coming. The right front wheel hits a rock, skids and digs into the road, launching the chair into a sideways cartwheel.

Lyle hurtles from the back and David, strapped in, is at the mercy of the chair, as it rolls and lands on its side, scraping and sliding to a stop in the gravel along the edge of the road.

Lyle lies on the ground, and opens his eyes, blinking, to large chunks of gravel very near his face. He smells hot asphalt and dust. He feels like he's just awakened, though he knows he wasn't asleep, because he remembers every detail of what happened with precision-perfect slow-motion clarity. He struggles to get up, and Mrs. Maxfield leans over him.

"Is David okay?" Lyle asks, afraid to hear the answer.

The teacher helps him to his feet without a word. Officer Jenkins steps in, and assures himself Lyle is not seriously injured. He whisks him away to the squad car.

They ride in a heavy fog of silence. The police officer looks at Lyle's face. The distress is unmistakable; the boy is in torment. Their eyes meet.

"Is David going to be okay?" Lyle ventures again.

"He'll be fine," Officer Jenkins reassures him.

"Are you takin' me to juvey?" The boy's voice is tremulous.

"No, Lyle," the officer says kindly. "I'm not taking you to juvey. I'm taking you home. Your mom is waiting for us."

Officer Jenkins' car eases into the Hatchers' driveway, and the moment it stops Lyle climbs out and runs on shaky legs to the house. Mrs. Hatcher, in shock, meets him on the porch.

"I'm sorry." The words tumble out. "I'm sorry." He wants to bury his face in her arms.

"Sorry won't fix anything," she tells him, and points him straight to his room.

Lyle dives into the house, down the hallway and to his bedroom, throwing himself onto his bed. Lying on his back, he digs the apple from his jacket pocket. One entire side of it is injured and bruised, and a deep split runs up the center. He stares at it, then places it carefully on his dresser.

Mrs. Hatcher leaves him alone, waiting for her husband to come home. She hears nothing from Lyle for the entire afternoon, and when Mr. Hatcher walks through the door at four o'clock, she barrages him with what happened. Furious, he beelines for Lyle's room.

Mr. Hatcher enters, filling the doorway, and the space hardly seems big enough to contain him. For the first time in his life, Lyle is frightened of his father.

Mr. Hatcher is ominously subdued. "You *know* what your punishment is."

Lyle looks up.

"What ... is ... your ... punishment?" Mr. Hatcher demands.

Shaken, Lyle delivers the answer he's heard many times before. "I'm grounded and I have to go straight to school and straight home after school."

"And?"

"And," Lyle continues, barely audible, "no TV, and no ice cream, and no friends, and no phone."

"All right! Now, I want you to listen, and listen very carefully. I do not want you to talk, do you understand? Nod your head yes."

Lyle nods, and drops his eyes.

"Look at me!"

Lyle's head pops back up.

"It's one thing when you decide to do these daredevil stunts and put yourself in harm's way, but when you involve other people . . . when you get somebody else in the middle of your antics and put them at risk . . ." Mr. Hatcher takes a deep breath. "*That* is a whole different ball game."

"Dad, I—"

"I told you not to speak!" Mr. Hatcher's face is dark. "Your mother and I did not raise you this way and I guarantee you things are about to change. Now, you can either decide to make it happen the moment we're done here, or we can take this to the next level, and believe me . . . you're not going to like it. And I don't want to hear 'I'm sorry' and I don't want to hear any pathetic excuses. There is somebody who *does* have an apology coming, and you know exactly who I'm talking about. And you make that apology face to face, eye to eye. That's how a real man does it. It's time for you to start growing up."

Mr. Hatcher waits, to be sure Lyle knows the importance of what he's about to say. "The only thing I want to hear from you are the words 'Dad, I will change.' And then I expect to see it happen."

Lyle's voice is thin and broken. "Dad," he begins, "I will—"

"Speak up!" Mr. Hatcher thunders. "And stand into it!"

Lyle trembles, but he stands tall, as tall as his body will allow, and he makes his speech strong and deliberate.

"Dad, I will change!"

Mr. Hatcher spins and leaves the room, punctuating the encounter with a close of the door that leaves no room for doubt. He storms down the hallway and shuts himself in his own room, and the rest of the family sees neither of them for the remainder of the night.

Monday, October 25
16 days to Parent Night

David isn't hospitalized and there are no broken bones, but the scrapes and cuts are severe. Dr. Brewster orders him to stay in bed for however long it takes him to heal, so until then he can't attend school.

Lyle does as ordered: he goes straight to school and returns home immediately after. He spent most of the weekend in his room, working on the bug collection and building his upper-body strength for the hand-walk he believes is upcoming. These two things are all that matter to him now.

During recess and lunch hour, he works out with Mr. Merrick in the boiler room. He does chin-ups on the pipes, and push-ups against the concrete floor. Afterward, Mr. Merrick shows him ways to improve his technique for balancing on his hands.

Mr. Merrick doesn't lecture Lyle about what happened on the Monroe Street Hill. He can see something has changed in the boy and figures on the big issues—like this one—he's smart enough to learn his own lessons in his own way.

"You're awful quiet today," Mr. Merrick drops casually. "Problems?"

"Nope," Lyle responds, starting on his handstand push-ups.

There *is* something bothering him, but he's not going to tell Mr. Merrick about it, or anyone else. It's something Miss O'Donnell said, only moments before. She was visibly upset when she took him aside for a word.

"I've called your parents and the Dahlkes, Lyle," she informed him in a tight, stern voice. "I have scheduled a meeting with everyone for the day after tomorrow, and you and David will be there. Whatever is decided, you can be sure nothing like this will ever happen at my school again. Never! And I'm not leaving it up to chance. Do you understand me?"

Lyle isn't at all sure what she meant, but he knows it isn't good.

Tuesday, October 26
15 days to Parent Night

Given the strictness of Lyle's punishment, the boys are forbidden contact, and in that a new problem takes shape. Lyle needs a way to get over to David's, to fetch the rest of the labels and finish their bug collection. He also needs to see David for a more important reason: to apologize.

He plods into the kitchen and stops dead in his tracks in the middle of the floor, nearly causing Linda to trip over him.

"Oh, no!" he announces loudly.

"Oh, for Heaven's sake, what now?" his mom asks.

"I totally forgot. I gotta call David!"

"I am not going to say this again. He's in no condition for company. You know that! And you heard what your father said. No phone."

"We barely have two weeks left, Mom!"

"You should have thought of that before. You're grounded!"

Mrs. Hatcher turns her attention to Steve. She scribbles a note and hands it to him. "Steve. I'm picking you up in front of the school at eleven o'clock. Now, don't forget. What time am I picking you up?"

"Eleven o'clock," Steve repeats back to her as he leaves.

Mrs. Hatcher frowns to see Lyle hasn't moved from the middle of the floor.

"Lyle, what on earth are you doing?"

"Mom, I don't feel so good."

She hesitates, every better instinct on alert, but tests his forehead. "You don't seem to have a fever," she notes.

"I just don't feel good."

She rummages through the kitchen cupboard and finds the thermometer. She rinses it, shakes it down, and hands it to him.

"Go climb back into bed. I'll check on you in a few minutes."

Lyle shuffles to his bedroom. He kicks up onto his hands and rests his feet against the wall for balance, doing push-ups. When he hears his mom approaching in the hallway, he jumps into bed and positions the thermometer in his mouth. She comes in to check it, by now in a hurry.

"Like I said, you're not running a fever," she tells him.

"But I don't feel good, Mom," he complains, sounding if not exactly ill, at least weak.

Mrs. Hatcher studies her son, and notices his cheeks, flushed from the handstand. "You look a bit feverish," she admits. She tucks him in. "Your timing is terrible. It's finals week and I've got tests I can't miss. And in the middle of all that, I have to get Steve to the dentist."

"It's okay, Mom. I'll be fine by myself."

"I'll be back by four. Your dad will be home then." She pauses. "I'll let Betty know you're here," she adds as a warning.

Mrs. Hatcher starts to leave, but the expression on Lyle's face stops her. It's his "sad dog eyes" look, as she calls it.

"What?" she says, trying not to sound exasperated.

"Mom? What's wrong with me?" Lyle asks her.

"You probably have a flu-bug."

"No. That's not what I mean."

Mrs. Hatcher sits down on the bed next to him. She listens.

"I'm always gettin' in trouble. I'm tired of bein' grounded! Tell me what to do and I'll do it! I mean it, Mom, just tell me!"

Mrs. Hatcher searches his eyes, and chooses her words before she speaks. "There is nothing wrong with you. Nothing at all. You just have a little extra. A little more than other people. You know what I mean. You need to channel it into something positive. Something good, that's all you really need to do."

"I want to give my extra to David," he laments. "He really needs it. I don't want it. If I could give it to him maybe we'd both be normal."

"Honey, I wish it were that simple. But it's not. All you can do for David is be the best friend you can be. I've told you this before." She leans her forehead against his.

"You have a good heart. Not everyone does, but you have a truly good heart."

She smiles. "And you know what?"

Suddenly, without warning, she pins his arms down on the bed so he can't struggle and puts her face up to his.

"No, Mom, no, no, no!" he screams, squirming and wagging his head back and forth.

She holds his head so he can't get away and quickly licks his eye. He wiggles and howls until she lets him go.

"Yuck, Mom. That's disgusting."

She gets up and walks to the door.

"Mom?"

"Now what!"

"Am I ungrounded?"

"No, you are *not* ungrounded. Ask again and you'll be in this room the rest of your life."

"I love you, Mom."

"I love you more."

She slips out the door, leaving it open.

"More," Lyle whispers.

"I heard that," she calls from down the hallway.

Lyle lies in bed until he hears the front door slam. He crawls from the covers and peeks out the window, watching her back her white '61 Corvair out of the driveway and speed away.

Lyle checks Betty Miller's house. No apparent activity there. He yanks his backpack from underneath the bed and hightails it out the door. Dino is delighted. He's been waiting a long time, days in fact. Mrs. Miller hears the dog bark and spies from behind her curtain blinds, standing away from the window where she thinks Lyle can't see her through the glass.

"I know you're there," he whispers to himself.

He has more important business to take care of, and Mrs. Miller squealing on him—he knows she will—is the least of his concerns. He swings the backpack into position and runs his bike down the driveway, leaping onto it and riding away, through the neighborhood streets.

Lyle pumps hard all the way to the Dahlkes'. He cruises across the lawn and slides to a stop under David's bedroom window. Leaning the bike against the house, he climbs onto it and stands on the seat. He peers through the window, hands cupped around his eyes. At first he can't see anything, but as his eyes adjust, he can make out the shape of someone in the bed, lying under the covers.

Lyle taps softly on the window. The person doesn't move, so Lyle lifts the window and climbs right in. He creeps over to the bed and finds David, on his back with his eyes closed, a peaceful expression on his face.

Lyle studies the road rash on David's face, and he feels a pang of guilt. Long scrapes run deep, along the left temple and down his cheek, where the skin was torn away. His ear is red and swollen. Lyle reaches out to touch it and decides instead to plug David's nose, squeezing it between his thumb and forefinger. David's body jerks awake, as he gasps for air through his mouth. He's groggy and weak, and he speaks with effort, his words sounding thin and raspy.

"Lyle . . . ," he manages with relief, "what are you doing here?"

"I need those labels!"

David thinks for a moment, blinking slowly and then closing his eyes.

"They're down in the basement by the Wizzard," he mumbles, struggling to come out of sleep. "My mom's skimming the pool. You can sneak down there."

"Sneak down there?"

David nods, and opens his eyes again.

"Did you plug my nose?"

"Maybe."

"Don't turn the light on or she'll know you're there."

"I'll be right back. I need to tell you something," Lyle tells him, postponing his apology for when David is fully awake.

Lyle slips from the room, makes his way down the hall, and rounds the corner into the kitchen. He can't see Mrs. Dahlke in the Bubble, but he hears the sounds of the pool vacuum. He ducks down below the window and tiptoes to the stairwell. Hanging above the stairs are several mounted birds: two pheasants, a dove, and a crow in full flight. They look creepy in the dark, like they're guarding the entrance to a dungeon.

At the bottom of the stairs, he hears mice scuffling to hide as they sense his approach. Out of the corner of his eye he catches a quick motion he knows to be the lizards, slipping beneath their sawdust for safety.

His heart beats fast. In the darkness, everything in the basement is bizarre and eerie, and he can't be sure what will move and what won't. He steals past the enormous terrarium and the two boa constrictors stir. He talks out loud for confidence; it helps to hear a friendly voice.

"Gypsy. Arthur," Lyle whispers. "What're you guys doin'?"

He passes under an expansive pair of wings, the familiar shape of the stuffed trumpeter swan.

"Giant duck."

A dark form with bucked teeth and beady eyes glares at him from the darkness. It's the stuffed beaver.

"Hi, Fred."

Not a minute too soon, he spies the bag of plaques leaning against Huge's terrarium. He treads slowly and cautiously in that direction. A big ball of fur scurries across his feet and nearly makes him scream.

"Dang it, Puff. Don't ever do that!"

Stupid badger! And Charlie the puppet isn't on the shelf where he belongs. That's just great! I wonder if Mr. Dahlke would think I was a robber and shoot me right in the guts if he caught me. I'd have to say, "Mr. Dahlke, don't shoot! It's me! It's me in the dark in your basement during school hours." And then . . . Bam! Right in the guts.

Lyle tiptoes up to Huge's terrarium. He doesn't want to be surprised by the giant tarantula.

"Huge? Hew-oooge . . . Come out, come out, wherever you are."

There's no sign of the arachnid. Lyle silently lifts the bag of plaques. A giant spider looms before him, hanging from the glass behind the bag, separated from Lyle's hand by a quarter-inch of sheet glass. Lyle yanks back his hand and drops the bag, and the plaques jingle softly as they fall onto the table and spill to the floor.

Lyle scrambles for the labels on his hands and knees, scooping them back into the bag. As he starts to get up he's suddenly, *horribly*, face-to-face with a monster—skin torn from its skull, dead and sunken eyeballs bulging, a wide-open mouth of needle-sharp, flesh-ripping teeth looking for a meal, waiting in the dark, lurking, hungering, thirsting.

Clutching the bag of labels, Lyle stumbles and falls over backward, against the wall. Hyperventilating, he finds his feet and shoots up the stairs, streaks through the kitchen, darts past a startled Mrs. Dahlke, and barrels out the front door. He charges through the front yard, forgetting about his bicycle, and tears down the street. Dino races after him, whimpering and glancing behind them. Lyle hears a quick blast of a siren but he doesn't slow down or look back.

Officer Jenkins drives up next to him and rolls down his window. "Pull over!" he commands.

Lyle stops.

"You'd better have a darn good excuse for skippin' school, Mr. Hatcher! In the car!"

Lyle climbs into the front seat. Officer Jenkins looks out the window at Dino who stands a few feet from the car, quizzical eyes locked onto him.

"Does the dog need a ride?"

"If it's okay."

The officer nods and Lyle opens the door. Dino scampers around the car and climbs onto Lyle's lap, burying him.

"Officer Jenkins?" Lyle's muffled voice comes from the passenger seat. Officer Jenkins glances over as he drives, and can only see the dog, with just the top of Lyle's crew cut sticking up from behind.

The voice behind the dog continues. "See, why I'm skippin' school is 'cause we're doin' this science project together, me and David, and we only have exactly fourteen days left and since David can't get out of bed right now and I'm grounded, there's no way for him to get me these . . ."

Lyle hoists the bag of plaques above Dino's head, so the officer can see them. Just to make sure, he gives the bag a vigorous shake.

". . . so I pretended I was sick so I could sneak over to David's house and get 'em, 'cause if we don't finish this Miss

O'Donnell won't let me walk across the gym on my hands to raise money for muscular dystrophy so they can find a cure for David because that's the only thing I could come up with to help—"

"All right, all right," Officer Jenkins interrupts. "I think I have the gist of it."

"I'm in big trouble, aren't I?"

"Yes, you are!"

Officer Jenkins lets Lyle digest the information. He parks his car in the Hatcher driveway and then pretends to write up a report in an official-looking notebook, with a Police Department logo on the front cover. Lyle waits nervously, Dino still comfortably parked on his lap.

Officer Jenkins looks up from his task. "Why don't you let the dog out?" he suggests.

Lyle opens the door and Dino jumps out of the car. The officer goes back to writing and once he feels Lyle is sufficiently distraught, he puts the notebook down.

"Tell you what."

He pauses to lend the moment more importance.

"You promise me—and I mean it—you promise me, you'll behave yourself 'til I retire, and we'll keep this between us."

"Really?!"

Officer Jenkins offers his hand, and they shake on it.

"And I'm going to hold you to it. I'm not foolin' around here. You just shook hands with a police officer. Next time it *is* gonna be juvenile hall!"

"Holey smokes. Not juvey!"

The officer nods his head, a stern expression on his face.

"Officer Jenkins?" Lyle ventures. "Could you come to my hand-walk on Parent Night? Mr. Merrick said I need someone official and you're the most official person there is. Can you come? It's exactly fifteen days from today and my thing is at eight thirty."

"So now what are you doing exactly?"

"I'm walkin' across the gym on my hands to raise money to find a cure for David."

Officer Jenkins can't help but smile.

"I'm happy to help the Dahlkes any way I can. Meantime, you keep your nose clean."

"This is great! Remember, I'm last. At eight thirty. And everybody's gonna be there," Lyle says, vigorously scratching his nose. He clambers out of the car and peers back through the car window. "Officer Jenkins, can you do the siren?"

The squad car backs out with a short siren blast. Next door, Betty Miller peers out the window from behind the drapes. Lyle waves to her. He's in a good mood even though he knows he's probably in big trouble—not to mention she no doubt called the cops. He scoots into the house, delighted, clutching his bag of labels.

Mrs. Hatcher arrives home well before her husband, and Betty has been waiting for her all afternoon. Before she even has a chance to get out of the car, her ears hurt, as Betty fills her in on the details of what occurred in her absence.

Mrs. Hatcher enters the house and goes straight to Lyle's bedroom, where she finds him asleep on his bed. On the floor is an enormous wooden box filled with neatly arranged bugs of every type, size, and color. She bends her knees for a closer look. Meticulously placed below each insect is a small brass label engraved with the correct English and Latin names. It's colorful, impressive, and it's a work of science and a work of art.

She thinks better of waking him and closes the door, a smile forming on her face. She knows she won't be telling her husband the story she just heard from Betty. She reflects on how he gets up at three thirty each morning, six days a week, so he can be out the door by four. He puts in a full day of milk deliveries and arrives home twelve hours later, bone-tired. It's better for everyone if she keeps this one to herself, she decides. It's the balance of family responsibilities.

When Mr. Hatcher does come home, a short while later, she takes his hand and draws him down the hall.

"Come here. I want you to see something."

When he realizes she's leading him into Lyle's bedroom, he groans, "For cryin' out loud! What'd he do now?"

Lyle is a lump on the bed.

"Shhh . . ." Mrs. Hatcher gazes down. "Look at him. He looks just like when he won that baby contest . . . with those blue eyes and silky blond hair," she reminisces.

"It was second place, and let's not let him sleep too long. He's recharging his battery," Mr. Hatcher grumbles.

Mrs. Hatcher smiles and points to the bug collection. Her husband moves closer, amazed.

"Now, that is something else!"

He crouches down, and examines every detail.

"Holey smokes, will you look at those labels. This is impressive. Did he do all this?"

"David Dahlke helped him with it. That's what those two have been up to ever since school started."

"I had no idea."

They gaze for a moment at their sleeping son, messily sprawled out on top of the covers. Mr. Hatcher puts his arm around his wife's shoulders.

"Maybe it was worth it," he says, as they leave the room. He's only half joking.

Lyle hears the door shut and cracks open one eye. He springs from his bed and starts his workout: one hundred regular push-ups, and then the handstand push-ups. He can't do a hundred of those yet, but he's determined to accomplish it before the big day arrives.

Wednesday, October 27
14 days to Parent Night

The next morning, Lyle stands at the foot of his bed, staring at the bug collection in horror.

It's in shambles.

Many of the bugs are missing parts and others are missing altogether. Lyle lifts a dead mouse by its tail from the corner of the box.

"Mom!" he screams, in agony.

She hurries into the room. "What in Heaven's name?"

"Mom, you won't believe it," he moans.

Lyle points at the remains of the bug collection, the mouse dangling from his fingers.

"He was eatin' our bugs and the carbon tetrachloride musta killed him."

Mrs. Hatcher is visibly crushed.

"Oh . . . I'm so sorry, honey . . . I really am. I know you boys worked so hard on this. I promise we'll talk about it later and figure out what to do, but right now we've got our meeting with Miss O'Donnell."

She suddenly processes the mouse swinging from Lyle's hand.

"Good grief! Throw the poor thing in the garbage and go wash your hands!"

"Mom?"

"What?"

"I know I'm grounded and everything, but I was just wonderin' if it would be okay if I don't come straight home from school next week, if I start runnin' a couple miles first? Jack LaLanne says to exercise every day."

"Running where?" his mom asks.

"I was thinkin' from school to the fire station and then straight home. Like that."

"You're not stopping anywhere along the way? Straight to the fire station and straight back home? That's it?"

"That's it, Mom. I think I need to run more, that's all."

She considers the request. "Okay, then. But it doesn't change anything else. Are you listening? You're still off ice cream, television, phone and friends."

"I know that, Mom. But that doesn't include David, does it?"

"You can visit David if it's okay with Mrs. Dahlke," she tells him. "Now put your shoes on. Your dad's waiting. And remember, this is going to be an adult conversation and I don't want you to say one word. Not one!"

Lyle feels a rush of anxiety.

CHAPTER TWENTY-TWO

DOD ALMIGHTY

*If you think the problem is bad now,
just wait until we've solved it.*

~ ANONYMOUS

Mrs. Hatcher has a vise-like grip on Lyle's leg. There is a repertoire of signals she can send through the subtle hand on his knee. A gentle squeeze is a warning, which simply means, "Better simmer down." A single pat says, "You're doing well" and "Continue to stay this course." If she draws a slow circle on Lyle's leg, and punctuates it with a quick pop, it means if he moves another muscle she's going to choke the life out of him.

The iron grip is something new, a clear indicator of the enormity of what is about to happen. She promised him a bowl of ice cream if he can hold still until the verdict is read, and she intends for him to have that ice cream. Lyle nervously yanks on his shirt and wipes sweaty hands on his pants.

The Dahlkes and the Hatchers have gathered in Miss O'Donnell's office, and the principal seems catlike and agitated. She paces behind David, seated between his parents, as though fearful of leaving him unprotected.

Mr. Hatcher, respectful of the principal's authority, is silent, and maintains constant eye contact.

"As you all know," Miss O'Donnell begins, "we've had an ongoing problem. One thing after another, after another. I'm sure you've been as frustrated as I have. We've been lucky, up until now, nothing catastrophic has happened. But things have progressed from bad to worse, and after giving this a great deal of thought, I realize there's really only one option remaining.

"What I'm requiring is this: we must separate the boys completely. I will see to it this is strictly enforced here at school and on the school grounds. I recommend you do the same at home.

"It is unfortunate, but I feel it's for the best this relationship is halted before David is irreparably harmed, and Lyle is forced to live with the consequences for the rest of his life. I know this seems harsh, but it's the best thing for both of them. This much is clear.

"If what I am suggesting is not satisfactory to you, I have already spoken with Sister Birgitta, the principal at St. Thomas More, and they will take Lyle for the remainder of the year on a sponsorship program, so there would be no cost to you for the private school.

"I've prepared a simple agreement for both families to sign. It simply states the terms of this arrangement, so there's no question should any difficulties arise."

Miss O'Donnell hands a single typed page to Mr. Dahlke, and another to Mr. Hatcher. Both men glance at the paper, see nothing objectionable, and pass it to their wives. The big flourish on the bottom where Miss O'Donnell has already initialed it is the first thing to catch Mrs. Hatcher's eye:

DOD

Dorothy O'Donnell

There is absolute silence in the room. Lyle glances over at David, eyeing the scabs on his face and arms.

If he doesn't wanna see me, I don't blame him.
I'm kinda glad it's over. David doesn't deserve this.

Miss O'Donnell thinks I'm the worst kid in the world, ever. Somebody's breathin' funny. Nose whistle alert! Cork it, Mr. Dahlke! David sure looks like he's mad at me. Those scabs look like moss. I'm gonna call him Mosshead—David Mosshead Dahlke.

"Excuse me, Miss O'Donnell. May I say something?" Mrs. Dahlke interjects, bringing an end to the silence.

Miss O'Donnell nods agreeably, relieved, as they all are, that someone has finally spoken.

"As you know, David's only been in public school for a couple of years. And it was wonderful you accepted him here. We appreciate it so very much."

Mrs. Dahlke pauses to gather her thoughts. She didn't come prepared to speak.

"When we were home-schooling him," she continues, "we didn't have to deal with this sort of thing. He never got hit in the head with a snowball, never got shot with BBs, and he didn't need a tetanus shot every six months. I admit it's been a challenging adjustment to make." She smiles faintly in Lyle's direction.

"But he used to just sit by our picture window and watch the world go by. A boy needs to be a boy. Now, one of my greatest joys is when he comes home with chickweed in his hair, smelling like the outdoors. Then I know he's having a life like other boys his age. So, what I'm trying to say . . ." Mr. Dahlke puts his arm around Mrs. Dahlke, and she folds her hand into his. "What *we* are trying to say, is we don't want the boys to be separated. And we still want Lyle to be David's navigator. We accept full responsibility for what might happen. They're friends, Miss O'Donnell."

A thick silence hangs in the air.

Miss O'Donnell breaks it, her voice appreciably tense.

"Friends or not, this is not at all what I was expecting to hear. I am strongly opposed, and I suggest you take some time to consider what I've said, as well as the recommendations I have made."

Mrs. Dahlke addresses Lyle's parents. "We'd like to try again, Mrs. Hatcher. Mr. Hatcher."

Mrs. Hatcher beams at her. Her husband, utterly convinced by Miss O'Donnell's presentation, hasn't quite shifted gears yet.

"I believe we can work it out," Mrs. Hatcher says.

Miss O'Donnell steps away from David's chair, a signal of defeat. "I hope you know what you're doing." She proceeds to straighten papers on her desk.

If it's a hint they should go, they don't take it. Mrs. Dahlke leans over to Lyle and whispers, "And Lyle, there's one thing we need from you. And that's to slow down. Just a little bit." She indicates what she means by "a little bit" with gently held thumb and forefinger. "This much. Okay?"

Lyle nods vigorously. "Okay, Mrs. Dahlke. I will. I promise."

Miss O'Donnell repeats herself. "I am not comfortable with this arrangement. But," she acknowledges in resignation, "I'll have to leave it up to you."

Lyle tries to get up from his seat; he wants to go over to David. Mrs. Hatcher clinches his leg.

"Hold your horses," she murmurs. "Let's let David's parents take him home today. He won't be back in school for a while, but you can stop by his house after school on Monday. If it's all right with the Dahlkes. Okay?"

They say their goodbyes. As Mrs. Hatcher leads Lyle through the doorway, he angles back and waves to his friend. "Hey, David. I'll see you on Monday."

David manages a wave, and a nod.

Monday, November 1
9 days to Parent Night

On Monday after school, Lyle and Dino race straight to the Dahlkes' house. They approach the front yard, and

Lyle spies David through the picture window, in the dining room, eating. He knocks on the door. David's voice carries from inside.

"Come on in."

Lyle lets himself into the house and bounds from the sunken living room up into the kitchen.

"Whatcha doin'?"

"Eating a bowl of soup."

Lyle notices Charlie, the puppet, propped up against the sewing box, staring at him.

"What's he doin' up here?"

He does not like that puppet. Charlie is no less disturbing in the brightly lit dining room than sitting on a dark basement shelf.

Why is he always starin' at me like that?

"My mom's making him a new jacket. He fell off on the floor and Puff chewed his old one and ruined it."

Lyle spots the new yellow-plaid jacket hanging on a doll-sized hanger, hooked over the back of the chair.

"I don't like it. It looks like mustard!" Lyle wrinkles his nose, as though it has a nasty odor.

"I thought you were colorblind," David shoots back.

"Good gravy, David. That doesn't mean I don't like mustard!"

"What?"

"You're mad at me, aren't you? I tried to stop the chair. I couldn't. You think I didn't try? I did, you know. I tried my hardest!"

"I'm not mad. It wasn't your fault," David tells him, and he means it. He hadn't been thinking about this anyway.

"What do you mean, it wasn't my fault? Yes, it was! Don't you know? It's always my fault. It was a stupid, stupid thing to do."

David puts down his spoon and his eyes meet Lyle's. "Look. I'm the one who couldn't stop the chair. Me, not you. I knew you couldn't reach the brakes. You should've bailed. Why didn't you bail?"

Lyle stares at David in disbelief. He delivers his heartfelt message.

"Because, David . . . friends . . . don't . . . bail. That's why."

There's a period of awkward silence. Mrs. Dahlke comes up the stairs from the basement.

"Excuse me, boys, I don't mean to interrupt. Lyle, would you like some tomato soup?"

"Yes, please. I would, Mrs. Dahlke."

She opens the cupboard for a bowl. "Large or small?"

"Large please," Lyle tells her politely. "And can I have some crackers?"

Lyle watches, as she removes a pan from the stove and ladles out the last of the tomato soup. She opens a sleeve of soda crackers, and sets the bowl and crackers on the table..

"There are spoons on the table and milk in the fridge. Help yourself," she tells him.

"Thank you, Mrs. Dahlke."

She smiles. "I'll be downstairs if you need me," she says, and disappears into the stairwell.

David grins at Lyle. He screws his face into an imitation of a sniveling infant and mimics Lyle's voice, making him sound like a crybaby.

"Cun I hab sum cwack-uhs?"

"What did you just say?"

"Mummy, cun I hab sum cwack-uhs?" David repeats, exaggerating it even more.

Lyle laughs, snorting out a bite of soup.

"Dang it, David! You made me snarf. I just snarfed!"

"Say it, don't spray it."

David picks up his spoon and it slips from his fingers and falls onto the tray.

"Do you need help with that?" Lyle offers.

"No. I can get it."

Lyle checks to make sure no one else is around, and then picks up his bowl, tips it to his lips and takes a large slurp, purposefully making as much noise as possible. David laughs and tries to imitate him but he can't lift his bowl.

In the basement, Mr. and Mrs. Dahlke sit on the floor, sorting through unsold items from their garage sale. Puff, the badger, observes them, haughty but curious.

"How was it going up there?" Mr. Dahlke asks.

"When I left they were staring each other down."

"Who was winning?"

"I don't know. They'll work it out, though. They're too good of friends."

Mr. Dahlke listens. "It's awful quiet up there. Maybe you'd better go check on them," he suggests.

"You go check on them."

"I'm not qualified. I don't even know the kid."

Mrs. Dahlke climbs up off the floor and starts up the stairs. "Good point," she agrees. "That's why I keep you around."

"Because I'm underqualified?" he puzzles.

"No," she tells him, "because you realize you are. It's so endearing."

She jogs up the stairs and rounds the corner into the kitchen. Lyle's back is to her, blocking her view of David. She intentionally makes noise, so they know she's in the room. Lyle turns. He holds a soup bowl in his hands, and a ring around his mouth hearkens of sloppily applied clown makeup. When she notices that David sports a similar marking, and realizes Lyle helped him put it there, she successfully suppresses a laugh—recognizing the boys are in the middle of a private moment.

"How are you boys doing?" she asks.

"Fine, Mom," David grins.

Lyle leaves David's house, and runs the two miles to the fire station like he told his mother he would. Dino is delighted, since Lyle being grounded has cut heavily into his activities.

When they reach their destination, they pause to catch a drink from the sprinkler, then Lyle heads into the firehouse. He finds three firemen in the bay, washing the truck. Surprised, they stop what they're doing as soon as he comes through the door.

"My name is Lyle Hatcher and I need to talk to you guys. I need some firemen," Lyle declares.

The men are impressed and amused, but they hold a straight face.

"Well, Mr. Hatcher, I'm Captain Roy Robinet. This is Stu and Buck." They nod their hellos. "If it's firemen you need, you came to the right place. What can we help you with?"

"I'm gonna walk across the Linwood gym on my hands to raise money for muscular dystrophy and help my friend David Dahlke, and I need you guys there . . . to make it official. I ran all the way here to ask you."

"Are you talking about Ernie Dahlke's boy, David?" Captain Robinet inquires.

Lyle nods.

"The Dahlkes are great folks. They taught my Becky how to swim."

"Yep," Stu says. "All five a' my kids learned how to swim in their pool."

"Shoot, half the kids on the north side did," Buck adds.

"Right, half a' the kids," Stu repeats. "My rugrats were in her kindergarten class. Great little school she's got goin' over there."

"What's all this about walkin' on your hands?" the Captain wants to know.

"I'm doing it next Wednesday at Linwood Elementary," Lyle explains eagerly. "It starts at seven thirty and my part is at eight thirty. I'm last on the program, I mean, last on the agenda. That's what Miss O'Donnell said."

Captain Robinet muses out loud. "I think we could drive a truck over there for the event. What do you guys think?"

Stu nods his agreement. "I'm in, Captain."

"Show us a handstand," Buck says.

Lyle, confident from Mr. Merrick's instruction and the hours of practice, swings up into a handstand and holds it.

"Impressive," Captain Robinet observes. "Would you like to stay for a while and help us reel hoses? Good workout for those arms."

"Thanks, but I'm grounded," Lyle replies. "I'm only allowed to do my run."

"Then you'd better get running," the Captain remarks.

Buck opens the main doors to the station, and the firemen step outside. Dino sits on the driveway, waiting patiently.

"What's your dog's name, Lyle?" Buck asks.

Dino can't get a handle on the three large men staring at him. He wriggles his way closer to Lyle, leans against him, and then sits on his foot. Lyle reaches down and scruffs the dog on the back of the head.

"He's really the neighbors' dog two doors down, but—"

"Who plays with him?" Captain Robinet asks.

"I do."

"Well, who feeds him?"

"I always give him part of my lunch after school. I save it for him. Mostly peanut butter and homemade jam. He likes strawberry."

The Captain smiles. "He doesn't like peach or grape?"

"Mostly strawberry," Lyle repeats.

"Who do you think he'd say he belongs to?"

Lyle looks at the dog he loves, and leans down to scratch him again. Dino licks him on the nose, and Lyle smiles at the dog, as if no one else is around.

"So what's your dog's name, then?"

"Dino. Right, Dino?"

Dino crouches down and barks.

"I gotta go," Lyle tells them.

He and Dino start down the street toward home. He yells back over his shoulder. "Thanks a lot! See you next Wednesday!"

The firemen watch him for a while.

"Think he'll make it?" Buck asks.

"I'll give him three to one," Captain Robinet says, sizing up Lyle as he runs down the street.

"Three to one," Stu repeats, thoughtfully.

Tuesday, November 2
8 days to Parent Night

The next day, after his run to the fire station and a quick exchange with the firemen, Lyle carries the large display box to David's house to show him, firsthand, the damage to their bug collection.

Lyle positions the box on the dining table, and David pokes around in it with his finger.

"Not again," he despairs. "This is a disaster!" He holds up a wing. "Where does this go?"

Lyle plucks it from him and holds it over the box, moving the wing this way and that as if it were a puzzle piece.

"It goes," he ponders, "somewhere."

"This June bug only has one antenna. And what's this?" David holds up a bug-part, shrugs and tosses it back in the box.

"Oh, wait a minute. Let me see it again. That's ahhh . . . oh yeah, it's a gypsy moth caterpillar," Lyle tells him.

"Caterpillar? Oh man-oh-man, what are we going to do?"

"Let's not panic!" Lyle orders, in a panic-stricken voice.

Dennis hears the noise, recognizes it as one Lyle would make, and sticks his head into the room.

"Hey, Lyle," he says. "You wanna see what I'm workin' on?"

"Heck, yeah," Lyle replies, immediately forgetting the bugs. "Let's go."

In the taxidermy room, Jenon is perched on a stool, reading, and glances up when they come in.

"Hi, Lyle. Oh, and hello, Mr. McCartney," she says.

David blushes. Lyle's eyes are fixed on Dennis' worktable. There stands the *monster*—the one Lyle came face-to-face with when he was in the basement with the bag of labels. The skin on its skull is peeled back, baring the marble eyeballs and the razor-sharp teeth. The exposed jaw and skull appear to snarl and grin at the same time, sinister and demonic. Even in the bright light of Dennis' workroom, it's nothing short of disturbing.

"Say hello to my coyote," Dennis says. "Obviously, it's not done yet."

"That thing scared the daylights outta me!" Lyle exclaims.

He spots the wind-up drummers on the shelf. "And I *told* you those were bears, David. You keep tryin' to tell me they're *dogs*."

"They are dogs," David corrects him.

"You know where we could get some real drummers, Dennis?" Lyle asks.

"Drummers? What do you need drummers for?" Dennis stops work on the coyote and leans over the back of his chair, interested.

"We need a drum roll for when I walk on my hands across the gym. A really, really good drum roll."

"I've got a couple of friends who play in the Shadle High School marching band. You want me to ask?" Jenon offers.

"That'd be great!" Lyle replies.

Dennis nods his approval. He has friends in the Shadle band as well, but he recognizes Jenon will get a more favorable response than he would.

"Hey, Dennis, can we use your coyote for our science project?" Lyle shoots, going for broke.

"No, you can't," Dennis laughs. "But I'd be glad to stuff you two jokers and enter you in the county fair next year. That'd be a grand prize ribbon for sure."

"We definitely should've done a volcano," David sighs in resignation.

"Are you kiddin' me?" Lyle exclaims. "Volcanoes never, ever win!"

CHAPTER TWENTY-THREE

HOPE

*The natural flights of the human mind
are not from pleasure to pleasure,
but from hope to hope.*

~ DR. SAMUEL JOHNSON

Wednesday, November 10
Parent Night

A large, smoldering volcano rests prominently in the center of a banquet table in the gym, a blue ribbon pinned to its side. Lyle and David stand rooted before it, not conversing, not commenting, just staring. But it isn't the volcano that has their attention. It's a pathetic arrangement of moss and mushrooms next to it.

"Fungus. We entered a fungus collection," Lyle complains, distressed. "That's the lousiest science project I've ever seen."

"Hey, look. We got Honorable Mentions. One for you and one for me!" David picks up a certificate and waves it at him.

"That's not an Honorable Mention," Lyle corrects him. "It's a Certificate of Participation. Big deal. Everybody gets one. And this is nothing but sprouts and mushrooms and spores and lichen. It's just a big giant salad."

Melvin Schmeck stands at the opposite end of the table, beaming at them. Lyle's eyes travel to the big beautiful *blue* first-place ribbon Melvin snatched from what should have been the jaws of defeat. He nudges David, and they continue along the row of display tables, checking out the other students' efforts.

Derek presides over his magnet display, and they entertain themselves with it for a while, lifting the large tubular magnets and trying to push the positive ends together. Their hands force into a rolling motion, which they find pretty funny.

"Cool, huh?" Derek says. Lyle and David nod in agreement.

They wander past Johnny and Doug, with their partially dissolved nail in a bottle of soda pop; play with Paul's electromagnet display; and watch, amused, as Greg's motorized version of an avalanche crushes a small mountain village, resets itself and does it again. Sharon Anne and Francine stand confidently beside a three-panel poster, upright on the table, brightly painted in a realistic depiction of the solar system.

David pauses in front of it and studies it for a long time.

"All right, all right," Lyle whispers, "I know you have a crush on her."

David grins. "Someday, Lyle," he says, "I'll be zooming from planet to planet all over the galaxy. I can hardly wait. You know there's other life out there. Things we can't even imagine."

"I'll tell you what I can't even imagine," Lyle says. "I can't even imagine you zooming around the galaxy in that wheelchair. It's not for racing, you know."

"Maybe it is and maybe it isn't," David grins, rocking his chair like a dragster at the gate.

The boys continue along the tables until they arrive back at their own project. Mr. Merrick works his way over to where they're standing, expertly swishing his dust mop on the floor. He stops dead in his tracks, before the volcano.

"Oh, for cryin' out loud! There's another spider. This place needs fumigatin'," he says.

A black widow crawls out of the lichen on the boys' fungus collection, and she has a pin, with a shiny black ball on top, sticking straight out of her back.

Lyle jumps. "Holey smokes! That's not another spider. It's the Queen! My mom's been lookin' all over for her!"

Mr. Merrick leans in, putting his face up close to it. "What in tarnation . . . ? She's got a pin stickin' out of her!"

"I know, I did that!" Lyle stresses. "What are we gonna do?"

"Do?" Mr. Merrick raises an eyebrow.

He lifts the black widow by the pin and holds her high in the air. The boys stare up at her, straight at the red hourglass on her belly. Mr. Merrick flicks his hand, and the spider comes loose from the pin and falls into the dustpan.

"Can you believe after everything, she's still alive?" David asks, incredulous.

"Everybody's got somethin' pinnin' 'em down," Mr. Merrick cracks. He winks at David. "I'm puttin' her outside, where she belongs."

Gingerly, Mr. Merrick carries the dustpan to the exit. He may not be fond of spiders, but the boys have made it clear, this one deserves special consideration.

As more and more families arrive for Parent Night, Mr. Merrick wheels out the extra folding chairs from under the bleachers. Miss O'Donnell's surprise grows as the gym fills— so many faces she's never seen. She wonders at the unexpected and unprecedented community interest in Linwood Elementary Parent Night.

Mr. Merrick brings out the last of the folding chairs, and even then there aren't enough seats. Mrs. Thompson steps up to the microphone, and the crowded gymnasium quickly hushes.

"My goodness, what a great crowd we have here tonight," she chirps. Her eyes are bright, and her stance a little giddy. It's a dream to be in front of a large crowd of people with a microphone. She lifts her hands, palms upward, and says, "Everyone! Please stand for the pledge of allegiance."

The crowd rises to its feet, and all turn in the direction of the flag, permanently hung on the stage. The rumble of three hundred voices—men, women and children, every pitch and every timbre—resonates through the gym, a tower of sound, as they speak the words in unison.

"I pledge allegiance to the Flag of the United States of America, and to the Republic for which it stands, one Nation, under God, indivisible, with liberty and justice for all."

Mrs. Thompson waits for the rustle to die down.

"Thank you," she says. "As I'm sure you all know, Parent Night is an event we hold only once a year, and it provides our students with the opportunity to demonstrate some of their accomplishments . . ."

While Mrs. Thompson speaks, Miss O'Donnell makes a perfunctory check of the hallway. She pauses. What sounds like a very large vehicle pulling up to the front entrance of the school pricks Miss O'Donnell's ears. She always investigates anything out of the ordinary, and tonight certainly will not be an exception.

She traverses the length of the empty hall and turns the corner toward the entrance. A ladder truck from the Fire Department idles outside at the curb. Instinctively, Miss O'Donnell reaches for the fire alarm on the wall, hooking her fingers over the switch and applying downward pressure— then stops, thinking. The Fire Department is already here . . . so if it were an emergency involving the school, they would be inside by now, evacuating the building.

"It must be a house across the street," she calculates. She approaches the door to confirm, just as three firemen in work uniforms clomp their way through the entrance.

Surprised, they respectfully remove their hats. Stiffly, Miss O'Donnell offers her hand to the one nearest her, and notices another carrying several silver buckets.

"I'm Miss O'Donnell, the principal. Is there a problem?"

"Pleasure to meet you, Miss O'Donnell. Captain Roy Robinet," the man shaking her hand responds politely. "We're here for the big event. This is Buck and Stu."

Miss O'Donnell puzzles as to why they're in uniform *and* why they brought a ladder truck to Parent Night, but she is, despite her awkwardness, socially adept.

"Fabulous," she says to her guests. "Right down the hall to the gym. So glad you could make it. Come along, I'm on my way there myself."

"Thank you, ma'am," Roy replies. "Really a pleasure to meet you."

As they make their way toward the gymnasium, Miss O'Donnell's radar privately beeps loud warnings. Something is not right about this.

"I'm curious about the buckets," she remarks to Stu.

"We thought it would be a nice touch . . . for the quarters"

"The quarters?" she queries.

Stu laughs. "I meant the change. I say quarters because it's what the little man always calls it. The quarters."

"Ah, yes," Miss O'Donnell responds. *Little man?* she wonders. *Who is he talking about?*

As they enter the gym, Mrs. Thompson is in the middle of another announcement. "Next on the program, we have a lovely dance prepared by Mrs. Maxfield and presented by Sharon Anne Wilson, Francine Hoffsteader, Derek Milney, and Paul Schneider."

Miss O'Donnell encourages the firemen to find a seat. They can see no seats are available, so they elect to stand. She spots Lyle approaching, and in one, sudden, jarring realization, understands *everything*. She quickly moves to intercept him.

"Lyle," she states quietly, in a tone of voice he has never heard before, from her or anyone else. "You and I need to have a talk."

Lyle fixes his gaze on her, but he's not moving.

"Outside," she orders. "Right now!"

She moves resolutely toward the exit, and Lyle knows he'd better follow. Mr. Merrick puts his hand on David's shoulder, and David looks up at him quizzically. The janitor shakes his head as if to say, "I got a bad feelin' about this."

Miss O'Donnell urges Lyle into the hallway, and closes the door behind them. She takes a deep breath, but before she can begin, more noises interrupt from the entrance to the school, followed by the sound of footsteps.

"What now?" she muses, unaware she does so out loud.

Around the corner and into the hallway step four teenage boys, moving with the confidence of seasoned performers. Dressed in bright red band uniforms, they pace four-abreast down the hall, habitually and unintentionally stepping in unison. One wears a marching snare; one, a set of three marching toms; and the others, shiny brass cornets as though permanent extensions of their hands. Even to Miss O'Donnell, it's a strangely riveting sight.

"The drummers are here!" Lyle utters, excited.

Miss O'Donnell would never make guests at her school feel uncomfortable, particularly through no fault of their own, so she waits for the musicians to reach them, and greets the four newcomers cordially.

"Where would you like us?" the first cornet player inquires.

Lyle starts to respond, but Miss O'Donnell squeezes his shoulder to silence him. "Just go on in and make yourselves comfortable," she tells them. "I'll be with you in a minute."

"Yes, ma'am."

They slip through the door to the gymnasium.

"Lyle," Miss O'Donnell begins.

And again, the sound of the front door opening and closing echoes down the hallway. She puts her head down, in the palm of her hand, for the briefest of moments. Then she directs her eyes to the hallway, where Officer Jenkins rounds the corner, striding in their direction. She whips back to Lyle.

"All right, what is going on?" she hisses.

"What do you mean?"

"Lyle Hatcher, you heard me, and I'm not going to ask you again. What is going on?"

"I told you. It's what we talked about. I'm going to walk on my hands to make money for muscular dystrophy."

Officer Jenkins slows to a halt nearby, and listens. Miss O'Donnell likes having him there and he knows it.

"What are you talking about? I honestly don't know what to do with you. Do you think the rules don't apply to you? Do think you can always push hard enough that at some point you'll win? Is that what's going on here?"

There's a pause as Lyle digests this. He speaks tentatively.

"Win? Win what?"

"You know exactly what I mean!"

Lyle clenches and unclenches his hands, fidgeting. His toes curl in his shoes and he feels his teeth biting down.

"I'm afraid to say anything."

"Well, then, I guess we're finished! And you were already finished, except for apologies and explanations. Do you want me to discuss this with the musicians and the firemen and Officer Jenkins, or are you going to do the mature thing and handle it yourself?"

Lyle knows when his back is against the wall. He realizes, clearly, he must try something—anything.

"What I was talking about was . . . running," he says in a small voice.

"Running! What on earth does running have to do with any of this?"

"David said that he was gonna run. This is our last chance." Lyle's face contorts into a frown. There's an awkward moment of silence.

"He said he was gonna run," Lyle summons the nerve to go on. "He said that. He said that he was gonna run . . . with me! And now I know that'll never happen unless they find a cure. And they need money for that."

Miss O'Donnell is speechless, but it's clear from her expression she is anything but swayed.

"Miss O'Donnell, I only did what you told me to do," Lyle whispers, not wanting Officer Jenkins to hear. Desperation grips him as realization dawns—she isn't going to let him do his walk.

"What I told you to do? I wish you would, just once, do what I told you to do. You have ignored the rules and undermined my authority for the last time. Right this minute, there's only one thing I need to know from you. Are you going to explain this to these people, or am I?"

With that, the haze clears for Lyle. He knows. He knows what he says in the next moment will change the course of his life forever; he knows this is his last chance; and above all, he knows no matter what he chooses to say right now, he has absolutely nothing to lose. He takes a deep breath, and launches into his final and greatest effort.

"You said you liked my idea and that it was grandiose, I know what that means, it means magnificent, noble, and brilliant, because my grandma looked it up with me, she even used it in a sentence, two sentences, actually, and you said we just needed to finish our science project and do a good job on that, and we would've won the blue ribbon if the mouse hadn't eaten our real project, it was a big bug collection with brass labels, way better than that giant salad, and you said I had to stay outta trouble on school grounds, and I did that, the donut wasn't at school so I didn't think that counted, and we did the presentation to Mrs. Thompson, David did all the papers, okay, there was only one paper, but he did it, and we gave it to her, we gave it to Mrs. Thompson exactly like you said, and I would have told you about the drummers and the firemen and Officer Jenkins, but you said you didn't want to hear another word about it, and you even said it was last on the agenda, which is how we knew when the firemen should be here and the drummers and Officer Jenkins were s'posed to uh . . . um . . . ahh . . ."

Lyle stops because Miss O'Donnell's face is bright red and there's a vein bulging out on her forehead. He's never seen anything like it. It's moving and shifting, like it's alive. He's worried. It doesn't look good.

"Miss O'Donnell," he says, more than a little freaked. "Are you . . . mad?"

She snaps her wrist in the direction of the gym door and flicks out her finger, and Lyle scurries, terrified, back into the gym.

Miss O'Donnell touches Officer Jenkins on his arm and holds up one finger, the universal sign for "Please give me a minute."

She hastens into the girls' restroom and when the door closes behind her, she leans on the little sink and puts her head down again. Only this time, her face is crimson and a loud snort escapes her lips, made louder by the immense effort she exerts to hold it in. But once the first sound escapes, she's unable to hold back, and the dam breaks.

At first the noises are not identifiable. It's quite possible she doesn't even know what they are, or what they mean. But soon it's apparent—even to her—she's laughing. She laughs so hard she clutches her stomach in pain. Howling with laughter, she crouches, balancing herself against the sink. Tears stream down her face, and she struggles to get enough air.

Officer Jenkins hears the strange, animal-like sounds coming from the restroom. He knocks on the door in concern.

"Miss O'Donnell? Are you okay?"

Inside the gym, Lyle hovers by the door, confused. Mr. Merrick catches his eye and signals him over with a wave of his hand. Lyle worms through the crowd and over to where Mr. Merrick stands, next to David.

"What's goin' on, Sparky?"

"I don't know, Mr. Merrick," Lyle replies. "I think there's something wrong with Miss O'Donnell."

"What did she tell you?"

Lyle tries to remember something she told him. Nothing comes to mind. "Nothing," he says. "She didn't say anything."

"Are you walkin' or not?"

Lyle shrugs his shoulders, uncertain.

The second-to-last event ends, and under Mrs. Thompson's direction, the firemen set up the silver buckets along the exit columns of the bleachers.

Miss O'Donnell enters the gym with Officer Jenkins, straightening her dress and smoothing her hair. She's slightly tousled and disheveled, her face is flushed, and her eyes are red. All attention turns to them, as they come through the door.

"For our final event this evening, we have a little surprise," Mrs. Thompson announces. "Lyle Hatcher, one of our fourth-graders, would like to issue a challenge to everyone here in this gymnasium. Lyle will attempt to walk across the floor on his hands. He says he can do it. If he makes it, he is asking for your pocket change to help find a cure for muscular dystrophy. And we have a couple of our local firemen with their buckets ready! What do you say, Linwood?"

The crowd explodes with applause, hoots, and cheers. The musicians—having received no specific instruction but knowing all about events of this type—let loose with a rousing audience-pleaser. The crowd claps in time to the music.

From across the room, Lyle's eyes meet Miss O'Donnell's. They gaze intently at one another. Finally, she inclines her head slightly forward and to the side, in a gesture which seems to say, "Well, young man—let's see what you've got."

Lyle points to himself and raises his eyebrows, requesting confirmation, and she nods.

He steps out onto the floor, moving the way his mother always tells him, head high and shoulders back. He positions himself at one end of the gym, paying attention to the world around him, focusing, not pretending, feeling humbled by new realizations: He wants to please Miss O'Donnell. He wants to succeed and help David. He wants to impress Sharon Anne. He wants his parents to be proud of him. But above all, he knows how lucky he is to be standing out here, and how many reasons there are that he shouldn't be.

The music ends with a ripping flourish, the crowd sits down, and the gym grows quiet once again.

"We are honored to have Officer Jenkins here this evening to make sure no shenanigans are involved in the execution of this near-impossible feat," Mrs. Thompson belts out, quite swept away by her role. "And now, for tonight's final event—"

The gym resonates with applause, and Officer Jenkins positions himself near Lyle, signaling the drummers, who begin with a sharp accent, commanding everyone's attention. Amid the suspenseful chatter of a drum roll, Lyle crouches to the floor.

Inhale . . . exhale . . . inhale . . . exhale.

He kicks himself up onto his hands, and balances there.

CHAPTER TWENTY-FOUR

THE ANSWER

More tears are shed over answered prayers
than unanswered ones.

~ St. Teresa of Avila

Lyle wobbles. He regains his balance, and walks: two feet, three feet, five feet, eight, twelve, fifteen feet. Officer Jenkins paces along nearby, adding to the drama with his presence. Lyle wavers and then stops, trying to steady himself again. He takes a couple of quick pumps backwards to keep from falling, and then another quick palm to the side. He seems to have regained control . . . but then suddenly he tips over, tumbling sideways onto the ground. The gym echoes with a low groan from the audience.

Terry jumps up in the stands and yells at Lyle, "Come on, Hatcher, you can do it. Come on!"

A chorus of cheers reverberates in support. Lyle hurries back to the starting line and begins again. And again, Officer Jenkins walks next to him. When he's about fifteen feet from the goal, Lyle falters. His heart thumps and pounds in his head, his ears roar, and he's positive he looks like one of Dennis' molly fish, *giant jelly eyeballs ready to splat!*

Officer Jenkins senses he's in trouble, and takes a subtle step to the side—right next to Lyle's legs. Lyle falls, but hits Officer Jenkins' shoulders, and is able to rest there for a few seconds.

Thanks, Officer Jenkins. I needed that.

Lyle can see the finish line. He breathes . . . and focuses all the attention he's ever had on this one all-important thing.

He pushes off, and the adrenalin in his arms propels him fast. He reaches the opposite wall! The applause and cheers are thunderous. The noise shakes the rafters; the place goes wild! Officer Jenkins puts his hands in the air in an attempt to silence the crowd. It takes time for the jubilance and whistles to die down.

Officer Jenkins makes sure it's quiet, before launching into his piece.

"We can't all walk on our hands—and personally, I don't want to—"

A chuckle ripples out from the crowd.

"But we can all do our part. If you want to support the cause, please, drop your change in the buckets. Our firemen are standing by."

Clink! Lyle turns in the direction of that beautiful sound. Francine stands beside Sharon Anne, waves shyly, and they both smile. Mr. Merrick proudly steps up, and empties his coin pouch into one of the buckets. Mr. Hatcher reaches deep into his pockets with a nod to his son. Soon, lines form, as people wait to toss their change into buckets in their orderly exodus from the bleachers.

The musicians break into another foot-stomping tune. Stu takes off his boot and uses it as a collection plate, moving down the line and speeding things up for everyone. The buckets fill quickly.

When the gym has emptied and most of the families gone home, the firemen give Lyle and David a tour of the ladder truck. Buck lifts David into the passenger's seat, and David straps himself in, ready for a spin around the block. An emergency call interrupts.

"Next time, David. A'right?"

David nods, as Buck lifts him down.

The firemen escort Lyle and David away from the truck and quickly pull away from the curb, lights flashing and siren blaring. Captain Robinet throws a salute in David's direction.

Mr. Dahlke loads the wheelchair into the back of the VW bus. Lyle pokes his head in.

"Pretty cool, huh?" Lyle brags to David—meaning the walk across the gym on his hands.

David grins at him. "Yeah, pretty cool," he says, thinking about how close he came to riding in that ladder truck.

The next morning, Miss O'Donnell is alone in her office, well before anyone else has arrived at the school. She listens to the news on the radio, optimistic. Everything appears properly arranged and under control, and her world has an atmosphere of ease, making her almost cheerful.

"Everything is in apple-pie-order," she muses with approval.

The front door to the school opens and closes. Miss O'Donnell stops her work, and watches as Lyle walks steadily into the school, balancing something in his hands. He enters her office, and places a napkin with three oatmeal raisin cookies, fresh out of the oven, on her desk. He lifts his face to meet hers, and looks her straight in the eye.

"Miss O'Donnell, these aren't because I want to be a teacher's pet or anything like that. They're to say that I'm sorry for disobeying you and not respecting you and for all the other things I did wrong. I know I've been really lucky and I don't want to just be lucky anymore. I want to be good. I'm never going to get sent to your office or Mr. Stratton's office, or the boiler room, ever again. That's a promise."

He leaves her office, closing the door behind. Her mouth moves in one unspoken word.

"Unbelievable!"

Lyle keeps his word to Miss O'Donnell and, while it wouldn't be quite accurate to say the rest of the school year is uneventful, neither would it be an exaggeration to say that he stays out of trouble, mostly.

Four months later, a warm gentle wind sweeps in from the South, and stays for several days. The piles of snow, accumulated along plowed roadways and shoveled drives and sidewalks, grow smaller by the hour. Within days, the hyacinths poke their bright green shoots through the remaining snow, as proof that winter is being pushed aside.

Dennis and Mr. Dahlke take advantage of the pleasant weather to dismantle the Bubble and clean it. They remove the weights that hold it in place, drag it onto the lawn, scrub both sides, dry it, fold it, and finally lug it into the garage. It's work, but a long winter's confinement makes springtime tasks almost pleasant. In a particular stroke of good fortune, it promises to be a warm season, so they decide to leave it down for the summer.

Puff, the badger, ever since her encounter with Matt Veale's dog, has been allowed to hibernate in the yard as she obviously prefers, and now, with the coming of spring, emerges from her tunnels in her full glory—hungry and cranky, and mean.

Mrs. Dahlke, eager to see her, thinks it would be appropriate to film her on the occasion of her exit from hibernation. Puff's winter coat is thick and luxurious and when she hunkers down and flattens herself out on the grass, as she loves to do, she looks like a beautiful little rug, or a fur hat that someone left lying on the lawn.

Unfortunately, Puff feels that being on camera before she's had any time to put herself together is both irritating and offensive. To make matters worse, the steady clicking of the camera sounds suspiciously predatory to her. Consequently, anyone watching Mrs. Dahlke's footage will see a badger staring in their direction, and then racing toward them at full speed. When the badger fills the entire screen, the camera angle jerks upward to a view of budding trees and blue spring sky, followed by an extreme close-up of the grass. Thus ends Puff's career as an actress and Mrs. Dahlke's foray into cinematography.

David and Lyle don't let up on their adventures, but Lyle minds Mrs. Dahlke's request and slows things down . . . just a bit. He increasingly perceives that his friend is losing strength—the natural course of his degenerative disease. At times David can't hold a cup, or even a spoon or fork. He drinks through a straw, and Lyle cringes as he throws his head forward at his glass, afraid he's going to poke out his eye. But David hits the straw dead-on every time. He doesn't lack coordination; it's only his muscles that are fading.

By early July, with summer in full swing, the Dahlke pool is once again alive with daily lessons and the excited voices of children learning to swim. The novelty of the Bubble can't compete with the clear skies of summer, which lend David and Dennis renewed enthusiasm for therapy sessions in the water.

Today, when Dennis wheels David out to the pool, Dena and Ella have the full attention of their class of tadpoles, and not one child notices as Dennis lifts David from the wheelchair and sets him into the water.

Dennis can tell David is lighter than usual, and weaker; his brother is recovering from the flu. Glad to get him into the water—the one place that, no matter his condition, David always feels stronger and better—Dennis helps him get situated with his feet on the underwater ledge. David hangs from the side, gazing up.

"Sit tight, little brother," Dennis says. He reaches down and musses David's hair. "I'll be right back. Just gotta move the sprinkler out front."

David smiles and raises his arm, wanting to straighten his hair, but he's too weak to lift a hand to his head. Instead, he angles his head toward his hand and manages minimal grooming from that position. When he looks up, Dennis is gone from view, already around the side of the house.

Dennis checks the front lawn for dry spots. A sprinkler runs along one edge of the sidewalk, and a noticeable brown area is forming on the other. He moves fast, as usual, so he leaves the water on and drags the running sprinkler by the hose. He pulls it across the sidewalk and flips the hose like a whip, to make the sprinkler hop to where he needs it. Satisfied, he trots back toward the pool.

As Dennis makes his way down the ramp and around the corner of the house, he startles to see that David is not where he left him. His pulse rockets, and his pace quickens. A half-second later, he's running. And midway there, he sees him.

David lies motionless, on the bottom of the pool.

Dennis flies across the yard and dives straight to the bottom. He hoists David into his arms and pushes off with his legs, leaping upward, reaching for the surface.

Dena sees Dennis give David mouth-to-mouth as he bursts up out of the water. She and Ella hasten the children out of the pool and usher them toward the basement. Dena races to the phone and dials zero.

"We need help!" she begs the operator. "My brother has drowned in the pool!"

Mrs. Dahlke, in the basement doing laundry, hears Dena's urgent phone call. "Call Dr. Brewster!" she shouts, as she drops the clothes to the floor and rushes out the back door.

Dena dials the Lidgerwood Professional Building and requests Dr. Brewster, her voice urgent.

"He's unavailable at the moment," the receptionist politely informs her.

"This is Dena Dahlke. Tell him that David's had an accident in the pool and we need him. It's an emergency!"

Dennis has David on the sidewalk by the pool, and continues his desperate attempt at CPR. Mrs. Dahlke dashes up to her sons and kneels on the concrete. While Dennis works feverishly to resuscitate David, Mrs. Dahlke prays in a frantic and fervent whisper. She gently caresses David's cheek as she prays.

Sirens wail in the distance. A fire truck dispatches from the Alberta Street Fire Station. A reporter for *The Spokesman–Review*, driving in the area, hears the dispatch on his shortwave. He swings his car around, and speeds in the direction of the Dahlke house.

Dennis tries with all his might to get David to breathe, but his efforts have no effect. Mrs. Dahlke lifts her face and sees the reporter, dressed in black, slip quietly into the yard. He stands across the pool from her, raises his camera, and lines up a shot. She shakes her head, eyes pleading. Slowly, he lowers his camera.

Mrs. Dahlke pours her gaze into her son and moves her hands over his body.

"Dear Lord. Not now," she prays. "Not this way. Please don't take him now. I don't want my children to have to live with this. It's not their fault. Please, Lord."

Suddenly, David's chest heaves as he sucks in a breath, moaning and sputtering, expelling water through his nose and mouth. He opens his eyes . . . and fixes his gaze on his mother.

"Mom," he whispers.

She clutches her son. David's eyes are bright.

"I was almost there. It was beautiful . . . and then He sent me back."

Dr. Brewster sprints around the side of the house and rushes up to them. Dropping to his knees, he takes David's vitals. Minutes later, the ambulance arrives and the paramedics administer oxygen.

The moment they finish Dennis scoops David up, cradling him in his arms as he walks into the house. Mrs. Dahlke hurries along beside them. For the first time in his life, Dennis' arms shake, as he carries his brother.

Later, after David has rested, Dena slips into his room and finds him awake.

She sits on the edge of his bed and tidies his nightstand, making sure things are within reach. Finally, she places a tender hand over his.

"What happened out there?" she asks. "I don't understand why you went down."

David manages a weak, but loving, smile for his sister.

"I was going to swim underwater and then pop up and surprise you. I don't know why, but I didn't float this time. And I tried climbing, to get back up to the top, and I couldn't get there either. Then everything went black."

"Were you afraid?"

"No. I just couldn't get to you."

"But I didn't see Dennis put you into the pool," Dena despairs.

"It's okay, I knew that," he nods, wanting to reassure her. For his benefit, she pretends to be reassured.

When Lyle hears the news, he's beside himself with concern. David requires a recovery period, and Mrs. Hatcher well knows that Lyle's presence isn't what he needs. She makes that clear, but nonetheless, her son hounds her daily, devising ever more complex and elaborate schemes to trick her into letting him visit.

Almost three weeks after the near-drowning, Lyle barrels into the kitchen. Mrs. Hatcher is busy cooking dinner, while Steve works hard on his yo-yo tricks. Lyle watches his brother, his head bobbing in rhythm with the toy, but Steve can tell Lyle is quickly getting bored.

"This is called 'Walk the Dog,'" Steve announces, trying to hold his audience of one.

He stands legs apart, trying to show off. He flings the yo-yo downward and it flies up, wraps around his leg and smacks him in the buttocks. He yowls, and runs from the room to assess the damage in private.

"Mom?" Lyle tosses out casually, like he's seen his dad do. "I'm gonna run down to see David. I'll be back by dinner time."

He starts toward the door. She stops him with her foot, both of her hands in use, occupied with dinner preparations.

"No, you are not. I talked to Mrs. Dahlke earlier today, and he's not ready for company."

"I know that. But I need to talk to him."

"As soon as he's feeling better you can go see him. I'll let you know when that is."

"When? It's takin' forever!"

"It's been three weeks. That's not forever. As soon as I know, you'll know. Now, call your dad and your sister and wash up for dinner."

Lyle stirs a pot that's cooking on the stove, even though it doesn't need it.

"Mom—," he starts in.

The phone rings, and Steve darts back into the room and grabs it. "Hello? Hatcher residence."

Steve listens. "Just a minute," he says.

He makes a face at Lyle as he puts down the phone, and sings at him in a teasing voice, "It's Sharon Anne. Pretty Sharon Anne."

Lyle snatches the phone from his brother, and scowls.

"Sharon Anne?" he says breathlessly into the receiver.

David's voice comes over the line, small and thin.

"Hey. It's me."

Lyle throws Steve a glare that threatens, *I am gonna pummel the life outta you the second I get off this phone.* Steve scrams.

"What are you doin'?" Lyle asks David. "You want me to come over right now?"

"No. My mom says no."

"Hey!" Lyle says excitedly. "My dad says we're gettin' a new lawn mower and that means you and me can use our old one."

"What are we going to do with a broken lawn mower?"

"I'll tell you what we're gonna do. We're gonna weld it to your wheelchair and put a glass pack on it. That'll make it rip!"

There's a moment of silence while David pictures it. "That sounds sort of dangerous," he finally comments.

"Yeah, maybe," Lyle says, hesitating. "What are you sayin'?"

"I'm saying I like it. That'll be great. We'll be flying! Hey, Lyle?"

"Yeah?"

"I have to go."

"Are you sure? 'Cause I can talk more if you want."

"Not now. But I'll see you later. 'Bye Lyle."

"Okay, see you later."

Lyle quietly hangs up the phone, disappointed.

Two weeks later, in the evening, David is at home in his bedroom, propped up in bed. Mrs. Dahlke sits beside him, a book in one hand, holding David's hand in the other. She reads from his favorite book, *The Prophet.*

In the living room, Mr. Dahlke stares at an open newspaper, aware only of the sound of his wife's soft voice, drifting from David's bedroom. He puts his paper down, and ascends the steps into the short hallway. Pictures hang along the wall— school pictures, family portrait, Christmas and Halloween, playing in the pool, vacation at Disneyland—and in the middle is a large photograph of David in his wheelchair, when he was the March of Dimes poster child. Mr. Dahlke gently touches the picture of his boy.

His wife's voice fades. Mother and son sit quietly, reflecting on the words of the text. Mrs. Dahlke closes the book and places it on the nightstand.

"Mom?" David says, speaking in a whisper, his voice shallow and labored. "Will you promise me something?"

"Of course, sweetheart. Anything."

"Promise me you won't cry when I'm gone. I know where I'm going. And I'm going to be okay. Tell me you promise."

A lifetime without tears is an impossible feat, but a profound and loving request. Mrs. Dahlke could weep simply from the knowledge that David's last thoughts are filled with concern for her heart. As she gazes on her son—this boy who gives her strength—she knows the truly impossible would have been to love him more.

"I promise," she says, smiling in her saddest hour.

She sees in his eyes that he is frightened.

"Momma?"

She takes his hand in both of hers, and squeezes.

"Don't forget me."

"Never," she whispers in his ear. "*Never.*"

In the hallway, Mr. Dahlke stands as a statue, listening, his head hanging, and a single tear falls to the floor.

The phone rings. Mrs. Hatcher and Linda are at the kitchen table, studying. Linda answers.

"Hello? . . . Yes, I'll get her."

Linda passes the receiver to her mom with a peculiar anxiety in her eyes. Mrs. Hatcher moves away from Linda and speaks into the phone in hushed tones. The conversation is brief. When she hangs up, she gazes out the living room window, where she can see Lyle sitting on the curb with Dino. She places her hand over her heart and holds it there, and then gathers herself together and moves through the living room, to the front door.

"Mom?" Linda inquires, concerned.

Mrs. Hatcher stills for a fleeting second, and raises her hand. Linda, fears confirmed, gazes after her mother.

Mrs. Hatcher approaches Lyle and lowers herself beside him on the curb.

Lyle feels it in her presence, and in her reluctance. He waits, scarcely breathing.

She wants to comfort him immediately, take away the sting that they both know is coming, but the words are just beyond reach. Silence hangs in the air.

"Mom. What's wrong?"

"Lyle," she manages, feeling her maternal strength return, "I just talked to Mrs. Dahlke."

Lyle tilts up his face, and meets his mother's eyes.

"David's passed away," she tells him.

Lyle waits. Frozen.

"What?"

"He's gone, sweetheart. His heart just gave up. He died this evening."

Lyle looks away, and a frown takes hold while he struggles with the weight of this information.

"His heart didn't give up. When I talked to him . . . he said he would see me later . . . that's what he said."

"I'm sorry, Lyle. I know it hurts, but he's gone."

"He's gone? But that's not fair, Mom. That's not fair."

He fights hard, not wanting to seem weak, but his face distorts into tears, and he starts to cry. His mother gently touches his face and hair.

"Listen," she tells him. "You know what I think?"

Lyle shakes his head, unable to speak.

"I think that right now he's running, and doing all the things he always wanted to do."

"He was supposed to do that with *me*. He said."

Tears roll down his cheeks. He can't stop them.

Mrs. Hatcher folds Lyle into her arms and holds him close. Close enough that her son can't see the tears in her own eyes.

"I did a bad thing," he sobs.

She holds him away and fixes her eyes on his. "Why would you say that?"

"I didn't pray for him, Mom. He prayed for everybody else. But who prayed for him? I should have prayed for *him*."

"Lyle, you still can, anytime you want." She pauses, choosing her words carefully. "I know that you will see your friend David again someday."

Lyle cries in muffled sobs. "Really, Mom?"

She holds him closer.

"Count on it," she whispers.

Mrs. Hatcher embraces him until he gently pushes himself away. He reaches down and picks up a stick, glances up at the clear blue evening sky, and throws the stick as hard as he can. He turns and starts down the street, first at an angry walk but then at a run. Dino leaps up and chases after him.

As he runs, Lyle feels as if he's moving in slow motion, like a dream. His feet are heavy, and he feels weak and lost.

Why didn't he tell me? He knew, he always knew. He said we were gonna do things, but he knew we wouldn't. He knew.

Dang it! We did stuff! He needed me. Who needs me now? Nobody. God came into his head, not mine. How am I supposed to know anything about God, without him?

Lyle runs to the Dahlkes' house. He slows when he reaches the yard, and treads silently up to the picture window that looks out from their living room. He cups his hands and peers in.

The family is gathered, huddled around Dennis, comforting him as he sobs uncontrollably.

Lyle turns and slides slowly down the outside wall of the house, slumping down and just sitting there. He feels out of place here now, out of place and far, far too late.

He can't understand how life can leave so quickly, in such an untimely gust. One minute there's a voice on the phone; the next, people are crying and the voice is gone. "Okay, see you later." That's what he said on the phone. Only he wouldn't. Not now, and maybe not ever. Not unless his mother is right.

He reaches out for Dino, wanting to remain there, huddled against the house with the dog close beside, but Dino steps back and pricks his ears.

"You run more than anybody I've ever seen."

"Oh, anybody can do that."

"Even me?"

"Oh yeah, you could do it."

Lyle closes his eyes, shutting out everything but the sounds around him—the wind blowing hard and the creaking and groaning of the pines. As he focuses on those sounds he becomes aware that the trees are murmuring, a patient and relentless susurrus, bearing a simple message carried to him by the wind.

Hurry!   Hurry!   Hurry!

In an unthinking answer to the call, he leaps to his feet and runs. Dino is already ahead of him, and he knows where they're going. Lyle and the dog run through the neighborhood streets, and Lyle pushes himself harder, trying to outpace his loss, his grief. The wind presses, lifting him forward and allowing him to feel hidden, concealed and isolated from the rest of the world. He can hear only his own pulse, his own breathing, as he races down the dirt road toward their destination.

He reaches the meadow of the Log, and he stops and bends down, hands on his knees, needing air but not tired. As he gazes over the wide expanse of grass, he remembers the sound of the wheelchair bumping across the field, a mechanical heartbeat keeping time with the rhythm of another soul.

"Are you with me?"

"Yes, I'm with you."

"Do you feel it?"

"I think so . . . is this really going to work?"

"Shhh. It's already working!"

Throwing his arms out wide, palms upward, he turns his face into the sun. The act floods his mind with memories.

"I asked Him if I would run—you know, no wheelchair, no braces, just like everybody else. I asked Him if I would ever run that way."

"What did He say?"

"He told me I would. With you!"

Lyle reaches out and grabs a wild sunflower, crushes it in his hand and breathes in the sharp aroma, wanting to remember that summer smell forever. He throws the flower to the wind, puts his head down and takes off. Dino barks and follows him. Lyle sprints directly toward the Log.

The faster he moves, the more the world around him transforms, changing in details that he can feel and see. He drives himself forward, and he sees a world composed of threads of true, brilliant *color* . . . weaving and flowing in all directions.

The sky is a rich, resonant blue; the trees encourage him with a wildly vibrant dance of every possible shade of green; and the ground below transforms into a fluid river of shapes and colors cascading beneath his feet. Yellow and red and brown and pink and purple. Lavender, lilac and violet.

"See? You're startin' to run!"

"Faster, Lyle . . . go faster!"

"Come on! . . . faster!"

Lyle's eyes fill with purpose as he throws himself forward and shouts, "You wanna run? Let's run!"

He moves so fast, he can no longer feel his legs churn beneath him. He perceives a wisp of movement nearby, something that stays with him, something keeping rhythm with his pace. Lyle turns his head, and sees David running at his side.

The tall boy smiles at him: a smile that speaks of a celebration of freedom, a celebration of the privilege and liberty of running—running with his friend as they had hoped, running with his friend as they had promised.

When they reach the Log, David, Lyle, and Dino leap onto it and launch themselves into the air. They fly above the meadow for that brief miraculous moment, and Lyle falls to the ground, rolling over and over, and comes to a stop on his back, gazing up at the sky.

He watches, as the colors fade and the world returns to normal, and the image of his friend washes away, mingling with the thin clouds that pebble the deep blue summer sky. And he smiles.

~ THE END

AFTERWORD

Mrs. Hatcher – Hazel did get her teaching degree, as planned, from Eastern Washington University in 1970. She enjoyed a rewarding teaching career at Otis Orchards Elementary for almost thirty years, which included a nomination for Teacher of the Year.

Mr. Hatcher – Ron was employed by Carnation for almost twenty years. He left in 1974 to work for Roundup and retired in 1993. Since his retirement, he has become an avid golfer and is considered by his children's children to be the best full-time grandpa ever.

Lyle Hatcher became chairman of the March of Dimes at Greenacres Junior High and wrestled his way through high school. Over the next 25 years, he divided his time between coaching soccer, raising his two sons, and working as a financial advisor. He retired in 2009.

Steve Hatcher attended Central Valley High School, where he was Athlete of the Year in 1976. He began work as a fireman with the Spokane Valley Fire Department in 1980, joined their paramedic team in 1985, and was promoted to Captain in 2009.

Linda (Hatcher) Thompson graduated in 1971 from Central Valley High School, and went on to earn a Bachelor of Arts in Liberal Studies from Eastern Washington University in

1995, followed by a Masters in Organizational Leadership from Gonzaga University in 2002. She currently serves as the Executive Director for the Greater Spokane Substance Abuse Council, in memory of her son Trevor (1982-1986) and in honor of her daughter Katie and her son Nate.

Mrs. Dahlke – Gloria taught swimming, preschool and kindergarten for over twenty years in her home, where she still resides, in Spokane. She specialized in teaching special needs children. She opened the first school for autistic children in Spokane in 1968, and is currently a grandma to the thousands of lives she has touched.

Mr. Dahlke – Ernie worked his entire career at Inland Hardware in Spokane, Washington. He alternated (with his wife) serving as President and Vice-President of the Muscular Dystrophy Association for a number of years, and died in September 1983 at the age of 69.

Dennis Dahlke graduated from Shadle Park High School in 1965. He received a Bachelor of Arts in Education from Whitworth College, and worked as a substitute teacher at St. George's School in 1982-83 as an Earth Sciences and Scrimshaw instructor.

He continued to work as a taxidermist, and currently owns and operates a bird farm in Spokane—with over three hundred emus, ringneck and golden pheasants, peacocks, and guinea hens.

Dena Dahlke received a Bachelor of Arts in Education from Whitworth College in 1972. She taught in Rathdrum, Idaho at John Brown Elementary for ten years beginning in 1980, as well as one year at the grade school in Rosalia, Washington.

She worked as the Director for Head Start for the State of Wisconsin for four years. She currently resides with her mother, Gloria Dahlke, in the home where she grew up.

Ella Kay (Dahlke) Solbrack graduated from Shadle Park High School and received a Bachelor of Arts in Speech from Whitworth College in 1971. She taught first grade and kindergarten for a year at Brentwood Elementary. From 1973 to 1981, she taught grade school in Rosalia, Washington. Since 1982, she has worked as a librarian for the Rosalia Grade School and as a teacher for special education children.

Mrs. Maxfield – Madge taught grade school for thirty years. Linwood Elementary was Mrs. Maxfield's last teaching position, and she worked there until her retirement in 1981. She still lives in the Spokane area.

Miss Dorothy O'Donnell died on July 15, 2000, at the age of 93. She was a grade school principal for thirty years, and hundreds of former students sought her out over the decades to thank her for the discipline that helped teach them how to survive in life. She received countless, humbly grateful thank-you's for the guidance she provided. Her niece Tootie Bell and her husband Bill Bell took care of her the last years of her life. They said she was one of a kind!

Lyle Hatcher, proudly wearing his
Tenderfoots Cub Scout uniform

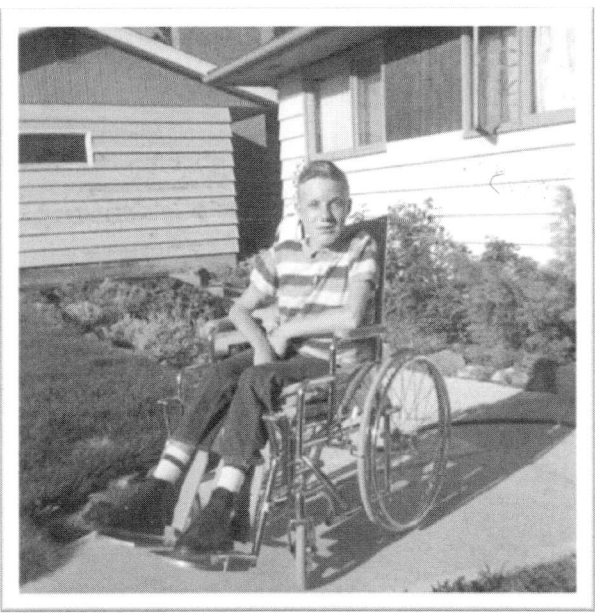

David Dahlke in his new wheelchair

The class at Linwood Elementary

David is seated in front on the far right.

Lyle is in the middle row, fourth from the left.

LINWOOD SCHOOL — MARCH 1965   CHATTEAU STUDIO SPOKANE, WASH.

Lyle giving Dino a bath

*Mr. and Mrs. Hatcher
(Hazel and Ron)*

The Hatcher children (left to right) Linda, Lyle, and Steve, ready to head out for Sunday school

The Dahlke family (left to right)
David, Dena, Dennis, Ella, Ernie, and Gloria

*Mrs. Hatcher with the television set she uses on
weekday mornings for her workout with Jack LaLanne*

*Jack LaLanne and his four-legged friends -
"A few minutes a day, that's all I ask!"*

David with Mr. and Mrs. Dahlke shortly after returning from Salt Lake City, where David was officially diagnosed with muscular dystrophy

He's showing his parents the scar on his left leg where the doctor took a muscle sample, or as David put it, where "the crocodile bit me."

David was three years-old when this photo was taken.

Mr. Dahlke and David setting out on their daily trek to Linwood Elementary

Mr. and Mrs. Dahlke (Ernie and Gloria)

Miss Dorothy O'Donnell (DOD Almighty), the principal of Linwood Elementary, in her office

Mrs. Maxfield, the fifth grade teacher and dance instructor at Linwood Elementary, displaying her original artwork on her dress

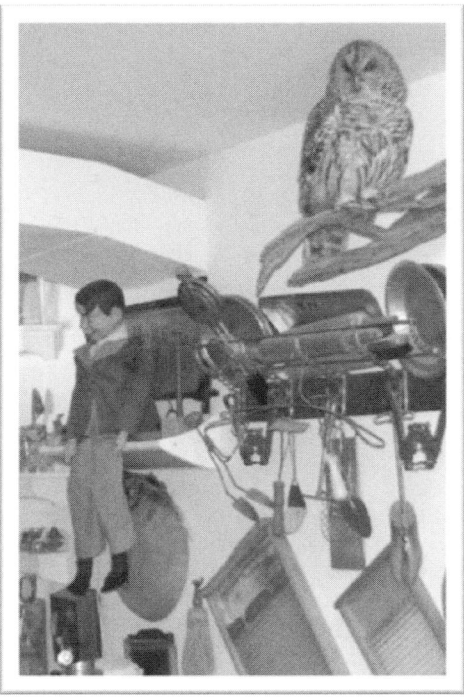

*Charlie, the puppet
under the watchful eye
of Dennis' prize owl*

*Charlie is surrounded by
some of Mrs. Dahlke's
antique (even in 1965)
kitchen and laundry
implements.*

*Dennis and Jenon at
the Snow Flake
Fantasy, 1964*

Dena teaching a class of tadpoles in the Dahlke family swimming pool

Dennis in his taxidermy room with a few of his stuffed and mounted birds

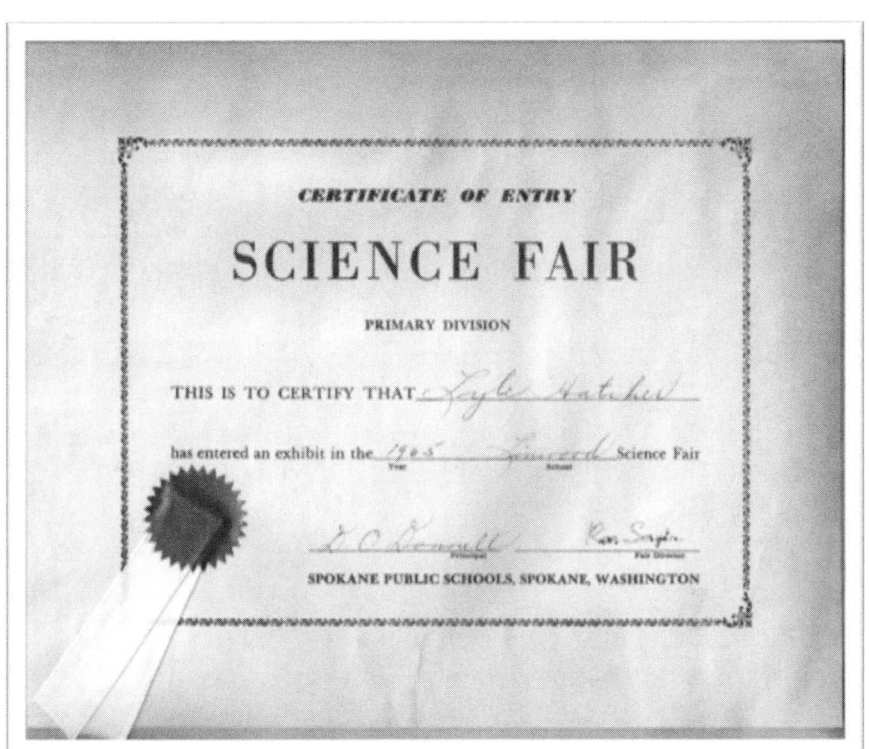

Steve and Lyle

Mrs. Hatcher's graduation

Dear David,
I hope you
get out of the
hospital. I know
how it feels. I
have been there
before. when I got

home. I ran and I
ate 5 bowls of
cornflakes. you
Your frend
Steve
Hatcher

Time

The time is passing ever so
                           fast —

Before you know it the days are
                    in the past —

So live every moment and

Remember this day —

And you will be very happy
                    and gay

David's Poem

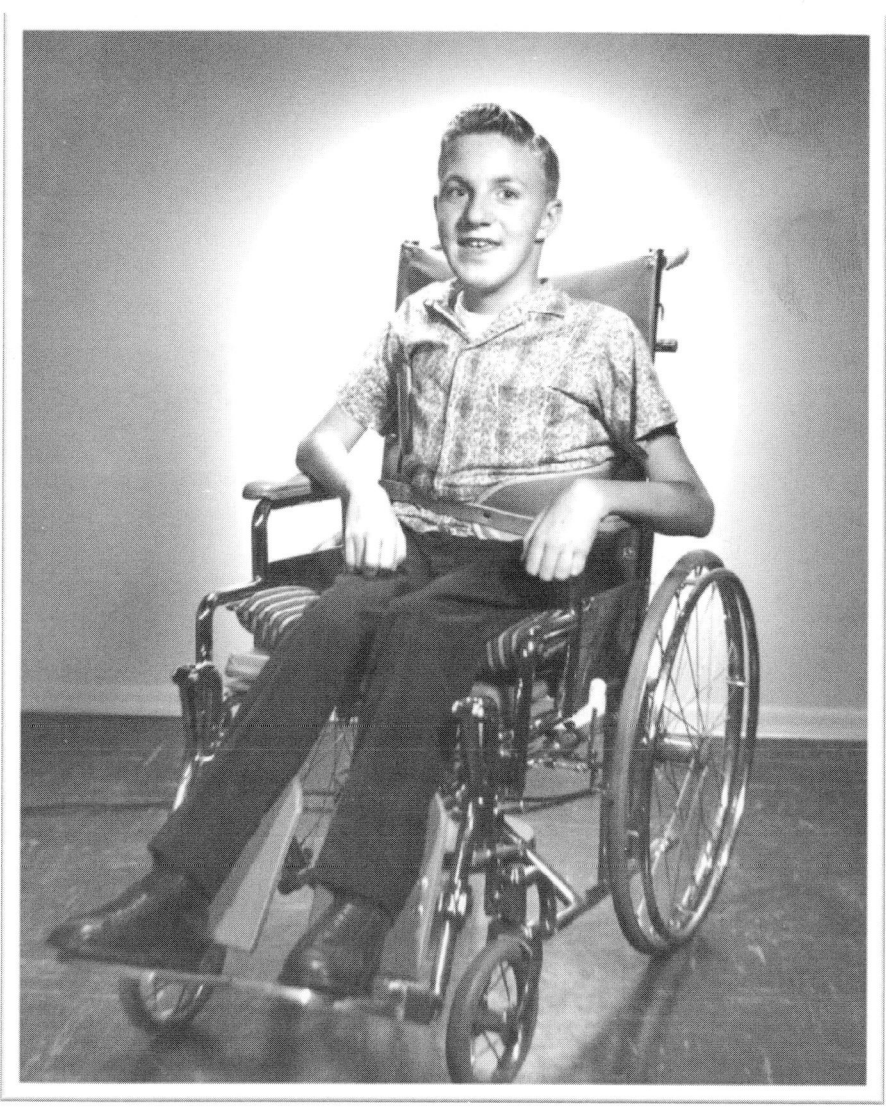

David Dahlke as the poster child for the
Muscular Dystrophy Association in 1965